The
Motoring Age

The Motoring Age

The Automobile and Britain 1896–1939

PETER THOROLD

P
PROFILE BOOKS

First published in Great Britain in 2003 by
PROFILE BOOKS LTD
58A Hatton Garden
London EC1N 8LX
www.profilebooks.co.uk

Copyright © Peter Thorold, 2003

10 9 8 7 6 5 4 3 2 1

Printed and bound in Great Britain by
Clays, Bungay, Suffolk

The moral right of the author has been asserted.

A CIP catalogue record for this book is available from the British Library.

ISBN 1 86197 378 0

For Marcus, Emelia, Daniel and Nicola

Contents

List of Illustrations

I. De Dion Bouton: an early advertisement (from Frostick, *Advertising and the Motor-Car*, Lund Humphries 1970)
II. Interior of a Rolls-Royce Phantom 1, 1927, with bodywork by Clark of Wolverhampton (National Motor Museum, Beaulieu)
III. Armstrong Siddeley: 1930 advertisement (from Frostick, *Advertising and the Motor-Car*, Lund Humphries 1970)
IV. René Vincent's poster for Georges Irat Cars (ADAGP, Paris and DACS, London)
V. Victorian tram: an advertisement for Huntley & Palmer Biscuits (The Robert Opie Collection)
VI. Poster by André Edouard Marty for the 1933 Motor Show (London's Transport Museum)
VII. Coach tour poster by L. B. Black (London's Transport Museum)
VIII. Salvador Dalí, *Apparition de la ville de Delft*, 1935—6 (ADAGP, Paris and DACS, London)

Acknowledgements for illustrations in the text
The author and publishers are grateful to the following for permission to reproduce illustrations in the text: Automobile Association, 40, 197, 198; Blackpool Central Library, 107; Cassell (from John Bolster, *The Upper Crust*), 27; Chrysalis Books (B.T. Batsford), 168; Curtis Brown, 33; Faber & Faber, 159; Getty Images, Hulton

Acknowledgements

I would like gratefully to acknowledge the help I have received from Peter Brears, Marguerite Evers, Jan Faull and her colleagues at the British Film Institute, Ian Hallums, Fiona Havergal, Christopher Humphries and David Shapiro. Andrew Lownie kindly introduced to me John Buchan's *The Island of Sheep*.

I am also most grateful to Madame Y. Odier, and to Olivier Paschoud, who made me aware of a number of important sources. The Paschoud family have the distinction of being the first to commission a working automobile powered by internal combustion.

I thank the Churchill Archives Centre at Churchill College, Cambridge, for allowing me to quote from the Hore-Belisha Papers; also the Random House Group Ltd for permission to quote from *Autogedden* by Heathcote Williams, published by Jonathan Cape and thanks too to John Murray (Publishers) Ltd for the extract from John Betjeman's poem 'Slough', taken from *Collected Poems*. I am indebted to Charles Kay of the Crawley Reference Library, Trevor Dunne of the Royal Automobile Club and Jonathan Day of the National Motor Museum, Beaulieu, for the particular trouble they have taken on my behalf.

1
Prelude

How vivid it was, London in the 1890s. The buses and trams, horse-drawn still, with their sparkling colours, blue and green, yellow and red, set off against the sober hues of the private carriages and cabs. And how elegant, particularly in the Season, with the myriad victorias and landaus and family coaches parading in Hyde Park, the horses sleek, the footmen in livery and cockades. And the hansom cab, 'swaying delicately in unison with the horse, the whip poised like a lance in its holder ... the cotton summer cover in colours or white with tassels, made in most cases by the cabby's wife, as the wives of the gondolieris still make covers for the cabin-tops of gondolas'. The trams too had their summer covers, drawn as they might be by mules, three abreast, the one in the middle with a canopy over its head hung with bells which jingled as it trotted along. People remembered the horse buses for the atmosphere, the friendliness, how driver and passengers chatted happily together as they rode along. Frederick Willis, a south London child, recalled how an 'old lady waving her umbrella on the pavement would bring the bus right up to the kerb' and how the conductor would dextrously lift her aboard with an almost affectionate hug.

That at any rate is one side of the story, the one perpetuated by cinema and television. The other is much less enthusiastic. Take the cabs. Often enough they were old 'growlers', their frames, as a writer of the time put it, 'afflicted with innumerable gaps, chinks and

The start of the Emancipation Run to Brighton, 14 November 1896. Harry Lawson, the moving spirit, dressed like a 'Swiss Admiral', is at the tiller of the car on the right.

crevices ... neither wind nor water-tight'. (And their horses, he went on, were miserable creatures, and their drivers little better.) The trouble with the cheery buses was that there were nothing like enough of them. In 1890 only one person in twelve in the south London suburbs commuted to work by any form of public transport. It was too expensive. There was also the noise of the traffic. Thomas Burke, writing in the 1930s, agreed that by then the volume of noise was greater than in the horse age, but declared firmly that modern traffic was less cruel to the ear: 'We have a concerted drone in place of random artillery.' H. B. Cresswell, an architect writing in the *Architectural Review* in 1958, went further. The din, he said, 'was beyond all imagining', with the multitude of iron-shod hairy heels hammering on the road and the deafening side-drum tattoo of the wheels. Cresswell also described the filth.

> An assertive mark of the horse was the mud that, despite the activities of a numerous corps of red-jacketed boys who dodged among

the wheels and hooves with pan and brush in service to iron bins at the pavement-edge, either flooded the streets with churnings of 'pea soup' that at times collected in pools over-brimming the kerbs, and at others covered the road-surface as with axle grease or bran-laden dust to the distraction of the wayfarer.

As somebody else put it, if, while crossing the street, you had the misfortune to get too close to a passing cab, you would emerge looking like a Dalmatian dog, spotted with thick, black, viscerous mud (much of it simply horse dung).

It was against such a background, elegant and friendly, noisy and filthy, that the motoring age in Britain came into being. The birth-date is usually taken as 14 November 1896, the day the Locomotives on Highways Act took effect, removing at last the legal barriers to motoring. Two days before, H. O. Duncan, well known as a racing bicyclist, arrived at Dover from France with the eminent French car builders Léon and Camille Bollée to take part in a celebratory motor rally from London to Brighton. To get to London at all was not easy. The petrol in the tanks of their three three-wheeler motors had been emptied out in Boulogne and it was difficult to lay hands on any replacement fuel at Dover. Eventually they tracked down some benzine (petrol) at a chemist's shop which Léon Bollée's hydrometer registered as satisfactory. Arriving by train at Victoria Station on the morning of 12 November, the three of them, with their motors, were surrounded at once by an excited crowd. A police inspector pushed his way through to declare, 'You are not to drive those instruments through the streets.' But the new act is passed, protested Duncan, and we are taking the cars no further than Holborn. Still, it was no use arguing, technically there remained a couple of days to go under the old regime, and anyway there were now half a dozen policemen on the spot whom the inspector ordered to accompany the 'things' to the Central Hall in Oxford Street (then the Holborn skating rink) where entrants for the rally were to be garaged. After much trouble, Duncan managed to hire some broken-down old hacks from a livery stable. Ropes were attached to the cars and off they started, escorted by an uproarious and jeering crowd. When the towing rope snapped in Piccadilly and the three old horses simply plodded on regardless, the joy of the crowd knew no bounds. It was indeed a comical sight, conceded Duncan wryly, the only consolation being that the Bollées understood no English.

Charles Jarrott, later a well-known racing driver and the man principally responsible for the founding of the Automobile Association, takes up the story with a description of the Central Hall on the morning of the rally:

> I shall never forget the scene which met my eyes when I entered. French mechanics and German inventors, with enthusiasts of all nationalities, were mixed up in indescribable confusion. Huge flares were being carried about from one machine to another to assist in lighting up the burners for the cars, which at that time were innocent of electric ignition. An occasional petrol blaze was seen through the fog which filled the hall, making the scene resemble a veritable inferno.

According to enraged neighbours, the din made by tuning the engines went on all night.

There is no doubting the significance of this, the first Brighton Run, and more than that, the first motor rally of any sort to be held in Britain. It proclaimed the new age, and did so with true late Victorian exuberance and bravado. Gluttony, or what we would consider gluttony, was unabashed. The day started with a 9.30 breakfast (washed down by Rudesheimer 1886 and/or Château Bechevelle 1889) at the starting point, the Metropole Hotel in Northumberland Avenue. Anyone still hungry could stop off at the White Hart Hotel in Reigate, where a substantial lunch was laid on. (In Brighton a suitably lavish dinner was waiting to round off the day.) 'Plutocracy', new and flashy money, another characteristic feature of the time, was represented, indeed personified, in the organizer Harry Lawson, the partner in some recent business deals with the 'modern Midas', Ernest Hooley. Lawson was very controversial, but no more so than another participant, the American inventor and salesman Edward J. Pennington, of whom it was said that 'it seemed impossible for any sane person to disbelieve anything he stated'. They were rash indeed, however, if they did not.

The day was foggy, turning to rain, with a gale building up at Brighton for those who made it. Of the fifty-eight cars at the starting line, only thirty-eight (or, according to some accounts, only thirty-two or thirty-three) succeeded in getting under way. They were a diverse lot: three-wheelers, four-wheelers, some powered by internal combustion, some by steam, some by electricity. Since

4

Britain's motor industry was in its infancy, apart from some esoteric home-made examples not intended for sale commercially, the
vehicles were all of foreign make. Crowds of onlookers thronged
the streets and balconies and house-tops, and perched on lamp-
posts around the starting point. In fact, there were crowds everywhere along the route. In the first car off were Harry Lawson and
his wife. They were followed by Frederick Simms, the original
chairman and managing director of the (British) Daimler Motor
Syndicate, accompanying the eminent Gottlieb Daimler, to whom
it has been said, 'without question belongs the title of inventor of
the [petrol-driven] automobile'. Then there were H. O. Duncan and
the Bollées, Charles Jarrott, and Evelyn Ellis — his Panhard-
Levassor is now in the Science Museum in South Kensington. A
younger son of the very wealthy Lord Howard de Walden, Ellis was
a former officer in the Royal Navy who had already fitted out two
of his Thames launches with petrol engines. Also in the procession
were a carload of French automobilists and, surprisingly, vans from
Harrods and Peter Robinson, another department store, carrying
parcels for delivery in Brighton.

The rally was also a race, for, after all, participants like the Bollées could not fail to see in it an excellent opportunity to advertise
their cars. Who exactly did what is not always clear. The Emancipation Run was improvised at the last minute and there was no
official programme to enlighten the journalists who went along —
they included Jerome K. Jerome, author of *Three Men in a Boat* —
about either the participants or their vehicles. What is certain is
that many of the cars failed to complete the course. Or at least by
road. A few, it seems, were simply driven from the starting line to
Victoria Station and loaded on to a train to Preston Park, a station
just outside Brighton, from where — having made themselves
plausibly dirty — they proceeded nonchalantly to the finish at the
Brighton Metropole. Some competitors missed the breakfast but
joined in part of the way along or tried to reduce the odds against
them by taking a short cut. Some were distracted by the Reigate
lunch. There was confusion about who actually won. The American Duryea team insisted they had and that they had been wrongly
disqualified by Lawson for commercial reasons. (And certainly
Lawson was not to be trusted: for instance, he pretended that the
majority of entries for the run were Daimlers, for which he owned

Armand Peugeot, a founder of the motor industry, in the 1890s. Monsieur Peugeot is in the passenger seat.

the British patent, rather than Panhard-Levassors.) The official judges were no use, since their car, a Panhard-Levassor and reputedly the fastest car in the world, had broken down and reached Brighton two hours after the first arrivals. Still, they did better than the van intended to rescue stranded cars — it did not arrive until the early hours of the next morning. Anyway, the Bollée brothers were generally accepted as the winners, taking both first and second places.

Why were the British so late into motoring? Why were the great names — Lenoir, Daimler, Otto, Benz, Maybach, Peugeot, Bollée, Serpollet — from some other country? As Charles Jarrott said, the people who really knew about cars on 14 November 1896 were foreign engineers and mechanics. How odd, since it was the British who had launched the Industrial Revolution and pioneered the railways, and it was to Britain that foreigners such as Gottlieb Daimler and Armand Peugeot had come to learn how to be engineers. 'The motor car should have been British', wrote Thomas Edison in 1901; that would have been natural, 'You first invented it in the 1830s, you have the mechanics and the roads.'

As it happened, the versatile and energetic engineers and businessmen of the early steam age had not overlooked the possibilities of self-propelled transport on roads. In fact, road locomotives predated the railways. Richard Trevithick, a Cornish mining engineer, set up his London Steam Carriage Company, which worked the streets of north London, as early as 1803. In the 1820s technical improvements made steam motoring more practicable. In the 1830s the Squire and Macerone Steam Coach ran daily from Paddington to Edgware and Harrow and was capable on level ground of cruising at 20mph. Walter Hancock, a remarkably determined operator, drove his steam car through the packed streets of the City of London in 1838. Then there was the Steam Carriage Company of Scotland, which ran a fleet of six steam carriages devised by John Scott Russell, designer and builder of the SS *Great Eastern*. This company operated a coach service between Glasgow and Paisley, with locomotives capable of carrying thirty or forty passengers inside plus a tender for six inside and twenty outside. Other pioneers were Sir Charles Dance, who ran four trips a day between Gloucester and Cheltenham, and Sir Goldsworthy Gurney. There was even, in the 1830s, an automobile periodical called the *Journal of Elemental Locomotion*.

One school of thought at about this time considered that the use of locomotives on roads might make the construction of railways unnecessary. A select committee of the House of Commons, reporting in 1831, concluded that steam power was likely to replace horses on the roads and recommended that discrimination against steam locomotives on turnpike roads should be prohibited. Yet by 1840 the first automobile age was to all intents and purposes finished. In 1859 there was a revival, but it petered out. One reason was concern over damage to roads and bridges, another the risk of boiler explosion and injury to people and property. A witness before an 1873 parliamentary select committee on locomotives on roads stated that he had once been involved with steam buses but had withdrawn following an explosion which resulted in loss of life. And the original recommendation to prevent discrimination, while accepted by the House of Commons, was rejected by the Lords. The turnpike trusts, which controlled the main highways, did discriminate, their proprietors claiming with reason that 'locomotives' damaged the road surface. Nevertheless, the difference in pricing was extreme: in one example, while a horse-drawn coach would be charged a toll of 3s (15p), a steam carriage would be obliged to pay £2. And very important was the antagonism of the railway companies. Their shareholders, having got rid of horse traffic — at any rate, all but the most local, which they did not want anyway — had no wish to see competition appear from another source.

Whatever the view of the House of Commons in the 1830s, it had changed a generation later. Parliamentary acts of 1861 and 1865 restricted the permissible speed for self-propelled road vehicles to 4mph in open country and 2mph in towns, and required that they be manned by a crew of two, with another person walking at least sixty yards in front displaying a red flag or, at night, a red lantern. For anything resembling a motor car, such conditions were impossible.

The profound effect of the railways on economic and social life, in a negative sense at least, was nowhere more noticeable than on the great highways, the old mail roads, which swept their way through the countryside of Britain. Deprived of the long-distance traffic, passenger and freight, for which they had been constructed, their purpose was gone. They resembled the Roman roads after the dissolution of the Empire. In the 1860s George Eliot could write:

> Five-and-thirty years ago the glory had not yet departed from the old coach-roads: the great roadside inns were still brilliant with well-polished tankards, the smiling glances of pretty barmaids, and the repartees of jocose ostlers; the mail still announced itself by the merry notes of the horn; the hedge-cutter or the rick-thatcher might still know the exact hour by the unfailing yet otherwise meteoric apparition of the pea-green Tally-ho or the yellow Independent; and elderly gentlemen in pony-chaises, quartering nervously to make way for the rolling swinging swiftness, had not ceased to remark that times were finely changed since they used to see pack-horses and hear the tinkling of their bells on this very highway.

In his *Uncommercial Traveller*, published in 1861, Charles Dickens described coming on a turnpike and finding it eloquent 'respecting the change which had fallen on the road. The Turnpike-house was all overgrown with ivy; and the Turnpike-keeper, unable to get a living out of the tolls, plied the trade of cobbler.'

There were enterprising tourists, such as Andrew Carnegie, who relished the horse-age version of the open road and were delighted by the emptiness. Carnegie, the immensely rich American steel magnate and philanthropist, wrote a charming description of rural England and Scotland in 1881. With family and friends he travelled in a hired 'four-in-hand' from Brighton to Inverness. His mood was buoyant, boisterous even; he enjoyed almost everything he saw. What a wonderful way to travel, he wrote: 'Everything of rural England is seen, and how exquisitely beautiful it all is, this quiet, peaceful, orderly land!' As to the roads: 'We bowl over them as balls do over billiard-tables.' In the north, travelling from the Lake District to Carlisle, the roads were as 'perfect as they can be made'.

The Hon. Charles Rolls in his first car, a ¾ hp Peugeot, before the Locomotives on Highways Act of 1896, with a compulsory red flag man out in front.

Most people, however, took a different view. Twenty years after Carnegie's trip, J. St Loe Strachey, the editor of the *Spectator*, remarked how gloomy it was to travel the once magnificent old mail roads and often to see no one for miles. Moreover, whatever Carnegie and later Edison may have said, many of them had undoubtedly deteriorated. 'It is well, perhaps, that the great supporters of our roads in years long since past cannot see them in their present altered and dilapidated state, looking almost like country lanes' was one comment. Another contemporary deplored the sad fate of the country posting inns, with their great empty yards and the windows of the upper rooms all shuttered. Once they had been 'the scenes of life and cheerfulness, but now [were] reduced to a tap-room and accommodation for a lodger or two'. The Australian S. F. Edge, perhaps the most flamboyant of motoring pioneers and a champion motor racer, remembered in the 1930s how even the Brighton Road in early motoring days was sometimes so narrow that not more than a couple of carts could pass each other. When a hole appeared in the road, 'a few shovels of stones were thrown into it and horses' hoofs and cart wheels were left to do the rest'. The turnpike trusts had gone into liquidation, leaving penurious parish authorities to cope with maintenance. In 1878 Parliament passed the responsibility to local districts and ten years later to the newly established county councils and county boroughs. The reorganization was clumsy and unsuccessful.

Descriptions and anecdotes are plentiful. No one perhaps is more illuminating than the travel writer J. J. Hissey, who belongs in a category of his own. In a series of books which included *An Old-fashioned Journey through England and Wales* (1884), *A Holiday on the Road* (1887), *On Southern English Roads* (1896) and then, as motoring gathered pace, five others culminating in the *The Road and the Inn* of 1917, he traces the process of change and its effect on the countryside. The titles — *An English Holiday with Car and Camera* is another example — give a good idea of his style and content. Not overly imaginative, more or less oblivious of economic causes, a bit of a buffer apt to invoke the shade of Dr Johnson — hardly an authority on rural matters — whenever he encounters what he regards as a change for the worse, Hissey is gregarious (a useful quality when extracting tales from locals), curious (especially about old churches and haunted houses) and even dramatic, as when, on one occasion, he writes of crossing Salisbury Plain at night. He loves the English countryside and what he calls its 'exquisitely finished, ever-changing, gemlike' nature. Once, years before, he had made a riding tour in California, but the dust and the inexorable sun displeased him. What he enjoys are tranquillity and leisure. And he is sentimental. Nobody can change anything without his noticing. He is always harking back, comparing past and present. Here, for instance, in 1887, lamenting the desolation of the roads and countryside, Hissey apostrophizes a crumbling milestone near Godstone in Surrey, where, at the White Hart in the old days, the horses were changed for the last stage into London. 'Poor old milestone!' he exclaims, 'now that road travellers

are so few and far between, your services are but seldom required.'
Again and again he refers to the decay brought about by the railways. 'The speed and convenience of steam', he says in 1896, 'has
[sic] robbed us of the poetry and picturesqueness of travel', and:

> We travel now in crowds, or rather are conveyed from place to
> place, for travelling proper seems to be a lost art, and to have dis-
> appeared with the post-house and the stage-coach; the very speed
> of the railway has robbed us of the real pleasure of travel ... The
> railways go where the country is most populated in search of traf-
> fic, so that only those who travel across country by road can form
> any idea how wild and desolate are some parts of England now ...
> The depopulation of rural England is becoming a serious ques-
> tion.

Twice in his early books Hissey records occasions when he bumps
up against the future. In one case, related in his 1896 book, he
remarks on the number of bicyclists, modest precursors of motoring
in the rejuvenation of the countryside. Hissey is approving if not
noticeably enthusiastic. It does grate on his prejudices, however,
when he comes across 'some of the small hostels by the wayside
[which] now rejoice in the sign of "The Cyclists' Rest" or the
"Cyclists' Arms"'. Whatever they may be, he notes sardonically.
The second occasion is dramatic and is related in the 1887 *A Holiday
on the Road*. He is on a country road. 'We had not proceeded far on
our stage when we met one of those rare blessings of our advanced
civilisation, a road monster breathing forth fire, steam, and smoke,
snorting as it crawled along like some dreaded devastating dragon of
children's fairy tales.' It was a steam traction engine of the sort
which dragged threshing machines and tackle for steam ploughs. To
Hissey this was 'about the most hideous machine that the inventive
genius of man has as yet contrived — a most dangerous one,
besides'. They were worse, a veteran traveller told him, more dangerous, than the mail coach you encountered galloping downhill in
the "olden time". But Hissey adds gloomily, 'Doubtless in years to
come, though, man's wonderful and fertile brain will improve upon
it, and produce something more uncouth still.'
These steam engines, huge and weighing up to fourteen tons, were
reminders of the past as well as harbingers of the future. They had
survived while lighter steam road locomotives perished, for they

could live with the stringent legislation. The speed limits mattered little since they moved very slowly, nor were the requirements on manning of much inconvenience to them, given their need anyway for a crew. (And after all in our day vehicles carrying particularly bulky loads are customarily preceded by an attendant car or van, or by a police escort.) Parliament, appreciative of the needs of agriculture — so long as they were not interpreted to include Corn Laws — had never intended to get rid of these heavy road locomotives. They might frighten the horses, but then, as somebody said during the debate on the 1865 bill, only low-bred horses are generally timid on seeing a road locomotive; high-bred ones 'had too much pluck'.

But these huge locomotives were a constant reminder that the roads were not wholly the preserve of horses, carriages and carts, pedestrians and bicyclists. Parliament had to accept that the problem of what to do about road locomotives would not simply go away. In 1873 a select committee was set up with the remit to examine the use of 'Locomotive Engines' on turnpikes, by then mostly in dissolution. It took as a premise that the use of these engines was daily increasing, and, most significantly, acknowledged that the large amount of capital by now invested in them was evidence of their importance. Moreover, they were used in industry as well as agriculture, being particularly evident at ports. There was discussion about the red flag. One witness, while not much bothered about the requirement for a man walking ahead, had little time for the rule that he should carry a red flag. It did not stay red for more than ten minutes and was totally black after two days, for the man who carried it also helped with the engine and had filthy hands. A particularly interesting witness was Commander De Lousada of Glasgow, owner of two locomotives which were entirely employed in transporting heavy machinery from one part of the city to another, chiefly to the shipyards. His engines, he said, used the roads all day and at any hour of the night and were capable of pulling six wagons apiece. De Lousada also opposed the red flag rule.

Eventually, in 1878, the motoring law was amended, for the first time making it more favourable to motorists. It was an improvement, but no more than a mouse of one. The man in front was allowed to drop back from sixty yards to twenty and he was no longer obliged to carry a red flag — unless a local authority required him to do so. The use of engines continued to increase, and it was calculated that — excluding those involved entirely in agriculture — there were by the 1890s something like 8,000 steam traction engines and steamrollers on the roads of England and Wales, with 800 smaller locomotives pulling tramcars.

If by 1896 very few people in Britain had actually seen a car or motor cycle, most of those with any level of education would have been aware to some degree of what was happening in France and Germany. A well-publicized reliability and speed run had taken place in July 1894 covering the seventy-nine miles between Paris and Rouen. A year later the committee responsible organized a more ambitious run of 732 miles, Versailles to Bordeaux and back to Paris. It was a clear-cut race, by day and night, the sponsors of which included the Americans W. K. Vanderbilt and James Gordon Bennett, proprietor of the *New York Herald*. Occasionally self-propelled vehicles made their appearance at exhibitions. Frederick Willis remembered riding in a 'horseless carriage' in 1893 at the Crystal Palace in Sydenham, which specialized in sensational shows, as for instance horses that dived into water. Willis said of the vehicle that it 'was like a wagonette, and progressed smoothly at about fifteen miles an hour in an offensive atmosphere of petrol fumes'.

It was left to a few individuals to lift Britain out of its supine attitude to an invention that could in common sense no longer be ignored. One of the most persistent was John Knight, who built a successful steam carriage back in the 1860s. He experimented with various fuels and devised a petrol-driven car which, in November 1895, he conducted through his home town of Farnham in Surrey at around 8mph. He was arrested for speeding, and for being without a traction-engine licence or a red flag man. In Birmingham, Léon L'Hollier was charged with driving without an escort in front. In both cases the magistrates were reluctant to impose heavy fines and the publicity helped bring home to the public the anomalous state of the law. Other early drivers got away with it. In July 1895 Evelyn Ellis and S. F. Edge undertook a drive of fifty-six miles from Micheldever in Hampshire to Ellis's house at Datchet, near Windsor, which took five hours, thirty-two minutes 'exclusive of stoppages'. It was, Edge claimed, 'the first ever made by a petroleum motor carriage in this country'. In this case, the police who occasionally stopped them were satisfied by the production of a carriage licence. Then there was Henry Hewetson, who obeyed the law but made fun of it. There was no rule about the size of the red flag, so Hewetson got his young son to march in front of his car carrying an inch of red ribbon tied to a pencil.

The man above all responsible for persuading Parliament to accept reality and to make the vital distinction between ordinary cars and the unwieldy and potentially much more dangerous traction engines was Sir David Salomons. He was a remarkable man, a lawyer and also an electrical engineer, who had built his own motor tricycle, constructed a telescope and invented a signalling system for trains. He also installed electricity at Broomhill, his country house near Tunbridge Wells, which, since manufacturers did not as yet exist, he fitted out with home-made equipment. Most important, Salomons carried social and political weight. He was a baronet, a Member of Parliament and a director of the South East Railway Company. He was the first Jewish Lord Mayor of London. Linked by family with the Montefiores, Goldsmids and Sterns, he occupied a prominent place in the Jewish community, but at the same time he was popular with non-Jews. Through his character and standing he was able to influence his fellow MPs. While automobiles had figured as curiosities in exhibitions, the 'motor show' which Salomons, as mayor of Tunbridge Wells, organized in the grounds of Broomhill in October 1895 was a far cry from the circus-like atmosphere of the past. It attracted an estimated 10,000 spectators, a creditable figure. Seven months later, in May 1896, he promoted another (serious) motoring exhibition at the Crystal Palace. (Not to be outdone, Harry Lawson organized his own exhibition at the Imperial Institute.)

Salomons stood apart from the flamboyant Lawson, whom he distrusted, and was not a participant in the Emancipation Run. He was far from being alone in his distaste for the commercial atmosphere which surrounded many of the early motorists. It was an atmosphere, however, which could hardly be avoided. For motoring grew out of old industry, particularly out of bicycles. It was the creation of practical working engineers, not of scientists experimenting in laboratories, of men with clear commercial interests. Even gentlemen amateurs quickly developed business links. Evelyn Ellis was a substantial investor in the (British) Daimler company and Lord Winchilsea, who presided at the Metropole breakfast, was closely tied to Harry Lawson. At the same time, the sheer enthusiasm and dedica-

tion are not for a moment to be doubted. Apart from journalists and a few other observers, it is improbable that anyone who took, or attempted to take, the Brighton Road that 14 November was indifferent to the sheer excitement of the new invention. Many were utterly passionate about it. But passion alone was by no means enough.

The Hon. Evelyn Ellis, a pioneer British motorist, at Sir David Salomons's Tunbridge Wells Motor Show in 1895. Mr Ellis's car, a Panhard-Levassor, is now in the Science Museum, South Kensington.

Charles Jarrott wrote, 'If there was one great quality which motorists in the early days possessed more than another, it was that of being philosophical.' They needed to be, for the early automobiles, the horseless carriages, required infinite time and attention, with their owners subjected to humiliation, to scoffing and abuse, and, both before and after the passing of the Locomotives on Highways Act, to sustained harassment by the police.

So, you needed to be philosophic, to have fortitude, 'grit' in the language of the day, and you would do well to have a sense of humour. Motoring in its initial phase is constantly entangled with broad comedy. Gottlieb Daimler, filling his room with old iron and — perforce noisily — constructing his motor, was suspected by his neighbours of being a counterfeiter. From one point of view the Emancipation Run to Brighton itself was a great joke. And there were the grotesque clothing, the broken-down cars which had to be rescued by horses, the memory of the futile red flag. One of the dottiest bits of fun surfaced in the week before 'emancipation' came into effect. Harry Lawson rode in a Cannstatt-Daimler as part of the Lord Mayor's procession, to end up with a charge against him (later withdrawn) of being improperly provided with an outrider.

Comedy had popped up too in the House of Commons. Henry Chaplin, the president of the Local Government Board, introduced the second reading of the crucial Locomotives on Highways Act under the impression that the red flag was still obligatory, whereas, as we have seen, it had disappeared from the statute book (if not from local authority regulations) eighteen years before. It is not clear whether members laughed at that particular lapse, but at any rate they let themselves go when Chaplin went on to say that motor cars might come to rival light railways.

Henry Chaplin was an original, an extravagant version of the late William Whitelaw. He successfully guided the bill through Parliament, and for all but the heaviest vehicles the requirement of an outrider was abolished and the speed limit increased to 12mph. The opposition was slight, for the pointlessness of pretending that light automobiles could be suppressed was becoming clear. Indeed, the Conservative government had inherited the bill in draft from their Liberal predecessors. If Chaplin was not himself a figure of fun, his position was ironic in the extreme. For this massive figure who delivered reform, who ushered in the new age, 'the Squire', the hero of the hunting field, steward of the Jockey Club, was the man of whom it was said he 'might have sat, body and mind alike, for a national statue of John Bull with his coach and four, his two packs of hounds'. 'I often think that Providence intended me to be a huntsman and not a statesman,' he once remarked. The paradox struck one of the few vocal critics of the bill in the House, Dr Tanner (Cork County), who regretted that 'the right honourable Gentlemen [sic] whom he had looked upon all his life as his idol, and as the soul of English sport, should have fallen to such a degree as to become a tout for these non-sporting machines'.

What, then, did people expect of the automobile? To some it was a joke that it could hope to compete with the railways; to enthusiasts such as Alfred Harmsworth (later Lord Northcliffe), its possibilities were almost limitless. According to Charles Jarrott, the public at large were for a moment carried away even before the Emancipation Run, believing, he said, 'that horses were to be superseded forthwith'. But the initial euphoria did not last. At the Brighton dinner after the run even some of those most involved were careful. Lord Winchilsea in his speech wondered whether what they had been taking part in that day was an interesting experiment or whether they had been founding a great national industry.

The *Illustrated London News* is a useful guide to how people felt, or at least those people who were wealthy enough to afford a car. To judge by its articles and advertisements, its readers were above all interested in royalty, military campaigns on the fringes of the Empire, liver pills and bicycling. It gave a short notice to Salomons's Tunbridge Wells exhibition, but in July 1896 an article about 'the rage' for bicycles in France stated that the horse was in danger of being swept away by the bicycle; 'autocars' make an appearance only in the penultimate sentence, with the observation that they might perhaps become a serious competitor to the bicycle. Four months later the journal reported the Emancipation Run but paid it much less attention than it did the National Cycle Show at the Crystal Palace. In December 1897 an article was printed under the heading of 'Motor-Car Meet'. It observed:

> The second meet or parade of motor-cars proved at least that a one-year-old institution could celebrate its first birthday sturdily, even though it had not so far carried all before it. The year that has elapsed ... has not brought the motor so triumphantly into vogue as was at one time expected ...

While the *Spectator* thought that at any rate the motor dray (the van and lorry) would turn out a success, it considered the fate of the motor carriage and motor cab to be uncertain. Even people whom one might expect to have formed clear ideas were cautious or heedless. In 1898 Ebenezer Howard, the highly influential planner and the originator of the project for garden cities, published *To-morrow*. It includes a chapter on 'social cities' and discusses the crucial importance of transport. However, while Howard is expansive about railways and electric trams, astonishingly he does not mention the automobile at all. As late as 1905, a royal commission examining 'The Means of Locomotion and Transport in London' was woolly about motor traffic. Surprisingly, since two years earlier a chapter in George Sims's *Living London* could declare:

> Slowly, but very surely, the horseless vehicle, devoid of nerves, muscles and sinews liable to shock and pain, has effected a revolution in the traffic of our London streets ... The time is not far distant when all utilitarian vehicles as opposed to carriages used by London Society for pleasure and ostentation will take the form of road machines.

And indeed two members of the commission, one of them citing experience in Liverpool, formally dissented from the majority report, insisting that motor buses (in competition with electric trams) were likely to have an important part to play in urban transport.

It is no surprise that the most imaginative prediction by anyone — certainly by anyone not directly engaged with motors — came from H. G. Wells, who in 1902 published his *Anticipations of the Mechanical and Scientific Progress upon Human Life and Thought*. Wells's appreciation of the future for automobiles is impressive. He discusses the sense of personal independence which they will foster, the effect of the motor bus and the lorry, and the interrelation with the railways. He anticipates the role of the automobile in the spread of large cities and how the regulation of urban traffic will be necessary. He foresees motorways, adding that no doubt they will first be built in the United States and Germany. The automobile, Wells pronounced, will mean 'the end of steam traction by land and sea; the end of the Age of Coal and Steam'.

2

Mr Toad and Kindred Spirits

Martin Harper was the son of the village postmaster and blacksmith at Therfield, in Hertfordshire. Like his two brothers, he loved working with machinery, even though most of their work was limited to the shoeing of horses and repairing of bicycles. Nevertheless, Martin knew something of traction engines, for, aged ten, he had been allowed to act as 'red flag man', keeping a lookout for panicky horses as he walked in front of one or other of the two great steam traction engines employed locally to haul ploughing tackle. One day in 1896, along with his father, he was busy sorting out harness before storing it away for the winter, when he heard

an unusual noise gradually making itself noticeable, sometimes louder, sometimes almost dying away. It was coming along the road, up the hills and then down into the hollows. I looked at my father and saw that he was listening too. The thought of what it was then struck me and, with a yell, I was up and away, dropping a spanner as I went, and sending the fowls flying and squawking in all directions. I made for the road, coming out just opposite the Horse and Groom ... just in time to see and hear my first horseless carriage ... The autocarist waved to me in response to my excited cheer, and on he went with a slightly uneven engine beat, tuff-tuff, tuff-tuff, and every now and then a strangled bang along with a little puff of smoke.

It was an epiphany such as many were to experience. Some were much younger than Martin Harper. A. F. C. Hillstead, later to work for the Bentley brothers, was of kindergarten age when he was besotted by automobiles as a result of seeing the local doctor in his Benz, in a cloud of blue smoke, laboriously climbing Putney Hill in what he described as a series of violent spasms. Even J. J. Hissey, of an older generation, who so delighted in the comfortable and easy travel provided by the horse-drawn phaeton, was almost equally affected. To put it mildly, he was no lover of novelty. But he confessed himself bowled over by the fascination of speed. He describes his sensation as he opens wide the throttle of his car:

> For a time a strange illusion took place; it was as though the car was standing still, and the country it was that went hurtling past. There is joy in speed, and poetry in it, and danger in it too. But a rush at full speed in a motor car over a lonely road, and through a deserted country, wide and open, is an experience to be ever afterwards remembered. Truly, for such a moment life is worth living.

Even those who lived for horses (that is, when there were no pheasants in the offing) were bitten. Osbert Sitwell remembered staying as a child at his uncle's house at Blankney in Lincolnshire. This was Henry Chaplin country, for the godfather of British motoring was master of the local foxhounds. (It was presumably at Blankney that Osbert's sister Edith disgraced herself by asking Chaplin, who was 'excessively startled', whether he preferred Bach to Mozart.) But Chaplin was not needed to promote motoring, for the younger generation represented in the house party — and some of the older one too — were passionate about speed and the opportunity offered by the car. Sitwell accompanied his mother and her friend, the famous Edwardian beauty Lady Westmorland, on an eleven-mile drive to Lincoln. It was hardly credible, they thought, that such a journey could be made in half an hour. They approached the towers of Lincoln Cathedral, he recalled, 'with the same sense of venture and modernity with which today [1946] the air-minded descend on Africa or America'. These drives were romance, to be compared to the night drives of King Ludwig of Bavaria.

The Sitwells, their cousins and their friends were rich; you had to be in 1903, the year of which he is writing, to afford a car. It was for this class that the Badminton Library published *Motors and Motor-*

Driving. While there were already motoring magazines in existence — the *Autocar* (established in November 1895), the *Automotor Journal* and the *Motor Car Journal*, for example — *Motors and Motor-Driving* was not trade press and it was a book not a journal. The Badminton Library had been founded to fill a gap, to provide an up-to-date encyclopaedia of British sports and pastimes. Since 1885 it had published books on hunting, racing, tennis, mountaineering, fishing, golf, coursing and falconry, among others. (One of them was *Driving*, edited by the Duke of Beaufort, which was about horses and carriages. In fact, that remained the word's connotation for years.) The Badminton book on motoring was to be the last in the series and was very successful: its edition of April 1902 was followed by reprints in May and December of that year, and again in August 1903, July 1904 and May 1906.

Motors and Motor-Driving consists of a number of articles, well written and very readable even today. The writers include familiar motoring names such as S. F. Edge and Charles Jarrott, who deal with mechanical design, and Charles Rolls writing on the petrol engine. The book opens with a survey of motoring history by, appropriately, a Frenchman, the Marquis de Chasseloup-Laubat. The press chief Alfred Harmsworth, more than anyone responsible for publication of the book, contributes an article on 'The Choice of a Motor'. Sir David Salomons writes on 'The Motor Stable and its Management'.

How to dress for motoring gets a lot of space. The Baron de Zuylen de Nyevelt, president of the French Automobile Club, reassures his readers that since he spends part of every year in England he knows what is and what is not acceptable to English gentlemen. He is aware, for instance, that they would not want to wear uniforms. Lady Jeune, a famous hostess, writes for women. She addresses a fundamental difficulty. Women, she recognizes, for most sports and pastimes, dress with a view to making themselves attractive; it is one of the reasons that has led them to take up outdoor sports so enthusiastically. Motoring is different, its rigours — at a time when most cars were hoodless and none insulated from conditions outside — made it almost impossible to find clothing which was both suitable and becoming. An accompanying photograph illustrates her point: it shows a woman with a veil to protect her complexion which is so opaque that it all but totally obscures her face.

Both Lady Jeune's husband, a distinguished lawyer, and J. St Loe Strachey write on how road speed — motorized speed — is quite different in its nature and in the sensation it gives from railway speed. For Jeune, the railway opens out to the traveller a great expanse of scenery but allows no sense of foreground. To the road traveller, on the other hand, foreground is everything, for he can perceive the thousand sights of beauty which lie right under his eyes. Strachey, with particular felicity, advances the same argument:

> No one can travel down fifty miles of an English road without coming upon a hundred beautiful and unexpected things, and seeing those things in the best possible way and as they ought to be seen. When we see scenery from the railways, or, at any rate, the near-at hand scenery, we are, as it were, looking at the brocade of the landscape on the wrong side. We see the pattern awry and upside down.

Years later, Osbert Sitwell pronounced tendentiously in one of his travel books that the constraints of rail travel were responsible for what he called 'that curious, slow inflexibility of mind' characteristic of nineteenth-century writers.

For Strachey motoring will bring into existence a new kind of travel. It is not, he says, that the car will be a rival or a destroyer of the railways: the train will be used for long journeys, the car for shorter ones. That was an illusion to be shared by government and public, not to say railwaymen, for a long time. Indeed, Strachey contradicts himself when he urges the advantage of the automobile for the seaside holidaymaker. Up to now, he says, how complicated and wearisome it has been taking the family to the seaside. There is the getting to the station, the transferring of household and luggage from main line to branch line, and the changing of transport over again before arrival at the final destination. A lot of trouble would be saved, Strachey asserts, if the householder were to engage a light motor car for himself, his wife and his eldest daughter, a motor brake for the children and servants, and a light steam van for the luggage, bicycles, buckets and spades, and perambulators.

Strachey's holidaying family is clearly affluent. John Scott-Montagu, shortly to succeed as Lord Montagu of Beaulieu and father of the present Lord Montagu, writes directly to the upper class. Like David Salomons, he was an engineer; like Salomons, he

was to become the spokesman for motoring and its leading representative in Parliament. It is inevitable, he declares, that every country house of any size, and nearly every private carriage owner in London, will have a car of some sort in the future. He is inclined to think that for town work it may be an electric car; there is probably nothing safer,

A luggage van with chauffeur at Polesden Lacey in Surrey. Careful preparation was necessary for transporting luggage to the railway station, given the high risk of breakdown on the road.

he says, on the streets of London today. However, his chapter 'The Utility of Motor Vehicles' is concerned with the country and the change in its way of life that will be brought about by the petrol-driven car. At whatever distance you may live from your station in the country, the motor is bound to shorten the time it takes to get there. What an anomaly it is, Scott-Montagu argues, that the country gentleman may travel by train from his local station to London, a distance, say, of 100 miles, in about two hours, but that the six miles from the station to his house may add another hour to the journey. In ordinary weather the car would cut the time by half, while with frost or snow the saving would be even greater. Moreover, the car permitted a much more interesting social life: 'Perhaps you are surrounded by a few near neighbours of whom you have seen almost too much ... [now] you can lunch with your neighbour five-and-twenty miles off as easily in 1902 as in 1892 you could meet your friend living seven miles from your door.' Scott-Montagu then turns to sport: 'You have often in Scotland a lodge near your forest where the stalking is good, and possibly a few brown trout in the burn below.' A car will extend your range so that it may now be feasible to reach that easy fishing which perhaps is there, ten miles further on: 'The new mode of locomotion will make river, loch, and forest accessible from the same centre.' For shooting game he recommends the purchase of a 6 or 12hp wagonette to carry loaders.

If you ate enormous meals, at least with a horse you could hope to work them off. Potential motorists might reasonably be worried about the effects on their health of a more sedentary life (sedentary, that is, so long as you employed a chauffeur/mechanic to do the cranking, to change tyres and carry out running repairs). It is a question addressed by Sir Henry Thompson, a distinguished doctor, who remembered the old steam vehicles of the first part of the nineteenth century. 'The easy jolting which occurs when a motor-car is driven at a fair speed over the highway conduces to a healthy agitation,' he affirmed; 'it "acts on the liver", to use a popular phrase, which means only that it aids the peristaltic movements of the bowels and promotes the performance of their functions ...' On the other hand, motoring could not vie with riding in exercising leg muscles, and sitting still in confined space could cause stiffness or cramp, particularly for older people. The eighty-one-year-old Sir Henry recommends his readers to follow his example: stop after twenty miles and run smartly for two or three hundred yards. He is reassuring too about psychological and physiological effects. He claims that motoring is an antidote to insomnia and that he has 'known instances of ladies suffering from defective nerve power who have derived great benefit from the invigorating and refreshing effect of meeting a current of air caused by driving in an automobile'. Some years later, the German *Meyers Grosses Konversationslexikon* made the same point, pronouncing that 'a highly advantageous effect on the nerves goes hand in hand with the beneficial relaxation caused by scenic landscapes and the unburdening of the internal organs'.

This, though, was controversial ground. To many committed motorists the excitement was less easy to come to terms with. For an impressionistic description, it is hard to beat Octave Mirbeau, the influential French novelist and critic, who recorded his reactions to a trip he made in 1906 with a companion and a chauffeur through parts of France, Belgium, Holland and Germany. His journal was first published in 1908, with drawings by his friend Pierre Bonnard, under the title *La 628/E8*, the licence number of the car, a 1904 Charron. The motor car, Mirbeau asserts,

> is all whim and fancy; it engenders incoherence, forgetfulness. You set out for Bordeaux and that evening you are in Lille ... The speed of travel confuses impressions, batters the mind and upsets one's balance. When you get out of the car after a twelve-hour drive, you feel like a patient recovering from a fainting fit who gradually resumes contact with the outside world. Objects are distorted and refuse to stand still. Your ears hum as though assailed by hordes of buzzing insects. With an effort, your eyelids blink open to reality, like a curtain slowly rising to reveal a stage set. So what has been happening? You retain only the vaguest impression of empty spaces ... You have to shake and pinch yourself to make sure there is solid ground underneath, that you are surrounded by buildings, by people talking and going about their business. Only later in the evening, after dinner, do you really come to.

And speed becomes an addiction:

> Motoring, it must be admitted, is a disease, a sickness of the mind. And it has a very pretty name — *la vitesse* ... [The motorist] cannot keep still — quivering nerves taut as springs, impatient to be off again the moment he arrives, in agony to be somewhere — any-where — else.

The novelty, of course, had its own appeal. That had much to do with the success of Percy Richardson, a pioneer car salesman recruited by the Great Horseless Carriage Company (an associate company of British Daimler) in 1897. It was August, and Richardson discovered that most of the people wealthy enough to afford cars were away in Scotland for the shooting. It was, he thought, an unpromising start, for to him Scotland was more or less a foreign country, lying somewhere near the North Pole and inhabited 'by bekilted natives, full of Scotch and haggis'. Anyway, after a week's training in motor mechanics, he set off in a Daimler from Coventry, settling at an hotel in Edinburgh, where he consulted the hall porter. Together they studied the *Scotsman*, ran down the list of the various shooting parties, selecting as most promising the house party of 'Sir Charles —' in that several titled people were among the guests. The house and estate were located in the region of Balmoral and took two long days' driving at 12mph to reach. When at last he arrived, Richardson brushed himself up, left the engine running — 'for to start an engine in those days was no light joke' — and rang the door bell. He told the footman who answered what he had come about, only to have the door slammed in his face. Richardson, a true salesman, waited ten minutes and then tried again, this time shoving his foot in the door and announcing loudly that the matter was one of extreme importance. Luckily Sir Charles himself heard the commotion and appeared in person. Richardson explained. 'Do you mean to tell me, young fellow, you've driven that contraption all the way from Coventry?' exclaimed Sir Charles, and called all his guests into the hall to hear. The upshot was a magnificent success. For two hours Richardson gave trial runs in the park and answered myriad questions. He stayed a week and ended up with deposits for four cars and a pocketful of introductions. To his boss in Coventry it appeared too good to be true, and he was summoned back by telegram to explain in person what was happening.

Most people, even if there was no question of their affording the new machines, were curious and, initially anyway, enthusiastic. One early motorist remembered that when he and his wife went out to dinner, the rest of the party invariably came to see them off. In 1897, a year after the Emancipation Run, Henry Sturmey, co-founder and editor of the *Autocar*, set out to publicize motors and to offer reassurance as to their reliability. He undertook a 1,600-mile tour from John o'Groats to Land's End, and then back to Coventry, driving a two-cylinder Daimler — tiller-steered with solid tyres — borrowed, along with a mechanic/co-driver (sustained by some driving lessons) from the Daimler Company. His account of the trip was published immediately afterwards under the title *On an Autocar … through the length & breadth of the land*. For protection — he started in October — he carried with him three heavy waterproof coats, thick mufflers, fingerless gloves and an umbrella. He also took a cycling guide and numerous spares for the car. Petrol stores were organized along the route. The car and its crew were a sensation. After a false start — ten miles out the engine was close to boiling over — and accompanied by valiant bicyclists striving to keep up, they set off in intense cold, with rain, intermittent at first, then coming down in torrents. Breakdowns were frequent but the crowds enthusiastic. News of their expedition went on ahead and at Inverness they found half the pop-

ulation waiting outside their hotel. Their experi-
ence with horses was mixed. In the traffic jams at
Edinburgh they found the horses around them
Early motoring scene as visualized by the anti-motoring press in 1902.

quite calm, and their noisiest encounters were with yelling juveniles
and 'hobbledehoys'. However, later on, there was more trouble and
on one occasion they were confronted by a furious driver of a pony
and trap who insisted that they should have been preceded by a man
with a red flag. 'Don't you know that *that* is a locomotive?' he
demanded. But the cheering crowds more than made up for such
upsets. At Bodmin in Cornwall, they were given a public reception:
'The whole town appeared to have turned out, and a big cheer went
up as we turned into the main street, the windows of the houses
being occupied by people who yelled and cheered, and waved hats
and handkerchiefs frantically.' In the later stages of the journey they
achieved around sixty miles a day.

Sensibly, Henry Sturmey had equipped himself in advance with
'Save Trouble' cards, which he handed out to the crowds who surrounded his Daimler and bombarded him with questions. They give
an excellent idea of how much, or rather how little, people generally
knew about automobiles at the time. In bold letters the card was
headed 'What is it?' and there followed a series of answers to the
most commonly put questions: 'It is an autocar', 'Some people call it
a motor car', 'It is worked by a petroleum motor', 'The motor is four

horse-power', 'No, it can't explode — there is no boiler', 'It can travel at fourteen miles an hour, but ten to eleven is its average pace', 'Speed is mainly controlled by the foot', 'The car can carry five people', 'It can get up any ordinary hill.' The card also explained that it was driven by benzoline and needed filling up every sixty miles, and that it was made by the Daimler Company of Coventry and cost £370 (nearly £25,000 today).

Breaking down as frequently as they did, automobiles provided the man in the street with a lot of fun. It was a real laugh when horses had to be fetched to pull them out of ditches or drag them home. However, after a short time a reaction set in. Motor organizations and writers needed to take pains to reassure the public and police and magistrates about the effect of their noisy machines on horses. After all, they argued, horses had soon accustomed themselves to bicycles. S. F. Edge, out with Evelyn Ellis on their pre-Emancipation Run, declared that out of the 133 horses they had encountered only two ponies showed signs of alarm. But it was clear that reassurance was not going to be easy. On another occasion, Edge, out with Charles Jarrott, was stopped by the driver of a dogcart who slashed at him with his whip. (The fracas ended in a fight won by Edge.)

It was not only the horses which were terrified. Less sophisticated human beings could have the same reaction. Lord Kingsburgh told a good story in one of the Badminton chapters. A Colonel Magrath claimed to have met in Ireland:

> an elderly woman on a quiet road, proceeding to market. She got dreadfully startled at seeing the car, and when she arrived in Wexford told everyone that she met a carriage from the other world, with a horribly ugly demon driving it, and she knew at once that the carriage was sent to take her to hell, but, thank God! she had sense enough to make the sign of the Cross, when carriage and ugly driver vanished.

One pioneer motorist declared that, in the country, he had seen 'timid women run right away to the very centre of a field perhaps a quarter of a mile distant, at the approach of a motor'.

Rudyard Kipling, a keen motorist, recalled real hatred. 'Earls stood up in their barouches and cursed us,' he said. Gypsies cursed them too. The foreign antecedents of automobiles were held against them, with the car labelled 'a foreigner's plaything'. One witness declared, 'Every old woman, in the country, all the old women upon the [magistrates'] benches, rural vicars, notoriety-hunting members of Parliament, those interested in the stable, farmers, horse-dealers, cab proprietors ... cried out loudly' for the suppression of motors. (In fact, the MPs did not need to be 'notoriety-hunting'; they were, it seems, deluged by mail from irate constituents.) Oddly, one of the most hostile groups was hotel keepers, people after all who stood hugely to gain from a revival of road traffic. One of them told Lord Montagu that he was not going to have one of those 'contraptions' near his place — it might blow up at any moment. In the popular mind, all automobiles were still steam-driven, a harking-back to the road steamers of earlier days. Even when cars were accepted at hotels and inns, they were liable to be discriminated against. The first edition of the *Guide Michelin*, published in 1900, and listing hotels and garages throughout France (particularly those which stocked Michelin tyres), noted that certain hoteliers had the cheek to charge for garaging cars while taking carriages in free. It urged motorists to refuse to pay and to invite the hotel to sue them.

The year 1902, when *Motors and Motor-Driving* was first published, marks something of a watershed. A novel *The Motor Maniac*, of the same year, saluted a new trend. Motoring, whatever the views of much of the population, was becoming fashionable. The book's heroine, eager to persuade her lethargic husband to buy a car, pronounces, 'Granted that, a year or two ago, only people in the trade and manufacturers went about on [sic] motor-cars; but all that is of the past. The King has set the fashion, and now even the smart set are waking up to thinking horseless vehicles the thing.' The conversion of that natural speed freak, King Edward, was of great importance. He had been given his first drive in the grounds of the Imperial Institute as Prince of Wales, but his real experience was due to Lord Montagu. In December 1901, the King ordered a new all-British car with twice the horsepower of his existing, foreign, car. It meant that he could cover the journey from Marlborough House to Windsor as quickly as by train, although it was another five years before he achieved a car capable of carrying him at 60mph. In the mean time, so the magazine *Car Illustrated* reported, he added to his 'stud' of cars a fourteen-seater Daimler intended to transport loaders for shooting. Special cartridge boxes were supplied with the car, to be fitted under the seats.

King Edward VII, when Prince of Wales, with Lord Montagu in the latter's 12hp Daimler, 1900. The King violently resented being overtaken on the road by other motorists.

Car Illustrated, a weekly, was founded by Lord Montagu in May 1902. He was also its editor. Even before that, Montagu had proved a tireless advocate of motoring, pressing its commercial possibilities on Arthur Balfour, the Prime Minister, who was anyway himself an enthusiastic motorist. While in Monte Carlo, Montagu discussed development possibilities for Bexhill, a Sussex seaside town, with its principal landowner, Lord De La Warr. The magazine, however, was directed towards private motoring and its target readership was high society. Advertisements from leading estate agents such as Hampton's promoted country residences especially suitable for motorists 'being within a speedy run of town, on good roads'. It showered on its readers photographs, with accompanying text, of the grandest of grandees. The King of course, who figured at the start of the first number, pictured in Montagu's car. There were Lord and Lady Wimborne at their country house, Canford, their cars in the charge of an engineer and four assistants. Lily Langtry was reported to be an ardent motorist who — in spite of Lady Jeune — wore lovely clothes for driving. A very enthusiastic 'chauffeuse' (which meant that she could drive herself) was Mrs Claude Watney, seen wearing a coat of sable-heads, 'a creation of Paquin's Paris house'. Later editions of the magazine showed the Countess of Carnarvon and the Countess of Dudley. (Women and women's clothes were a very important feature.) Sometimes things were taken rather too far: Lord Salisbury, for instance, appears, although it seems he had only been out in a car twice. There is also Marie Louise Hart, aged eleven, pictured taking a girl cousin for a drive on country roads around Luton in her electric run-about. Unsurprisingly, she is 'probably the youngest "chauffeuse" in England'.

In town and country, announced T. H. S. Escott, a well-known writer on society and fashion, 'the motor has become as much a part of a courtier's baggage as is the cigarette case'. The secret of its popularity, he said, lay as much in its intricacy as in its high cost. The *Sketch* announced in unctuous terms a new royal convert to motoring — this time the Prince of Wales, who up to then had been 'somewhat indifferent'. *The Motoring Annual and Motorists' Year Book*, in addition to the King and Queen and other members of the British royal family, listed the Shah of Persia and the King of the Belgians as keen motorists. The Empress of China, it reported, had been 'badly smitten with the motoring fever'. And the Kaiser, an even more likely addict than his uncle, King Edward, drove through Berlin, his horn sounding a distinctive 'tatoo, tata'. The annual's column 'Who's Who in Motoring' included some of the familiar pioneers, and others such as the Marquis of Anglesey, whose car, a 22hp Mors, it considered one of the most handsome in the country. No wonder, since its interior fittings were of solid silver and the exterior of silver plate. (In fact, Lord Lonsdale sent his Mercedes back to Germany when he found that its fittings were plated with chromium and not silver.) Sir Daniel Gooch had so reconciled his nine carriage horses and hacks to the motor 'that they will eat hay off the car while the engine is running'. Some, however, clearly did not relish this type of publicity. The Duke of Bedford, for instance, who in the 1920s and 1930s was to be famous for his retinue of cars and chauffeurs, allowed himself only a very cursory appearance. The duke was a wary motorist in the early days. About to make an unfamiliar journey, he sent out a chauffeur well beforehand to check how long it would take. When the time came to go himself, he took along two chauffeurs, since once he had been stranded a long way from home when his driver had broken a wrist trying to work the starting handle. The Duke of Portland may not have resorted to such thorough preliminaries but he did possess six cars serviced by twelve chauffeurs. Actually that was by no means excessive, since no gentleman, it was said, thought of having fewer than three cars.

Yet there is no doubt about who is the most famous Edwardian motorist. A character from a children's book, the fictional, outrageous Toad of Toad Hall. His name has entered the language to represent selfishness, self-indulgence and even, because of the resonance of his name, a self-satisfied nastiness. In fact, in Kenneth Grahame's *The Wind in the Willows* he is not altogether unpleasant, and turns out in a dotty way to be very enterprising. He resembles many of the real motorists of his time whom his creator sets him to satirize. Toad is a natural enthusiast, a dilettante, very conceited but with a sense of humour, and, when not carried away by some new whim, quite shrewd. He is rather touching. He lives in a large riverside house, and when Rat and Mole first call on him, they see, as they glide up the creek towards it, the remnants of his last passion but one — a number of fine-looking boats, slung from the crossbeams or hauled up on a slip, but none in the water. The place had an unused and a deserted air. What new fad has he adopted now, they wonder in trepidation. They discover quickly enough. Toad has taken up caravanning. So, with a smart new caravan led by an old grey horse, the three of them set off down the high road.

> They were strolling along the high road easily ... when far behind them they heard a faint warning hum, like the drone of a distant bee. Glancing back, they saw a small cloud of dust, with a dark centre of energy, advancing on them at incredible speed, while from out of the dust a faint 'poop-poop!' wailed like an uneasy animal in pain. Hardly regarding it, they turned to resume their conversation, when in an instant (as it seemed) the peaceful scene was changed, and with a blast of wind and a whirl of sound that made them jump for the nearest ditch, It was on them! The 'poop-poop' rang with a brazen shout in their ears, they had a moment's glimpse of an interior of glittering plate-glass and rich morocco, and the magnificent motor-car, immense, breath-snatching, passionate, with its pilot tense and hugging his wheel, possessed all earth and air for the fraction of a second, flung an enveloping

cloud of dust that blinded and enwrapped them utterly, and then dwindled to a speck in the far distance, changed back into a droning bee once more ...

The Rat danced up and down in the road, simply transported with passion. 'You villains!' he shouted, shaking both fists. 'You scoundrels, you highwaymen, you — you — road-hogs! — I'll have the law on you !' ...

Toad sat straight down in the middle of the dusty road, his legs stretched out before him, and stared fixedly in the direction of the

Toad of Toad Hall welcoming his guests in the drawing by Ernest Shepard for Kenneth Grahame's *The Wind in the Willows*. Fictional, but nevertheless the most famous of Edwardian motorists, Toad, like many of them, was a menace on the road.

disappearing motor-car. He breathed short, his face wore a placid, satisfied expression, and at intervals he faintly murmured 'Poop-poop!'

Toad is converted; he becomes, as he proclaims, the 'Terror of the Highway'. He wrecks a series of cars and, before his final redemption, is sent to prison.

Perhaps most people, at some period of their lives anyway, have something of Toad in them. His of course is a burlesque of road rage; a more common form was King Edward's extreme dislike of being overtaken by another driver. The motoring establishment, the Badminton writers and the organizations such as Sir David Salomons's Self-Propelled Traffic Association and the Automobile Club, formed to represent the interests of motorists, were fully aware of the lethal potential of automobiles roaring along roads animate with children and the old and infirm, not to mention poultry, dogs, cats, sheep and the like, none of them accustomed to anything which travelled at more than ten miles an hour. Regularly they urged motorists to be careful, reminding them how much they depended on the public's goodwill. Some pioneer motorists like Captain and Mrs Kenneth Campbell took pains to convert critics. You can usually get rid of their objections, Mrs Campbell wrote, 'by taking them for a spin of a few miles', but always, she said rather boldly, drive at high speed. It appears that the joys of speed could overcome misgivings. Largely, however, advice fell on deaf ears. There seemed to be a Toad everywhere. The excitement induced by speed, the prospect of the open road, could carry away even the most apparently conscientious and respectable citizen. Casualties from road accidents mounted. Even the highly sensitive Octave Mirbeau confessed:

> When I am in the car, possessed by speed, humanitarian feelings drain away. I begin to feel obscure stirrings of hatred and an idiotic sense of pride. No longer am I a miserable specimen of humanity, but a prodigious being in whom are embodied ... Elemental Splendour and Power. And given I am the Wind, the Storm, the Thunderbolt, imagine with what contempt I view the rest of humanity from the vantage-point of my car.

At the start, however, even the experts did not anticipate the pace at which motor technology would advance. In 1937, speaking on the

BBC, Charles Jarrott recalled a banquet given to celebrate Emile Lev-assor's victory in the 1895 race, Paris to Bordeaux and back, accomplished at an average speed of 14mph. At this dinner one of the speakers predicted that a speed of 20mph would be attainable in the course of the next few years. Monsieur Levassor's comment was, 'There's always *someone* at this sort of banquet who makes some ridiculous remark.'

Not only was the car exciting to drive, it was a dazzling status symbol. Unlike pictures, furniture, bank balances, even one's house, it displayed wealth so publicly. In this respect it was more like jewellery and guns perhaps: indeed, when car sales boomed, the demand for jewellery and guns dropped, and vice versa. How well the car suited people like the 'magnifico' Cyril Flower, Lord Battersea, generous and popular, and married to a Rothschild. His friend the writer E. F. Benson described him out on the road: 'On his motor there was a horn which when the bulb was pressed, emitted gay bugling sounds. He loved to tear about the country at sixty miles an hour, and sitting beside the chauffeur, to press the bulb on coming to a corner or passing through a village.' Then there was Field Marshal Sir Henry Wilson, who enjoyed driving his open Rolls-Royce about London, forcing taxi drivers on to the pavement. And the braggadocio that went with it all. The 'Motor Lie', declared one writer in 1904, was enough to make even a fisherman tell the truth in disgust. Or as another was to put it, 'I should pay little attention to eulogies by an archbishop if he happened to be the owner of a car.'

Gentlemen know how to behave and how to drive with consideration for others, claimed a correspondent to *The Times* in September 1907. The problem, as he saw it, was that so many cars were owned by people who were not gentlemen. Actually, though motoring mania and bad driving could strike anyone, it was true that so obvious a symbol of wealth was bound to be attractive to those intent on rising in the social scale. It was a reason for the suspicion with which many of the upper class treated motoring in the ever-snobbish Edwardian decade. Looking back from 1933, Mrs C. S. Peel recalled that the more established people refused to allow cars to be brought to their front-doors; the motoring visitor was required to leave his or her machine outside in the road. The arrogance shown by motorists became closely associated with the plutocrats, the new, commercial rich — very rich indeed, some of them — who loomed so large in late Victorian and Edwardian times, and were so resented by the old aristocracy enfeebled by the effects of the prolonged agricultural depression. G. W. E. Russell, a member of Liberal governments in the 1890s and no reactionary, described the plutocrat as wholly urban by nature. He would have a country house, but he did not often inhabit it and would anyway contrive to turn it into a larger replica of a London house: 'Bridge rages from morn till midnight; the telephone bell tinkles without intermission, and telegrams fall like autumn leaves.' The plutocrat does not really care for any sort of sport, but he may go in for shooting 'for it smacks so agreeably of wealth.' Russell goes on:

> What he really enjoys is motoring. For him the motor must have been invented. It combines every element of life which he most enjoys — luxury, ostentation, insolence, and the sense that he is envied and admired ... It brings the glare and noise and swagger of London into the 'sweet, sincere surroundings of country life.'

A younger Liberal politician, C. G. F. Masterman, wrote what is possibly the most significant book of the Edwardian decade. In *The Condition of England*, he warns of the political dangers associated with the motor car:

> Aristocracy in England has been kindly and generous. Even as in part transformed into a plutocracy, it provides little of that attitude of insolence to the less fortunate which is the surest provocation of revolution. The action of a section of the motoring classes, indeed, in their annexation of the highways and their indifference to the common traditions, stands almost alone as an example of wealth's intolerable arrogances, and has certainly excited more resentment amongst the common people than any extravagance of pleasure or political reaction.

A writer in the *Contemporary Review* in 1902 observed, 'it is only since the coming ... of the motor car that class distinction has been set up all over the earth.' Even the *Tatler* rebuked *Motors and Motor-Driving* for its apparent refusal to register the fact that there existed people with less than £10,000 a year. An MP declared that for the first time since the French Revolution the working class looked on

the wealthy as 'an intolerable nuisance'. In the United States, Woodrow Wilson, then president of Princeton, deplored the advent of the automobile as likely to incite socialism. And Walter Long, president of the Local Government Board, declared in 1907 that 'there was an embittered feeling in the general public against all persons who use motors, which as a dangerous class feeling is perhaps without parallel in modern times'.

Dust thrown up by car at a time when the roads, long-neglected, were unable to cope with motor traffic.

One problem of course was that there were inevitably a great many bad drivers. Apart from the professionals, mechanics and chauffeurs, few people had more than the vaguest idea about how cars worked. One country parson bought a second-hand Benz Ideal, imagining somehow that it needed no attention. He filled the petrol tank with water and dealt with lubrication by dropping a minute amount of bicycle oil on to the piston. Later motorists can get away with hardly more mechanical knowledge than the parson, but in times when cars were extremely unreliable and needed constant maintenance, such ignorance was wholly unrealistic and could prove lethal. Another serious drawback was the rudimentary state of the long-neglected roads. It was not necessary to drive as fast as Toad and his friends to throw up the clouds of dust, at least in summer, which affected both those in the car (more properly on the car) and those on the streets or highway. 'The difficulty and horrible discomfort of passing a car raising clouds of dust beggar description' were the words of man-about-town George Cornwallis-West. Dust in those days, once stirred up, could hang over the road for hours. The dust problem caused great resentment and was a factor in political debate on automobilism. Nor were early motorists endearing to look at: the elderly Irishwoman of Lord Kingsburgh's anecdote had been as much scared by the 'horribly ugly demon' of a driver as by the machine he was driving. They looked awful, with their heavy layers of protective clothing often reeking of oil and with their 'hideous goggles almost like a gas mask'.

There were, then, good reasons for employing a chauffeur, and, after all, the rich had always employed coachmen. Even an expert like Charles Jarrott sometimes took a mechanic with him, especially if he was driving an unfamiliar car. The most basic functions could be hard to deal with, anything could go wrong. King Edward was motoring in France when the gear lever of his car snapped off; it was not easy to find a replacement swiftly. Charles Jarrott remembered his alarm when his brakes failed on a hill while he was driving a tiller-guided car. Cars were difficult to start — it was a work of art, said one pioneer motorist. To put it mildly, the Duke of Bedford's chauffeur was very far from being the only person to injure himself while cranking the engine. Cornwallis-West, returning from Knole to London at night with his wife, Jennie (Winston Churchill's mother), drove by the light of two acetylene lamps. One burst into flames at once, the other followed suit, so they continued the journey by the light of a small electric torch. (It was the more tiresome since these lamps and the side and tail lamps were a great deal of trouble to light in the first place.)

Breakdowns and punctures were incessant. E. F. Benson described staying, along with other guests, for a weekend where the host's car was a 'hoarse tremulous monster of most uncertain gait'. The house was ten miles from the nearest railway station. When the time came for the party to break up, a cart, loaded with the guests' luggage, was sent on ahead an hour and a half before the time of the train. Twenty minutes later, it was followed by the car carrying those guests who, in Benson's words, were daring enough to trust themselves to it. A quarter of an hour after that, a brake set out, drawn by a pair of fast horses, so that if there was a problem with the car, the stranded guests could be picked up and delivered to the station. On this particular occasion, Benson noted, the car behaved surprisingly well, in spite of the fact that it had to stop each time a horse-driven vehicle appeared on the road.

Actually, the invention of the car had a marked effect on week-end parties, destroying, so some people argued, the old group spirit. It was difficult to know where you were; you could not count on guests staying the full course. 'The party is in a ceaseless state of metabolic flux', considered Lord Ernest Hamilton. You came down at breakfast and found that your charming neighbour at dinner the night before had already left for some other country house. A replacement of course might turn up, but she was only too likely to find it difficult so late in the day to adapt herself to the mood of the party.

For the motorist it was not just a question of putting up with abuse and ridicule. There were the police and behind them the local magistrates, who were likely to share many of the same prejudices. They indulged them freely, not exactly inhibited by the fact that fines for motoring offences alleviated the local rates. In the days before emancipation you could hardly blame them. For instance, Mr T. R. B. Elliot, the first automobilist in Scotland, was allowed by the chief constable of his own county, Roxburghshire, to use a car without undue restriction. However, one day, or rather one night, he drove to Berwick-upon-Tweed, arriving at 3 a.m. and settling down by the town hall for a picnic. He was interrupted by a posse of thirteen policemen, who charged him (successfully) for having driven without being preceded by a man on foot. (Although one wonders, given the hour, whether they thought he was drunk.) But even after the passing of the 1896 bill, police harassment of motorists continued unabated. In 1899 there was the case of Mr Lyons Sampson, charged at Slough for failing to stop — as the law required — when the driver of a horse and cart signalled him to do so. Sampson had slowed down but claimed he had not seen the driver's signal. It turned out in court that the cart had been waiting in the same place for three-quarters of an hour with a police constable in plain clothes standing by the horse's head. It was a put-up job. The magistrates had to dismiss the case, but they in no way blamed the police and refused to grant Sampson costs. Another case concerned Charles

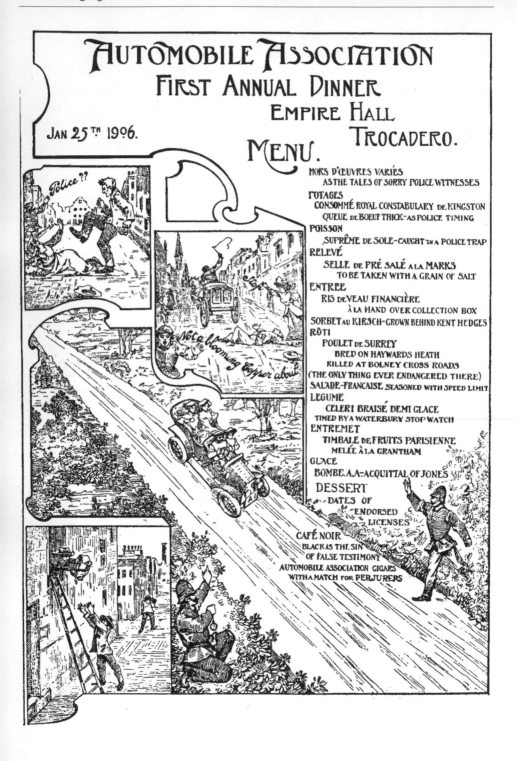

Jarrott, who was accused of driving at over 12mph in a remote part of Norfolk. The whole affair was a farce. The key witness, a policeman, identified Jarrott's solicitor (who was cross-examining him) as the driver of the car, while another policeman selected some harmless member of the public who happened to be present. In any case, Jarrott had been a passenger, not the driver, at the time. None of this stopped the magistrates from finding him guilty and imposing a fine.

In view of the vulnerability of motorists to what they considered persecution, several bodies came into being to protect their interests. The Automobile Club, founded in 1897, emerged as the most important. Socially, it was very grand. The Duke of Sutherland, at one period owner of four Rolls-Royces at the same time, and son of a Marquess of Stafford who had run steam coaches commercially in the mid-nineteenth century, was president. Sir John Ellerman, soon to be even richer than the duke, was a member, as were Lord Montagu, Lord Battersea of the 'bugling' horn and Hiram Maxim. Other members included royalty and two prime ministers, Rosebery and Balfour. The club established itself at Whitehall Court, and later in Piccadilly, and issued a handbook which *inter alia* reminded members that they were required to pay a tax of two guineas (£2.10) for armorial bearings portrayed on their cars and a licence fee of 15s (75p) for the male servant they employed as driver. The club organized exhibitions, lectures and tours, but in character it was essentially a gentleman's club of the old school to which women at first were not admitted. The women therefore set up their own organization, the Ladies' Automobile Club, with premises at Claridge's, which provided a Red Drawing Room and a White Drawing Room, and also a 'Silence Room' where members could conveniently work on their motoring accounts. In addition there were two bedrooms for the use of country members.

The Automobile Club was undoubtedly influential, but it was wide open to the charge made by the *Daily Mail* that it was almost as unrepresentative of the road as the Jockey Club was of the turf. Nevertheless, it set up the Motor Vehicle Users Defence Association to assist members brought before the courts on motoring charges, and through a subsidiary employed cyclists and later motor cyclists to act as patrolmen to

Opposite: The menu for the first annual dinner of the Automobile Association, formed above all to protect members against what was regarded as persecution by the police.

warn members of imminent police traps. But increasingly there was conflict between groups within the club, notably between those with commercial interests and those who were purely 'consumers'. There was disagreement as to whether the club should accept a fee to act as patron of the annual motor exhibition at the Royal Agricultural Hall in Islington. Some members wanted to support a rival Crystal Palace exhibition. Above all, with a membership which by 1904 had reached 2,500, there was friction on how far the club should go in appearing to oppose the law. In 1905 the split came: the patricians stuck to the Automobile Club and restrained opposition to public authority, while the remainder formed the more militant Automobile Association. The breakaway was an indication that the days of motoring as an exclusive, rich man's pastime were already coming to an end.

By then there were many more motor vehicles on the roads. The number of cars had doubled to 16,000 in a single year. By 1907 it had doubled again, and by 1909 the total had reached 48,000. In addition, there were now a substantial number of buses, taxis and goods vehicles. The spread of motoring was reflected in books on touring. An example is *Motor Days in England* by an American, John M. Dillon, which was published in 1908 and related to trip made a year or two before. It started with the usual troubles — breakdowns galore and a supposedly expert mechanic sent from London who knew nothing but nonetheless charged heavily for what he did not know. Dillon ran out of petrol on one occasion but managed to borrow some from another car. He complained about the difficulty in identifying the road he wanted, and throughout his trip got lost in any town of size. The roads, he reported surprisingly, were usually free of dust, and excellent though always twisting, but he strongly advised motorists from abroad to equip themselves with non-skid tyres and to fit chains to their rear wheels. Road surfaces were often greasy and slippery because of the frequent rain. But Dillon and his party enjoyed themselves. At Blenheim, they found the Duke of Marlborough had put his estate out of bounds to motorists, by reason, so Dillon gathered, of his dislike of the smell cars made. (Another duke apparently had closed his park after being coarsely and violently abused by a motorist.) However, Warwick Castle made up for any disappointment at Blenheim; Dillon was struck by the incongruity of seeing cars placed against the background of the 'ancient pile'. Even though views were sometimes spoiled by the tall hedgerows, the party was unperturbed, agreeing that they added variety to the landscape. Those members of the party who were already familiar with England were particularly enthusiastic about the motor trip, claiming that it enabled them for the first time properly to appreciate 'real' English life and customs.

Dillon made good time and reflected that a modern car of average power might be expected to cover 125 to 150 miles a day. He gives the impression that motoring had become altogether more comfortable. It is striking that at mid-decade, when cars were appearing in much greater numbers, he found the roads still astonishingly empty. He states, indeed, that he and his party came across no other cars at all, on the country roads or in the towns they passed through, during a seven- or eight-day journey from Bath to Brighton. But he adds that, according to an acquaintance who had made a similar trip more recently, 'nowadays motor cars are too numerous to count' and that it showed how popular 'the sport' had become in a very short time.

Certainly there is a sharp contrast with the experience of J. E. Vincent, who in 1907 set out on a tour of East Anglia in a powerful and lavishly equipped Rolls-Royce, accompanied by two daughters and a mechanic, and with Claude Johnson, a partner in Rolls-Royce, doing the driving. For the first 300 miles or so they were free of trouble, but after that they suffered continuous difficulties. Vincent commented ruefully that the old saying about troubles never coming singly, that it never rains but it pours, is never more justified than in relation to motoring. He was at one with Dillon in deploring the lack of signposting. He needed to take along a mechanic to pilot him out of Cambridge, which was not a particularly large town. The roads to Ipswich were shockingly bad and, unlike Dillon, he suffered from some 'foul' dust. Moreover, traffic was heavy (although of course it is difficult to be sure what rated as 'heavy' in those days) and he found it difficult to find anywhere to park in Ipswich. People in the streets were more sophisticated and, Vincent remarked, pedestrians no longer scurried out of the way when you blew your horn.

Given his numerous journeys, J. J. Hissey is the best source for comparisons. Back on the road again in the Edwardian decade, he recounted his experiences in three books, published respectively in 1906, 1908 and 1910. For Hissey, the car now rates as 'a thoroughly reliable conveyance provided it is a well-built model and properly driven and cared for'. He sees cars everywhere, observing, 'Wherever goes the road to any interesting or famous spot mentioned in the guide-book, there comes the conquering car ... The main roads are once more alive again with traffic, and the motor-horn is heard all over the country.' By now the days were past when a mechanic was a necessary adjunct to a journey. Not that Hissey had ever used one; 'a motorist,' he said, 'who takes with him that ever-present nuisance a mechanic knows nothing of the real charms of motoring'. Anyway, overcoming a breakdown was the spice of motoring for which 'the possibilities of an adventure lend a zest to a journey.' What impressed him most, he wrote, was that, unlike a horse, a machine never tired. Nor did it bolt if left unattended. He remarks early on the demographic changes induced by the automobile, which were later to be of such enormous importance. At Batemans in Sussex, the home of Rudyard Kipling, he observes that Kipling would never have bought so remote a place had it not been for the car. Indeed, he discusses the point with a local estate agent whom he comes across. The agent tells him:

> There is quite a boom in such property ... property of this class, that it was very difficult to deal with at all a few years back, is now readily saleable, provided it is situated in at all pretty country. Not long ago, nearness to a railway was almost an imperative condition of my clients; now, very often, the stipulation is, 'well away from the railway'.

In his autobiography Kipling supplies some background. When in 1902 he had safely signed up for Batemans, the man who had sold it to him asked Kipling how he expected to get to the station, which was four miles away. 'I've used up two pair of horses on the hill here,' the man said. Kipling's answer, as he pointed to his Lanchester, was, 'I'm thinking of using this sort of contraption.' 'Oh,' said the other, 'those things haven't come to stay!' Years later, the two met again and Kipling's predecessor confided that had he realized at the time what was going to happen, he would have asked twice the price.

There were drawbacks to the opening out of the countryside. Hissey stopped at an inn where there appeared a noisy party of six from Hastings in an equally noisy hired car. The landlord called their attention to the splendid view. 'We've come here for refreshments, not to see a view,' was the response, and, as they left, Hissey heard them question the driver of their car about how far it was to the next pub. He must have been the more dismayed since he adored old country inns; their recovery was to him an almost unmixed blessing. For finally the innkeepers and hoteliers had discovered which way their bread was buttered. In his 1910 book Hissey describes the process:

> The landlords of the country inns began to open wide their eyes with delighted surprise, and forthwith to refurbish their premises, not before they wanted it. Profitable customers had come again their way. The ostlers were at first none too sympathetic; but finding that the motor car meant money, and that soon the motor cars outnumbered the horses even at an increasing rate, they philosophically accepted the situation, touched their forelocks as deferentially to the arriving motorist as to the horse-driver, and pocketed their tips contentedly.

The accommodation in many inns and hotels needed bringing up to date for, as J. E. Vincent said, the motorist required baths and bathrooms. Hissey would no doubt have approved of that, but sometimes his conservative instincts revive. For instance, he is not at all pleased to find that the Olde Whyte Harte Hotel at Broadway in Worcestershire has changed its name to the Lygon Arms. However, he is not too unhappy when he comes across an old coaching inn now announcing in big, bold letters that it was the Motor House. Perhaps he recalled his scepticism of ten years before when he came on pubs called the Cyclists' Rest and the Cyclists' Arms.

In his 1908 book *An English Holiday with Car and Camera*, Hissey mentions stopping at an hotel in Exeter and finding the yard filled with cars and not a horse to be seen. Twelve years on from emancipation the automobile had come into its own. It was much more comfortable, it was easier to drive and it was reliable enough to do away with not only specialized mechanics but also the need for annual replacement. The significance of a charming book, *The Woman and the Car*, published in 1909, is that it can truthfully assure people — all people, though as the title shows, it is intended primarily for women — that motoring is no longer a mystery reserved for enthusiasts and those who positively enjoyed scrabbling underneath a car on the high road in the rain. Its author, Dorothy Levitt, famous for her lunch parties, was a 'bachelor girl' living in a flat in what was described as a quiet but fashionable part of the West End, with housekeeper and maid and small dog. She was a keen rider to hounds, an excellent shot and an inveterate first-nighter, pretty and 'modest almost to the point of bashful'. She was also a champion motor-boat racer and in 1906 had broken the women's land speed record, driving a car at 96mph. What is notable about her book, commissioned as a result of articles she had written for the *Daily Graphic*, is its simplicity, its naturalness. Motoring is represented as an enjoyable pursuit open to everyone, without the encumbrances of chauffeurs and mechanics. The book is not bland: for instance, she recommends that her readers follow her example in keeping a revolver in their car; also a hand mirror — not as protection against human predators but in order to check from time to time whether there is another car behind you. There is no talk of 96mph; she suggests that women start their driving life with a small car, an 8hp, single-cylinder De Dion voiturette, which combined simplicity with reliability. It was cheap to run, with a petrol consumption of 28—32 miles to the gallon. They should join the Automobile Association because of police speed traps; they should beware of car salesmen and second-hand cars. She is reassuring about dress for women. Only on long roads when travelling at speed are goggles and masks necessary; normally what the 'motoriste' requires is an overall with long sleeves. Women, she adds, can learn map-reading and mechanics just as quickly as a man. Starting the engine is a matter of getting the knack.

Towards the end of the book Dorothy Levitt allows herself more latitude:

> there is no country in the world in which woman may be seen at the helm of a motor-car so frequently as in England. Whatever the cause — whether it be due to a greater sense of security from annoyance on public roads or simply to superiority of pluck, the fact remains that women in England excel their sisters in other countries as greatly in motoring as in horsemanship.

If in some ways Dorothy Levitt seems to herald the freer spirit of the 1920s, here she speaks as an unmistakable representative of her time. And, in the same frame of mind, she desires to reassure her readers how respectable (i.e. fashionable) motoring has become. Nevertheless, while a member of high society, she shared fully in that spirit of camaraderie which, not only in Britain but everywhere, so infused enthusiasts and gave such impetus to the development of motoring. The inventors and designers, the manufacturers and assemblers, the chauffeurs, the racing drivers, professional and amateur, and ordinary car buyers — worked in close cooperation. John Moore-Brabazon, one of the most remarkable of early motorists, wrote in his autobiography, 'I think we were all a little mad, we were all suffering from dreams of such a wonderful future.' Rudyard Kipling declared that everyone was learning together. Nobody knew anything about anything. When his Lanchester broke down, there was a furious exchange of telegrams with the manufacturers; but then the two Lanchester brothers would come down to see him and his wife as friends —'we were all friends in those days,' he said — and would sit round the hearth speculating on what the problem could be. (Lanchester's after-sales service was excellent. The Campbells broke down on a trip to Scotland, needing replacement parts. They were on the road again within something like twenty-four hours.)

The racing drivers were particularly important. S. F. Edge, a friend of Dorothy Levitt — he spotted her during her first competition drive and enrolled her as an (amateur) works driver for the manufacturing firm of Napier — was a highly successful racing driver as well as a formidable salesman, and never doubted that the spectacular driving possible on the race track provided marvellous publicity. To Charles Jarrott, motor-racing in its early days was the greatest sport evolved by man. Particularly exciting were the great continental road races, which came to a sudden and disastrous end with the projected race from Paris to Madrid in 1903. Two hundred and sixty-eight cars started. There were appalling casualties, with fourteen people killed and many more injured, both among drivers and spectators. Jarrott remembered 'cars in fragments, cars in fields, some upside down, others with no wheels'. The French government stopped the race at Bordeaux and insisted that the cars be taken to the station by horses and sent back to Paris by train. From then on, racing was confined to circuits, of which the most famous in Britain was at Brooklands at Weybridge in Surrey, established by a local estate owner, Mr Locke-King, with the support of an influential committee chaired by Lord Lonsdale and which included the dukes of Beaufort and Westminster. It is worth noting, though, that the sense of fellowship at Brooklands was not wholly uninhibited. Except for Montagu and Jarrott, the committee knew nothing much about motoring. They were horse-racing grandees and originally insisted that drivers, like jockeys, should wear coloured shirts and caps, and should not be allowed into the club-house bar.

Motor-racing provided enormous excitement to drivers and spectators. But its importance in the longer term lay in the publicity and in its influence on car design. The underlying intention was 'to prove to the world that that motor-cars would go, and that they were capable of travelling long distances in a reliable and speedy manner'. The pressure on manufacturers was intense. New cars were built for each event; technical improvements appeared one after another, with the racing car of one year becoming the touring car of the next. In Jarrott's words of 1906, 'There can be no question but that the motor-car of today owes its very existence to racing.'

Motoring altered human life so swiftly that generalizations are often valid for only a very short time. (Hence the lavish sprinkling of dates so evident in this chapter.) What was true in, say, 1902 was likely to be out of date by 1905. The automobile itself was transformed in a mere ten or twelve years from the primitive 'horseless carriage' — a third of the entrants could not even get started on the Emancipation Run to Brighton — into the type of vehicle which, internally and externally, was the obvious precursor of the automobiles we have today. Yet however profound its consequences, then and throughout the twentieth century, the place of motoring at the forefront of technology lasted no more than a few years. Aviation took over. Less than twelve years after the Emancipation Run, John Moore-Brabazon became the first Briton to make a powered flight. As a schoolboy at Harrow he had cut school to watch the Automobile Club's Thousand Mile motor trial pass by. At Harrow too he witnessed his first fatal accident: a car, braking too fast as it came down a hill, capsized, with the driver killed and the passenger badly injured. Moore-Brabazon 'with pride' turned off the burners and the ignition, and stopped the engine. He went on to Cambridge to study engineering, acquired a motor bicycle, and spent the vacations working as a mechanic for Charles Rolls. He was a highly successful racing driver and winner of the 1907 Circuit des Ardennes. As it happens, his comment, quoted above, about all being 'a little mad' was made with flying particularly in mind; but he would have regarded it as applying equally to motoring. The affinity between motoring and aviation was close — most obviously in the common use of the internal combustion engine, but also in the ease with which devotees slipped from one to the other.

Lord Montagu and the outstanding automobile designer Edward Lanchester were closely involved with aviation, and indeed in 1905 the former offered land on his Beaulieu estate to embryo aeronauts. Brooklands was an airfield as well as motor-racing track. Charles Rolls, Moore-Brabazon's mentor, was killed flying. Lord Northcliffe was an enthusiastic supporter of the Wright Brothers (described by Moore-Brabazon as inventive and imaginative, typical of technicians of the sort you could find almost anywhere). Claude Johnson of Rolls, Montague Napier and F. W. Lanchester were enthusiasts, while the wine merchant Frank Hedges Butler, the original treasurer of the Automobile Club, founded the Royal Aero Club in 1901. He reckoned that in the next seven years he made 100 or so balloon ascents. Among the motoring grandees listed by Dorothy Levitt was the Hon. Mrs. Assheton Harbord, a Rolls-Royce driver, who had, by the date of the book, competed in seven races in her own balloon, 'The Valkyrie'. Winston Churchill, who was to be much embroiled with motoring and motorists in the 1920s, told Wilfrid Blunt in 1909 that he was sympathetic to his complaints about the 'motor car tyranny'; but anyway, said Churchill, flying machines will have superseded cars in ten years' time as an amusement for the rich.

Such was the force of the scientific and technological revolution of the time that it was difficult for anyone to forecast what would happen. Some of the changes, in physics and medicine for example, were for the moment at any rate more or less wholly benign. So, without the qualification, was the introduction of wireless telegraphy, electric power and streetlighting, and the modest vacuum cleaner. But the advantages of the revolution in transport, the advent of the automobile, the aeroplane and the submarine, were more debatable.

There was much more resistance to Lord Montagu's Motor Car Bill of 1903 than there had been to its predecessor. It was accused of promoting 'government of the rich, for the rich and by the rich'. In the House of Lords, one speaker, complaining that speed limits were simply ignored, quoted a story in the press about two foreigners in a Mercedes who enquired at a police station how far they were from Birmingham. Told they were thirty miles away, one said to the other, 'Then we shall do it in about half an hour.' A Scottish member, Mr Weir of Ross and Cromarty, though, was sensible enough to understand possible advantages and asked the minister to see whether motor cars might be placed on the roads between Carloway and Stornaway and between Ullapool and Ross 'for purpose of assisting the fishing and other industries'. The bill went through, providing for an increase from 12mph to 20mph in the normal speed limit, with provision for stricter local limits. Other clauses introduced driving licences, and an increase in the weight limit for automobiles, a matter of great importance since it made motor bus and freight services more practicable. The new law also stipulated that motor road vehicles should be registered and numbered. Until then, the car had been identified by the name — sometimes painted on the car — given to it by its owner. Kipling, for instance, called his steam Locomobile 'Coughing Jane' and the Lanchester which replaced it 'Amelia'. It was seriously suggested during the passage of the bill that such a system was adequate and should be made permanent.

The Motor Car Act recognized that the automobile was here to stay and that the law affecting it needed adjustment. The general election of 1906 marked a further step forward. The *Motorist and Traveller* magazine declared that 'the predominant feature in connection with the General Election has everywhere been the motor-car' — a wild claim perhaps, given the particular importance of that election in British politics. Nevertheless, the widespread use of cars to encourage voters and to bring them to the poll attracted a great deal of attention. (One of the few Unionist gains, that at Hastings by Harvey du Cros, was attributed by the *Daily Mail* in large part to the eighty cars he mobilized.) Another event, or rather a non-event, showed how strong the momentum was. In 1908 the Local Government Board sent a circular to county councils and town councils, 'prompted by the numerous representations ... respecting the danger and annoyance not infrequently caused by the driving of motor cars'. The board (of course) acknowledged that many of the complaints were justified, but insisted the answer must lie in a stricter enforcement of the existing law. That was happening, it claimed, though nobody seemed to notice much change. Otherwise, authorities should look to improving roads and modifying dangerous corners. Nothing much there to disturb the motorist. In fact, nothing much anywhere, except in the Swiss canton of Graubünden, which in 1900 prohibited automobiles altogether and continued to do so until 1925.

By the time war broke out, the automobile was triumphant and the Automobile Club was now the Royal Automobile Club. The number of cars on the road had continued to increase rapidly. From 1909's 48,000 it had risen to 88,000 in 1912 and 106,000 by 1913, to reach 132,000 in 1914. This description of holidaymakers on the Whitsun Bank Holiday in 1913, published in the 'Automobile World' column of *Country Life*, might have been drawn from the 1920s:

> Thousands of motorists seemed to have made up their minds to do a tour at Whitsuntide, whatever the weather might be, and, so far as the West Country is concerned, I have never seen more traffic on the main roads nor more crowded hotels at the popular stopping-places. To sit for a few hours outside some big hostelry in any of the country towns in the West and watch the arrivals and departures afforded the best possible illustration of the change which the motor has made in the habits of a large section of the population.

There was disquiet. Wilfrid Blunt was not alone in his hostility to the 'motor car tyranny'. Most articulate among the intellectuals was G. Lowes Dickinson, who wrote an article under that heading in the *Independent Review* which was timed to coincide with the tenth anniversary of the Locomotives on Highways Act. To quote from it:

> For some ten years the people of this country — as of all countries — have been groaning under a public nuisance which increases day by day until it has reached a malignity and magnitude altogether unprecedented. Their property has been depreciated; their senses offended; their comfort destroyed; their security invaded. The amenity of the country has been indefinitely impaired; the discomfort of the town indefinitely increased. The citizen who does not motor has become a kind of outlaw on his own highways.

Lowes Dickinson quoted as witnesses an estate agent who declared that the herbage near the Bath Road in the neighbourhood of

Windsor was ruined, and an 'author', Miss Everitt-Green, who complained that dust had ruined all her plants, inflamed her eyes and throat, and wrecked her typewriters.

But Lowes Dickinson, Fellow of King's, Cambridge, and a distinguished and charming humanist scholar, was ill-fitted to lead a counter-attack. He was a man who was always 'theorizing about life; never living', said Virginia Woolf. Unsurprisingly, his article, despite its clarion call of a beginning, petered out, for Lowes Dickinson did not really know what to suggest. Nor, it seems, did more practical men who worried about the effects of motoring; if they did, they kept very quiet. When it came to it, no one really thought that the automobile could be disinvented. Yet people were conscious that there was a price to pay for the undoubted benefits it conferred. Some regretted the loss of the picturesque carriage parade in Hyde Park. Many lamented the demise of the horse: Lady Jeune, the Badminton contributor, could write wistfully that there would always be 'a soft place in our hearts, and a saddened memory, of the faithful horse'. Her turn of phrase for its conqueror is apt and vivid — 'a monster in the stable who has to be exercised'. For some (as Dickinson said) the penalty was a drop in the value of their houses, for others it was the effect on the countryside, the introduction of that urban vulgarity, personified to J. J. Hissey by the pub-crawlers from Hastings. Then there were the figures for road accidents. In 1910 the number of fatal accidents caused by mechanically propelled vehicles was 644; in 1911 it was 844. It was the mortality rate and the dangers of the road generally that prompted *The Economist* to ask in its motoring editorial of 11 October 1911, 'has the invention of motors brought with it a balance of profit or pleasure? Would the nation as a whole be richer and happier if motor vehicles of all kinds had been absolutely prohibited?'

There was, though, one possible penalty about which the country needed to worry less than it had a few years before. Motoring seemed no longer likely to cause civil unrest or even revolution. If, in 1913, there were 132,000 cars on the road, there were also 51,000 charabancs and motor coaches. The opportunities and freedom offered by motoring were spreading, were becoming available to people lower down the social scale. Yet if this new form of mass transport symbolized relief from social tension, it symbolized too a price that would have to be paid. One returns to Osbert Sitwell's Blankney, to the heedless upper class, people who in the years before the First World War enjoyed a previously unimagined luxury and ease, people made happier, if not necessarily richer, by the motor car, and to whom it seemed

as though this world, new born, would last for ever. One thing alone in this panorama might have suggested — though only then to those prescient to an almost prophetic degree — its coming disintegration ... One object alone might have given them a vision of a civilisation falling to chaos, and of the cities they loved laid waste: the motor which sometimes tinnily vibrated and steamed in the frost outside the door; for this was the first appearance of the internal combustion engine which was to destroy them.

3
Upheaval

Motoring provided new pleasures and new opportunities, and, as the industry grew, employment which had not previously existed. However, there was one obvious penalty: the plight of those employed, directly or indirectly, in looking after horses and in the manufacture and maintenance of the vehicles they propelled. While the census of 1901 is not very helpful, that of 1911 allows a breakdown of employment figures. From a total of 471,000 vehicle drivers, it shows 404,000 employed with horses, 17,000 working with trolleys and trams, and 50,000 on motor vehicles. The surprising numbers still working with horse transport — surprising given that there were by then so many motors on the road — is explained partly by the difficulties experienced by business in conversion, particularly by farmers and hauliers. A better measure by which to establish the trend from horses to motor is the amount of money spent on new horse-drawn vehicles. In 1900 £1.2 million went on new carriages, in 1902 £800,000, in 1907 £400,000. By 1911 the figure had sunk to £200,000. After the war, from 1919, when there was a heavy burst of car buying, the figure for new carriages had statistically ceased to exist.

In 1902 a Dr Bruce Porter contributed an article to the *Car Illustrated* in which he calculated from his own experience that while the annual expense of renting and feeding a pair of horses, plus the rent of a brougham and the wages of a coachman, came to about £320, his car — reckoning on a four-year life — cost him £305. While he

supplies no figures, it is clear that his earnings have gone up, since he is now able to visit more patients. Indeed, the *Spectator* stated that a rural doctor, with a motor costing no more than a single horse and carriage, could cover a district that would tax the resources of well-filled stable. Dr Porter, however, is not a typical motorist. To start with, given his

The mud and discomfort of a tyre change. On his knees is S. F. Edge during the 1,000 Miles Trial of 1900. Edge, 'one of the great heroic figures of early motoring', was, like others, originally a racing bicyclist.

profession, he covered a lot of ground; for someone driving fewer than forty miles a week a horse and trap came out cheaper than a car. Moreover, he was competent to drive himself and even to carry out much of the demanding maintenance that a car required. Had he needed to employ a chauffeur, the car would have proved much more expensive than the carriage.

As the present Lord Montagu has pointed out, almost without exception, the people who bought the first cars were those who kept a carriage. Their attitude to automobilism was entirely shaped by their experience with horses and very few knew anything about mechanics or electricity. The houses they lived in were heated by open coal fires and lit by coal gas or oil lamps. They were woefully ill prepared to deal with complicated machines, and as yet they were unlikely to have near to hand any local garageman who could help. (Though it is worth mentioning that drivers on the Emancipation Run came upon an enterprising blacksmith at the village of

Albourne Green who advertised 'Motor Cars Repaired while You Wait'.) So their coachmen and grooms and footmen, and sometimes their gardeners, were enrolled, taught to drive and, as far as possible, to absorb the rudiments of car maintenance. While the motor manufacturers might be willing to help with training, these often involuntary recruits found it difficult to drop old habits such as shouting out 'Whoa!' when they wanted to stop. And frequently, as Martin Harper found, they were far from enthusiastic about their new responsibilities. After his inspirational encounter with the autocarist, Harper rushed off to Cambridge to learn about motoring. One day he was summoned to help with a Locomobile Steam Carriage which had broken down on the Huntingdon Road. The owner had departed, leaving his coachman/driver in charge. The poor man could drive the machine but he could do nothing else. He described to me, recalled Harper, 'the tremendous advantages of horseflesh over these new-fangled, smelly and dangerous contraptions, and predicted an early return to commonsense by his master, and all others caught up by this rage for horseless carriages that seemed to be overtaking so many young gentlemen nowadays'.

Some of those who switched jobs adapted easily, busmen from the old horse buses being an example. They were used to heavy traffic and able to come to terms with their new machines after a month's training. The economic historian Sir John Clapham remembered one busman explaining to him that he and all his colleagues were from the horse buses 'with their whiskers shaved off because of the oil'. Drivers of horse cabs were not so fortunate, and in 1909 Lord Rosebery initiated a fund to provide relief for those left without work. They were 'a stiff-necked, sporting class of men' not given to compromise and change. Some did learn to drive motor cabs, but most went down 'with their whips flying'. And clearly, whatever the merits of the coachmen and grooms, and whatever the genuine attachment that often existed between them and their employers, it must have been difficult to cope with the new demands. For one thing there were the unremitting breakdowns. Writing in July 1900 to Lady Elcho from Downing Street, A. J. Balfour reported driving back to London from the country. His car suffered 'a mild breakdown about every three miles, and finally when we arrived within striking distance of home, we betook ourselves to hansoms, leaving the little French chauffeur in tears of mortification'. French chauffeurs were supposedly experienced and provided one solution. Another was recommended by Alfred Harmsworth, in the form of a motor engineer, someone who — perfectly — was a combination of gentleman and engineer. Martin Harper became one of these, employed for many years by Lionel Rothschild, one of the pillars of the Cambridge Automobile Club, which was founded and financed by undergraduates at the university. Harper's job was to accompany Rothschild in his car and to carry out immediate repairs when it broke down. Sometimes he acted as a spare driver. How 'motor engineers' fitted into the overweening snobbery of Edwardian England, which held professional engineers to be grubby, oily members of a lower order, is not entirely clear, and certainly the Automobile Club — the London one — recommended owner-drivers never to wear peaked caps in case they should be mistaken for chauffeurs.

So a new breed of employee emerged, men who had little in common with either Balfour's 'little French chauffeur in tears' or the gentlemanly 'motor engineer', let alone with the remoulded coachman. An example appears in Bernard Shaw's *Man and Superman* of 1903 in the shape of the chauffeur Straker. The notes to the play describe him as being cool and reticent and not at all deferential, keeping his employer and his employer's friends at a distance while giving them no excuse for complaint. He gives the impression of knowing the world well from the seamy side. Straker is proud that he has been educated at a polytechnic as an engineer, and remarks sardonically, 'Very nice sort of place, Oxford, I should think, for people that like that sort of place. They teach you to be a gentleman there.' He loses some of his aloofness only when he hears that an American steam car has got ahead of him on the road. Another version, a rather rougher one, of what Octave Mirbeau called 'a new zoological species' was Mirbeau's own driver, Brossette:

> Brossette is pure motor trade. He can't distinguish too well between what is mine and what is his, and deliberately mistakes my purse for his own ... He is an excellent travelling companion, amusing, resourceful, attentive without being servile and, apart from his fanciful bookkeeping, utterly loyal.

'Chauffeurs,' said Mirbeau, 'exert a magic on the minds of cooks and housemaids that is almost as irresistible as a soldier's. This magic has noble roots: it stems from the nature of the job, which they regard as heroic and dangerous, just like war itself.' Brossette is very efficient in his work. 'At a crossroads he raises his head, studies the horizon, sniffs the breeze, then resolutely takes one of the half dozen roads ahead — and it is always the right one.'

These two portraits are reasonably sympathetic. The general reputation of motor drivers and the motor trade, in Britain and in France, was very poor. There was the story of a potential buyer going out with a salesman for a trial run in a Daimler. Suddenly the car caught fire, with flames shooting upwards to the height of a lamppost. The salesman blandly assured the would-be buyer that this was merely a clever device for warming up the engine. Hard-featured and sharp-tongued, was Osbert Sitwell's opinion of the trade's representatives. One experienced British motorist of the day declared, 'No industry in the world has given birth to such unscrupulous rogues as the motor-industry.' Mirbeau's view was, 'The motor trade is still on the fringes, with a reputation akin to that of the gambling den and the brothel.' In much moderated form, the poor reputation has lingered. For instance, there is the case of the affair between Wallis Simpson and Guy Trundle which has recently come to light. Mr Trundle, according to *The Times*, was well bred and charming, yet 'he may have rented a Mayfair flat next door to where the present Queen was born, but he was still in the motor trade'.

However, as the industry became more organized, as automobiles proved more reliable and customers more experienced, and as trained mechanics and drivers became more numerous, so was the need for the 'new zoological species' less urgent. The law of supply and demand reasserted itself. The days were gone when 'any youngster who hung about a motor factory and picked up a little driving knowledge was sure, sooner or later, of a "job" upon a car'. In his 1910 book J. J. Hissey reported that a crowd collected around him once when he stopped for petrol in a small Shropshire town and that it took 'as much interest in the car as though it were not the common object of the road it has become'. On a similar occasion in Sussex the younger members of the village crowded round, calling out to each other 'a motor-car, a motor-car'. Hissey reflected, 'In the old times the youthful population of places who watched with eager eyes the coming and going of the coaches all desired to be coachmen; today the height of their ambition is to be motor-car drivers.' (In one way, though, the car did not replace the old mail coaches: it was not as they had been, the bearer of news, through whom villages first heard of war and peace, of battles and political crisis.)

So the trade had no choice but to turn more professional in its attitude and behaviour. Mr A. E. S. Craig of the Putney Motor Company was one of a number of people to offer their services. His company could provide technical advice and help with arbitration, and, if required, expert evidence. Craig also advertised mechanical and driving tuition 'for a limited number of pupils'. He even wrote a book entitled *Motor Driving for a Living.*

In his book Craig sets out the types of job available. One category of course comprises chauffeurs to private motorists, another drivers for commercial travellers — an employment, he warns, which may entail living in lodgings for six days a week. His pupils can qualify as lorry drivers or bus drivers, they can take charge of delivery vans or motor boats. There is a category for 'professional work': Craig specifies doctors and, a period touch, 'theatrical and music hall artistes, who use a motor to crowd more turns into a night's work than they are able to do with a horse cab or brougham'. Another, very separate, category is that of the 'fiercely-goggled fiend, the racing man'. While this particular employer may be prepared to pay £10 a week, beware. His chauffeur can find himself travelling at 100 miles an hour at the mercy of a man who may have had too much champagne the night before. Craig has some other useful advice about drink: when filling out a job application, if possible write in 'a life abstainer', or if that is going too far, try 'abstemious all my life'. He insists on the dignity of the driving profession. Dress should be restrained: goggles, for instance, are only necessary — this being 1905 — in summer in a fast car; the fact that some car owners dress up to look 'something between an overgrown goat and a door mat' is irrelevant. A chauffeur should be careful not to accept a job which involves part-time work as a valet or gardener. 'Such positions', says Craig, 'should be left for Chinese or other amiable aliens.' And thinking of foreigners, he is able to report that the craze for foreign drivers is noticeably diminishing. A good thing too, he feels, making no bones about that — 'their chief occupation is the consumption of cigarettes and their principal solace to complain of the climate and the cooking'.

The French might be on their way home, but they had already left their imprint on the language of automobilism. 'Garage' was one of their words and so was 'chauffeur', which derived from the man who stoked — *chauffer* — the steam cars of the 1880s. Like a modest version of the Académie Française, the Automobile Club strove to defend the language: 'chauffeur' was not a word used in their publications, and as far as 'garage' was concerned, what was wrong with 'motor stable' or 'motor house'? There was the same problem in Germany. Ford Madox Ford remembered (or said he did; he could be unreliable) sitting in a hotel at Boppard on the Rhine when the local garrison commander, arriving with great flourish, pointed to the hotel's sign of 'garage'. He declared that if the objectionable Gallicism were not removed he would put the hotel out of bounds to his officers. That would have ruined the innkeeper, who, however, came up with a good riposte: the new sign read 'Kraftwageneinstellraum' — 'power-wagon-standing-in-place'.

Of course, each nation adapts what it inherits from another: 'chauffeur' came to be pronounced 'shuvver' in Edwardian English. Martin Harper heard the engine of his first car as 'tuff-tuff'; to the French, car engines went 'teuf-teuf'. (And to Toad they went 'poop-poop'.) However, the real source for nomenclature was the horse world. There were motorized (usually electric) broughams and victorias and landaulettes. 'Dashboard', 'boot', 'hind wheel' were inherited. It was not just a matter of borrowing names, for motoring relied on the past also for visual effect, for appearance. At the start, in 1896, the *Spectator* had forecast that 'the foolish conservatism which models the horseless carriage on the same lines as the carriage drawn by horses will disappear'. It took some time to do so. The cars of the 1890s were in effect carriages with motors and appurtenances added, just as a steam car used by Lord Caithness in the 1860s looked like a miniature railway locomotive with the engine facing backwards. Partly, the conservatism reflected designers' tastes, but no doubt apprehensive customers were reassured by what was familiar. Osbert Sitwell remembered the first motor charabancs (open-topped buses). The charabanc was built, he said,

> as though to be drawn by horses, it was the same height from the ground and, as one looked over the dizzy gap that hung above the almost invisible bonnet of the engine into space, one suffered the most violent feeling of disproportion, as though in a boat that ended flat, without a prow, for one missed the glossy animal extension of the carriage.

In 1897 the Worshipful Company of Coachbuilders and Harness Makers declared in the *Autocar* magazine that they saw no reason why anyone should expect a carriage propelled by a motor to differ in looks from the familiar horse-drawn model. That was not necessarily, however, the view of some of the leading carriage builders, of Mulliners, Barker, Hooper, and Thrupp and Maberley. Responding quickly, they prepared to diversify and to take the motor industry seriously. H. H. Mulliner in particular was alive to what was happening. He was present at the Emancipation Run breakfast, and became a director of Daimler and chairman of the London Electrical Cab Company. But the trade as whole was reluctant to change; understandably, since tied to the horse and carriage went a medley of usually small craftsmen such as blacksmiths, wheelwrights, spring makers, platers, brace makers, painters and curriers. What was more, the Boer War brought with it a surge in demand. Firms, especially those in saddlery and harness making, did very well. The time did not seem favourable to drastic change. To judge from the report of the annual general meeting of the Institute of British Carriage Manufacturers held in January 1900, neither the president nor any other speaker even mentioned automobiles. Two months later, there was at least a sign that the trade's eyes were not quite shut: the *Carriage Builders' Journal* (incorporating the *Wheelwright, and Saddlery & Harness Record*) carried a long article on the possible effects of automobiles on carriage builders. It was markedly patronizing.

The carriage builders believed — or many of them did — that the motor manufacturers were as dependent on them as they were on the motor trade. To an extent that was true. However, whatever they might look like, motor bodies were not the same as carriages: the strains and weighting were different. A test case occurred affecting the Lanchester Engine Company, manufacturers at the time of the most advanced British cars. Lanchester intended to buy their car bodies from outside but discovered that the body builders would not work to the very precise instructions formulated in the drawings and templates they supplied. When the body work was delivered, either it or the chassis to which it was to be fitted required alteration, with the result that production was held up. So Lanchester decided to make its own car bodies.

However unwilling to change many of these firms might have been, they were fortunate to have in the editor of the *Carriage*

Builders' Journal a man who was under no illusions. He insisted that 'every carriage builder [must] most closely study every movement of the motocar [sic] industry'. What did it matter if, as was alleged, car bodies were ugly — that should be regarded as an opportunity. The public was waiting to see how the trade would react. 'The policy of Mr. Micawber must be abandoned.' Anyway, in October 1902, fighting against the future as its members were, the journal changed its name to the *Automobile and Carriage Builders' Journal*. A couple of years later, recognizing reality in their turn, the Cycle Engineers Institution changed its name to the New Institution of Cycle and Automobile Engineers. Its first president was Herbert Austin.

Another section of society facing financial loss were those who actually owned horses and carriages. In fact, many of the owners were not individuals at all: they were firms. Dr Porter, the doctor who had written the article about the money he saved by switching to cars, mentioned that he had not actually owned his pair of horses or his brougham — he had hired them from a livery firm, usually known as a jobmaster. He wrote, 'nearly everyone now jobs horses as it is much less bother, and if the horse goes lame the jobmaster finds another to match the sound one'. The consequence, therefore, of this general trend was that much of the enormous investment in horses and carriages came not from consumers but from hiring companies. The largest jobmaster in Britain was Thomas Tilling, which provided horses and carriages and, if required, coachmen for dukes, clergymen, business firms — for virtually anyone, including the police and most of London's fire stations. Tillings also supplied forage and veterinary inspections. Some of their assets were in property, in stabling and in the south London suburbs, where they possessed a granary at Peckham and a clinic for sick horses at Catford. Tillings were also at risk as builders and owner-operators of horse buses. In 1897 they owned 4,000 horses and by the time they became a public company six years later the number had risen to 7,000.

When, in 1897, Tillings first altered their status, converting from partnership to limited company, the directors were prescient enough to reserve the right 'to introduce any present or future automatic inventions when (if ever) they may become of practicable utility'. Tillings is an example of a firm successfully adapting to new conditions, but doing so at great expense. While carrying on with their existing business, they invested heavily in taxis and motor buses. By

1905 they had twenty motor buses working the London streets. In theory, while the initial expense of 'motorisation' was considerable, running costs were less, for a horse bus or tram required ten to twelve horses to keep it going sixteen hours a day, with the horses requiring replacement every four years. Moreover, horses simply could not pull anything like so many passengers. Unfortunately, practice did not bear out theory. The running costs of the motor fleet proved heavy, for the first motor buses turned out to be notoriously unreliable and thus very expensive to maintain. Tillings' profits collapsed and nearly vanished. From a yearly average of £35,870 over the period 1900 to 1905, they fell to £28,000 in 1906 and to a dire £3,220 in 1907. From then on, however, Tillings began to reap the benefits.

One of the heavier costs of diversification into motor transport for Thomas Tilling was the conversion of stables and coach houses. Private individuals were faced with the same expensive problem. Dr Porter approached it with aplomb; he simply put up a 'car house' in his garden and rented out his stable. For the more fastidious, that would not do. Sir David Salomons, for instance, observing that a car was far more delicate than a carriage, undertook at his country house of Broomhill a comprehensive rebuilding which involved fire-proofing, improved insulation — coach houses were usually badly ventilated — the installation of electric light, the construction of an inspection pit and, along with it, a platform to allow the cars to be lifted off the ground. Stable doors everywhere were likely to need widening. With new houses of course, and many were built during the Edwardian decade, one could start from scratch. At Fulbrook, a country house at Elstead in Surrey, designed by Edwin Lutyens for Gerard and Ida Streatfield — she was a passionate motorist — there was a carriage house with an immense glass cover to allow for car washing. On the whole, though, new or old, there was seldom much flashy about these country-house garages. The spirit of toadism was largely absent; in fact, the spirit was often positively 'olde worlde', with the buildings dressed up in half-timbering and thatch. At Marsh Court in Hampshire Lutyens disguised the garage as a barn, and placed the electric power house in another barn behind.

In London in particular reminders of the horse world abound — occasionally in street names such as Cheval Place in Knightsbridge, Horse Shoe Alley on Bankside and Shoe Yard off Bond Street;

sometimes in resurrected horse troughs. In the mews they stare us in the face. These narrow, cobbled, pavementless alleys, with their dapper and expensive urban cottages, once provided the stables and coach houses of the affluent. They were also residential, for alongside the horses and carriages existed a community of attendants and hangers-on. In the middle of the nineteenth century, a French visitor observed how in London rich and poor lived in separate districts; when, in the wealthier areas, you came across the poor they were tucked away in the mews so that their unbecoming squalor should not upset the inhabitants of the grand houses to whom they were an indispensable adjunct.

It was a world in decline even before 1898, when Captain Sampson of Hyde Park Gate built himself a 'motor car house' in Queen's Gate Mews, just south of Kensington Gardens, and before the Grosvenor Estate in Mayfair was faced with a flow of applications from leaseholders who wanted to convert coach houses and stables into garages. This decline of the mews, at least in their original form, was the result of rising land prices in central London, and of improved public transport. It was influenced too by the widespread use of jobmasters, which entailed a greater centralization of stabling and coach houses. The arrival of the car, which required less space and fewer servitors, merely accelerated a trend.

If many of London's mews survive, occasionally as with the extensive Lancaster Mews in Bayswater in almost pristine (i.e. shabby) condition, other appurtenants of the horse age have vanished from the maps. For instance, a large block of land next to Captain Sampson's Hyde Park Gate shown in 1874 as occupied by a riding school has by 1914 been replaced by streets and houses. The coach-building firms dotted about Mayfair have also gone. Nevertheless, just as motors inherited the mews, so did the motor trade sometimes settle on old carriage trade ground. From Long Acre by Covent Garden, since the eighteenth century a centre of coach building, Mulliners in 1913 were advertising that they could supply every sort of chassis for fitting to cars. At Great Portland Street in the old days, N. & F. Thorn were reputed never to have fewer than 300 carriages in stock. Between the wars Great Portland Street was to be the hub of the British motor trade.

The switch from horse to motor can at times appear almost seamless. Even in 1902, it seems that London was crowded with car distributors, at least if one goes by Mrs Kennard's novel *The Motor Maniac*. The eponymous heroine — 'her head full of nothing but motors' — having convinced her husband of the need to keep up with the times, sets off on a tour of the 'motor shops'. What adds to the book's charm is that the motor shops she mentions are real ones. At first she can find nothing but the most expensive cars. There are 12hp Panhards priced at between £800 and £1,000 (£53,000 and £65,000 today). She goes to the Motor Improvement Company on Holborn Viaduct, where, not unnaturally, the foreman pooh-poohs the brands she mentions but which his firm does not stock. At the 'celebrated' Daimler's premises in Shaftesbury Avenue she encounters only contempt for Peugeot and Decauville and other well-known makes. The people there suggest she spend 1,400 guineas (around £100,000) on one of their products. She carries on to Tottenham Court Road, where the cars are much cheaper, and by tube to Holland Park. By now the motor maniac is thoroughly confused. Then she spots an advertisement for a modest Benz Ideal going second-hand. There are two problems. One is that the second-hand models are fitted with only a two-speed gearbox, while the new Benzes have three speeds. The other is that the car in question is to be found in darkest Whitechapel, a part of London she has never visited and knows of only as the stamping ground of Jack the Ripper. Anyway, she goes there, buys the Benz and hires herself an exquisite but dead-lazy 'motor boy'. (Mrs Kennard herself, it should be mentioned, drove a 40hp Napier, very much top of the range.)

But while London was an obvious place to buy cars, the heart of the British motor industry was elsewhere, in the Midlands at Coventry. This was a city with a long and remarkable history. To start with, it was the setting for one of the most vivid of the very few legends that recall pre-Conquest England — that of Lady Godiva, wife of the Earl of Mercia, Coventry's overlord. It is celebrated too in a major work of literature as the market town in George Eliot's *Middlemarch*. During the Second World War it suffered the most intense bombing of any British city.

In the 1890s Coventry was a city of old churches and new factories, where visitors remarked on the juxtaposition of old and new. 'From the electric tram-car you step into the most magnificent and venerable of parish churches' was how the *Illustrated London News* put it. But the ancient churches were an ornament to a city which

above all, throughout its history, was firmly commercial and industrial. In *Middlemarch,* its inhabitants, with a couple of exceptions,
are strictly business. Rosamond Vincy, one of the exceptions and
daughter of a manufacturer of silk braiding, yearns for socially
higher things, for the style of life associated with the country gentry
of the surrounding countryside. By rights she should marry a son of
another of the town's manufacturers. However, she despises such
young men, for they had 'not a notion of French, and could speak
on no subject with striking knowledge, except perhaps the dyeing
and carrying trades'. Coventry was — and remained — short of culture, but in 1830, the date in which the book is set, it could look back
on commercial success that in all probability predated Lady Godiva.
J. B. Priestley set out its history: in the thirteenth century, cutlery; in
the fourteenth, cloth; in the fifteenth, gloves; in the sixteenth, buttons; in the seventeenth, clocks; in the eighteenth, ribbons. In 1830
'ribbons', the silk weaving, still had twenty or thirty years to run.
Then it collapsed under the effect of free trade, with its abolition of
tariffs on imports. Coventry once more adjusted. It became a leading
manufacturer of watches until it was increasingly challenged by
Swiss and American competition. It made sewing machines until its
manufacturers found it hard to resist the onslaught of Singer. So,
when in 1868 Rowley B. Turner rode into the works of the Coventry
Sewing Machine Company on a French bicycle, there was spare
capacity. Enough to respond once more, and for the company to
produce their own version of his bicycle, which they then exported
to France. It was the start of a great boom during which Britain
became the leading exporter of bicycles in the world.

The bicycle was, so to speak, a cultural precursor of the automobile. It gave people a taste for a new form of transport and, through
the excursions into the countryside which it made practicable, a new
way of living, but one which would be gratified more rewardingly by
the automobile. (Of course, not everyone enjoyed bicycle excursions; Lady Ripon, for instance, did not really want to 'trundle
through rough country lanes, and listen to the cuckoo'.) There were
also technical legacies. Experimental work on cars was supported by
bicycle profits; and the pneumatic tyre, invented for bicycles, was
early on adapted for automobiles. And pioneer motorists such as S.
F. Edge and William Morris were bicycle-racing champions.

In 1896, when motoring became a feasible proposition in Britain, the craze for bicycling was at its peak, as the *Illustrated London News* bears witness. In his autobiography, *A Victorian Boyhood*, L. E. Jones remembered 'Singer, Rudge-Whitworth, Peugeot — only from the middle nineties could the names of bicycle-makers be remembered. But for a few years people bandied these names about as they now bandy the names of motor-cars.' At the same time, for these bicycle makers there were warning signals, indications of the increasing popularity overseas of cheaper machines, to which Britain, with its particular engineering tradition, might find it hard to adjust. Drawn by the potential of motor manufacture and the opportunity for diversification, firms in Coventry — and elsewhere — were to shift some or all of their production from cycles to cars. L. E. Jones's Singer and Rudge-Whitworth, and also Humber, Hillman, Rover, Riley and Swift, were in the forefront. Manufacturers in other types of engineering were to follow suit. The French-born Léon L'Hollier of Birmingham, maker of perambulators, acquired the British rights to Benz patents. The always-enterprising S. F. Edge teamed up with Montague Napier, who made coin-weighing machines in London, to produce Napier cars. By 1914 the two largest watchmaking companies, Rotherham and the Coventry Watch Manufacturing Company, were manufacturing automobile components. In the United States, the piano manufacturer William Steinway bought the Daimler rights. In France, Armand Peugeot, critically important not least in that he attracted Panhard-Levassor into automobiles, headed a metalworking firm which had developed into a large bicycle manufacturer.

Outside investors were in a buoyant mood. Between 1893 and 1897 the annual registrations of new companies more than doubled, with engineering sharing fully in the bonanza. Interest rates on government bonds were unattractive and the agricultural depression deterred those who might consider land. What is more, the traditional bias in favour of overseas stocks had been dampened by experience on Wall Street and the Baring crisis. During 1896 and 1897 there was enthusiastic buying of stock in bicycle and bicycle component firms, and in automobiles. There was of course a big difference. In the one case there was a comforting track record of profits and dividends, in the other such rewards were only in prospect. No car had yet been produced commercially in Britain. But cars and motor cycles had glamour, and an appeal to investors excited by the possibilities of a new technology. In fact, the investors of the 1890s were in a mood resembling that which so exhilarated their successors of a century later. It was a pre-play of the TMT — technology, media, telecommunications — boom of 1999 and 2000. Ardent investment was followed by heavy losses.

The man out in front of the field, and ready to spend a lot of money to stay there, was Harry Lawson, the organizer of the Emancipation Run to Brighton. Born in 1852 in the City of London, his father a well-known nonconformist preacher, he was an engineer by training. He certainly did not look like one. On the Emancipation Run he and his circle affected a yacht-squadron type of uniform, embellished with amber and gold armbands — the outfit of a 'Swiss Admiral' was Léon Bollée's comment. His more usual attire was a velvet smoking jacket. Lawson looked as if he would be good at public relations, and he undoubtedly was. It was the gift that enabled him to take his place at the forefront of the motoring movement in the months leading up to the 1896 Locomotives on Highways Act. Lawson's mind, said a friend, was inventive and financial. As to the first, he built a prototype of the 'safety bicycle', in essence the model we have today and which in its manufactured form was to be very popular with women. And he registered a patent for an automobile back in 1880. His flair for finance enabled him to raise money from the public on the flimsiest of prospectuses. His trouble, the same friend said, was that he was ill-suited to the technical detail of engineering. He was also a poor judge of people.

In his day Harry Lawson had lost a lot of money in bicycles and was in need of the stock exchange boom. Things were looking up, and he and his partner Ernest Hooley did well in the flotation of the Dunlop Company. In 1895, again in conjunction with Hooley, he founded the British Motor Syndicate. He then set up manufacturing subsidiaries, Humber, Daimler, the Great Horseless Carriage and the New Beeston Cycle and Motor. These companies went separately to the public for money. There were warning voices. *The Economist* for one was sceptical, finding — in today's language — the prospectus for the British Motor Syndicate far from transparent. The *Stock Exchange Gazette* minced no words, stating, 'the fact that Mr. H. J. Lawson is the controlling Spirit is a very bad omen for the company, and augurs a speedy acquaintance with the Bankruptcy Court'. Lawson followed the custom of decorating his boards with glittering, if hardly expert, names such as those of the Earl of Winchilsea, the

Duke of Somerset and Prince Ranjitsinhji, a famous Indian crick-
eter. Evelyn Ellis was included, who, though no businessman, at
least knew about cars and was a considerable investor. For a short
while, Gottlieb Daimler was a director of (British) Daimler, but as he
never attended a board meeting or took any part in its management,
his experience can have been of little use. Lawson was decidedly prudent as far as he himself was concerned: he raised £100,000 for
Daimler from investors but limited his own participation to £250.

Lawson, in the words of a recent authority on the British motor
industry, was not the sort of man you would buy a second-hand car
from. Actually, even had you wanted to, you would have found difficulty in buying any sort of car from him. The Great Horseless Carriage Company, for instance, got no further than producing five
Pennington autocars, the rights to which had been sold to Lawson at
a vast price. The company soon had to be reorganized and renamed.
As the *Economist* had spotted, there was nothing in the prospectus
for the British Motor Syndicate to suggest that Lawson was really
serious about manufacture. His intention was to buy up the rights
from foreign manufacturers such as Daimler and De Dion Bouton
and to live on licence fees. He certainly did not want anyone else to
manufacture either. There were clear conflicts of interest. For
instance, the British Motor Syndicate boasted that it was importing
more cars from the Continent than anybody else, while at the same
time it was supposed to be manufacturing its own. It also unloaded
much of the cost of buying up the old Coventry Cotton Mills
(renamed the Motor Mills) on to one of the subsidiaries.

It all fell apart. The inexperience of the directors, and for that
matter of the engineers, the confusion of aims and the fact that the
patents accumulated at great expense were soon rendered worthless
by the technical advances in motoring technology all contributed to
disaster. Harry Lawson himself was jailed for fraud in 1902 in connection with another venture and died worth virtually nothing.
Daimler and Humber among his motor companies survived but for
some years were much weakened. The effect of it all was to delay yet
further the establishment of a strong British motor industry and to
damage the reputation of what there was.

The Lawson débâcle did not bring down Coventry. It was too
strongly established for that and well placed with its excellent
communications north and south. It lay close to the industrial

conurbation of Birmingham and at the extreme south of the great industrial region which occupied much of the northern half of England. But driving southward from the city in 1900, possibly by car, more likely by horse and carriage, you would have found yourself among market towns, furnished often enough with a brewery and a flour and provender mill, but innocent otherwise of more than the lightest of industry. Within a distance of fifty miles of Coventry only Northampton could rate as a fully-fledged industrial centre. The other important town — or city, as it was officially rated — within that radius was Oxford, a place with which, apart from fine churches and antiquity, Coventry had absolutely nothing in common. Spiritually the two towns lay at different poles. Oxford had once indeed been a vigorous Saxon borough but — to quote from Peter Snow's *Oxford Observed* — it had been reduced to 'the medieval equivalent of a company town' serving the wants of its prodigious university. It was much the same in 1900. Even the college servants, it was said, looked down on the ordinary artisans of the town. This was 'that sweet city with her dreaming spires', the home of scholarship, poetry and romantic — that is, lost — causes, where clergymen waited for livings and occasionally burst out in bitter theological dispute. Apart from that, it was wealthy undergraduates having a good time. If Town resented Gown, which of course it did, there was nothing much to be done about it. Anyway, the largest single employer was the University Press.

There had been one rude interruption. In 1865 the Great Western Railway proposed to build a carriage and wagon works at Oxford. The city council was happy and ready to grant a lease. But the university was firmly opposed and so were many influential people outside. *The Times* objected and *Punch* came up with an article entitled 'The Great Western Vandals and Oxford'. So the Great Western chose Swindon instead. All was again quiet.

Then in the first quarter of the twentieth century a third Oxford materialized. Manufacturing Oxford, a centre of the motor industry to be put on a par with Coventry. The man responsible, William Morris, a generation younger than Harry Lawson, was aged twenty-three in 1900. He was a mechanic rather than an engineer, an assembler and repairer of bicycles, and also a bicycle-racing champion. His business was one of a number in the town which bought in parts and put them together. The parts Morris bought came from Birmingham, from firms such as BSA and Charter Lea; he collected them himself by bicycle, a journey of some 120 miles there and back. He had started simply in a workshop installed in a shed in the garden of his parents' house, exhibiting his products in the window of their front room with a sign planted in the garden to attract attention. Then, like others of his temperament and bent, he was carried away by motors. He moved up in the world, renting first a shop in the High Street and then a large shed (which he shared at first with a fruiterer) in Longwall, facing the Magdalen deer park, where he set about assembling motor cycles and repairing cars. By 1903 his business was calling itself the Oxford Automobile and Agency Company.

There was a setback, but Morris soon recovered and branched into car hire. He then took two key decisions. One was to continue his policy of buying in parts rather than making them himself. (In Birmingham they were startled to receive orders for car components from Oxford of all places.) The other, to an extent a consequence of the first, was to construct cars for the cheaper end of the market. Success meant new premises and in 1912 Morris established his factory in the village of Cowley (where he had been partly brought up) in the long-empty military training college, two miles away from Magdalen Bridge.

Had the Great Western managed back in the 1860s to settle in Oxford the city would have become ... well, another Swindon. No, that is probably going too far. But the atmosphere of the town girdling the superb buildings of the university centre would have been Swindonish. Railway stations and workshops regularly degraded their surroundings. But automobile factories were to be established as a matter of course on the edge of their host cities, rather than in the cities themselves. The very size of the factories was one reason; another was tighter planning rules, and a third modern transport which made a more distant site practicable. So the direct effect at Oxford was limited, and so, to start with, was the indirect effect. But that changed drastically after the First World War. Oxford's population doubled as workers for Morris poured in from outside. The city boomed under the general commercial stimulus; wage rates climbed. By 1936 Oxford was to be one of the three most prosperous towns in England outside London. (The other two, Coventry and Luton, were also automobile manufacturing centres.) Oxford was now what John Betjeman called 'motopolis'.

Partly because the Morris works were outside the city, partly because the build-up was gradual, there was little fuss. Certainly the city council could not be considered as favouring motor vehicles, for as late as 1913 they turned down an application from Morris to operate motor buses — which by then had been running on London streets for years. The university's attitude can be illustrated with two examples, the first perhaps allegorical. A newly appointed university registrar, looking through the files, discovered a letter which he himself had written as a civil servant asking for the university's view on further development at Cowley. Scribbled on it was a note to the effect that such developments were of no interest to the university. The second is a book, *Oxford outside the Guide-Books*, published by Blackwells of Oxford in 1923 and written by a former Librarian of the Bodleian Library. While it is mainly concerned with the university, past and present, a section is grafted on to the end which deals with Oxford's commercial life. It is full of information about ancient guilds and merchants and it revels in cordwainers, hosiers, glovers and other extinct species. It even goes so far as to mention the 'rapid development that has been so marked a feature in the commercial life of Oxford during the last two decades'. But nowhere in the text is there a word about Morris or Cowley.

Morris is still a well-known, indeed resurrected, name, even though his company disappeared during the calamitous decline of the British motor industry after the Second World War. That is more than can be said for most of the car names so far mentioned in this book. Some of the manufacturers were substantial or quite substantial, like Bollée, Panhard (which like Morris survived as a marque into the second half of the twentieth century), Levassor, Duryea, Charron, Lanchester, Napier. Others were tiny. The Arnold Motor Carriage Company which constructed about twelve cars (derived from Benz, for whom they were concessionaires) between 1896 and 1898, was an offshoot of some agricultural engineers of East Peckham, Kent, who despite their modest place in the manufacturing hierarchy claimed to have introduced the world's first self-starter. Their 'dog cart', maximum speed 16mph, participated in the Emancipation Run. The car John Moore-Brabazon drove at Cambridge was a New Orleans (later called just Orleans), which survived until 1910 and was made at Twickenham. In East Anglia, Botwood's of Ipswich turned swiftly from building carriage bodies to car bodies and in 1900 sold

their version of the French Gobon Brillié, advertis- **A fashionable motor**
ing it as capable of running on alcohol as fuel — it **meeting, 1898.**
went equally well apparently on gin, brandy or
whisky. The engineers J. W. Brooke of Lowestoft manufactured their
own gearboxes and engines for their Brooke cars, which went into
production in 1902. Lindsay Motor Manufacturing of Woodbridge
assembled a voiturette between 1905 and 1908. In Britain alone no
fewer than 393 firms constructing cars started up in the period before
the First World War. Of these, 113 were still operating in 1914.

With such a choice, car buying was complicated and, given the
risk of company failure, hazardous. Moreover, car-buyers had to
resolve for themselves some basic questions. One, not too serious,
was whether you should buy at all, or whether it would be preferable
to hire in the days when cars were so very unreliable. At the beginning, there was a choice to be made between steering wheel and tiller.
A. J. Balfour thought it necessary in 1901, when the steering wheel
was emerging as the clear winner, to write to Lady Elcho:

> *Do* reconsider the question of *steering* on your new motor. The
> only advantage of the tiller steering which is ever alleged is that a
> beginner is less likely to give it the wrong twist in the excitement
> of the moment. I attach no weight to this. *Per contra* it is univer-
> sally abandoned on the continent where they turn out 20 cars to
> our one. Even in England I am not aware of any makers who

73

habitually employ it on large cars except the Mo-car* people. My advisers (14 Regent Street) in the person of W. Jarrott (whom you know and who has unsurpassed experience) tell me that it is exceedingly *dangerous*.

And what kind of car: should it be powered by petrol, by steam from coal or coke or other fuels, or by electricity? Lord Montagu originally had favoured a combination of two of these, seeing the advantages of electric vehicles for town use and petrol-driven vehicles for the country. Electricity was popular with women, who were less tolerant than men of dirt and rude shocks. Electric cars were quiet, clean and odourless, and required no cranking or prolonged warming up. However, they were slower, suffered from a limited range and were very expensive to run. Several of the pioneers, including Sir David Salomons, backed steam. Lord Northcliffe bought a Serpollet steam car in 1900, and so did the Shah of Persia, who in fact bought two. They were fast: Léon Serpollet, the leading European steam-vehicle manufacturer, broke the land speed record in 1902 in one of his cars. Four years later it was broken again, this time by an American automobile, the Stanley Steamer, at an average speed of 127.66mph.

By 1907, when J. E. Vincent published his *Through East Anglia in a Motor Car*, in which he compared a White steam car with a Rolls-Royce, steam cars were themselves fuelled by petrol 'ingeniously vaporized'. Vincent liked steam cars and rated highly their ability to climb hills, and, in common with most people, was delighted that they involved no gear changing or cranking. For what a relief that could be, witness the experience of a young French nobleman who took an elderly lady for a drive in his (internal-combustion-powered) car. When he changed gear the car juddered so uncontrollably that her false teeth fell out into her lap. He finished the day with his arm in a sling, not because she hit him — her response was purely verbal — but as a result of an accident caused when cranking the engine. However, by the time Vincent's book was published steam cars were on their way out. One of the biggest manufacturers, Locomobile, had already switched to internal combustion and in that year Serpollet himself died. You needed a special education to get the best out of them, declared one experienced motorist. And they were more

*Mo-car was a short-lived Scottish manufacturer.

suited to heavy work, as in agriculture and freight, since the weight of the engine and fuel supply prevented their matching the performance of an equivalent internal-combustion-powered vehicle. A great advantage of petrol was that as a liquid it was light, convenient to stow and easy to transport.

Beyond such fundamental decisions was the problem that cars were seldom sold complete. Mulliner, it may be remembered, was in 1913 advertising chassis to be fitted for any sort of car. A. J. Balfour wrote to Lady Elcho, 'My new motor is excellent qua machinery but the carriage is disappointing. I am having a new body made.' The chassis for the first Rolls-Royce came in four versions which ranged in cost between £395 (£26,500) and £890 (£60,000), and the body might cost nearly as much again. To buy electric lights for the Rolls-Royce Silver Ghost cost about £75 extra. S. F. Edge in his reminiscences wrote that cars were delivered minus lamps, horns, windscreens, hood, spare wheel, speedometer and other fittings one would now think of as essential. He said that these extra accessories usually meant the best part of a £100 had to be added to the cost. Dorothy Levitt recommended a small and cheap De Dion costing normally £230, but she warned about how extras would increase the price.

An article in the *Country Life* Supplement's 'Automobile World' column gives a good idea of basic costs of motoring. The subject is a lady who in 1908 disposed of her horses and carriages to buy a 20hp car. The chassis was by a 'first-rate French maker with a limousine body by a leading London coach maker'. The car was based in London but largely used for tours both in Britain and abroad. She employed a thoroughly experienced driver, who was also an excellent mechanic. He did the servicing and was backed up by another man who helped with washing and polishing. The capital outlay was:

Chassis	£600
Body	£290
Sundry fittings & spares	£69

That is £959, or roughly £64,000 today. There was also the expense of converting the stables. The driver was paid £2 10s a week (£165 today) and the handyman 5s. The car was sold in 1912 for £375. The owner's running expenses do not seem particularly high except for the tyres, which come out over a typical six-month period (with 5,260 miles covered) at £60 (£4,000 today). As *Country Life* noted in another article, 'Widely as opinions differ on the cost of motoring, it is universally agreed that tires [sic] constitute the heaviest item.' Considering the comments of Edge and others, the cost of the extra fitments look modest. However, the car, being an expensive model, would have been better equipped than most. Here was a problem for the makers illuminated by a journalist in the *Contemporary Review* who asked a manufacturer why certain fittings, common to all large cars, could not be added automatically to small ones. The answer, it seems, was that if they were, no one would buy a large one.

By the time the *Country Life* lady took up motoring, the numbers of cars on British roads had climbed from a few hundred twelve years before to over 40,000. Nevertheless, if the car could no longer be considered just a plaything of the rich, it was a long way from being a normal conveyance for the man or woman in the street. Economically it was reckoned as no more expensive to run than a carriage and pair, but as yet nothing existed to compete on running costs with a simple pony and trap. With increasing reliability and the redundancy of 'motor engineers', running costs were coming down. How far, though, was it true that car prices were sky high, only within the reach of the affluent? According to the official statistics, the average price of a new car in 1908 was £420, say £28,000 today. For a cheap and simple voiturette Dorothy Levitt quotes £230 plus fittings, say £300 (£20,000). But she also says that you could pick up a second-hand model for £120 (£8,000). On that side of the equation alone, we might say that the price was not inordinately high. Once, however, we turn to the other side, to the income of potential buyers, it is a different affair altogether. The average annual mid-Edwardian wage for the top 25 per cent of earners was less than £6,500 in today's terms. Even the top 10 per cent would have had to pay out something like a whole year's earnings for Dorothy Levitt's second-hand vehicle, which anyway would not have lasted long. And it is worth remembering that only a tiny minority of the population possessed capital of more than a few hundred pounds.

But if wages edged upwards — which they were doing — and the price of a *new* car could be fixed at something near that £120, then it would be a different ballgame. The metaphor is apt, for the solution was American, not French, not German and not British. While both the British and continental motor industries were flourishing, it was natural that the first steps towards mass production should be made in the United States, where the principle of standardization was already entrenched. The need for the interchangeability of components had been demonstrated on the battlefields of the Civil War. There was already a strong American machine-tool industry and, above all, there was a large domestic market.

While America produced Duryea and Pennington and other pioneers, its automobile industry had been almost as late to get started as the British, and its progress was delayed yet further by an early concentration on electric and steam vehicles. Indeed, in 1900 two-thirds of the automobiles manufactured in the United States were either electric or steam. By 1906, however, the United States had taken over the lead from France. It was fitting that the cardinal figure of the motoring age should be American. This of course was Henry Ford. So extraordinary was his reputation to be in his generation that it is hardly more accurate to say that Ford symbolized motoring than that motoring symbolized Henry Ford.

Ford too experienced a revelation at the roadside. In 1876, aged twelve, he was accompanying his father on the way to Detroit. They encountered a steam engine of the type used to saw logs and work threshing machines, and, as they drew up to let it pass, the young Ford jumped off his father's wagon to question the driver, who allowed him to shovel coal into the fire-box and to operate the machinery. Later Ford worked on steam engines at Westinghouse and then, during the 1890s, he turned to experiments with internal combustion. Ford considered electrically powered vehicles too, but was reassured by a conversation with the master himself, Thomas Edison, who granted his approval for the internal-combustion technique. 'Electric cars,' Edison told him, 'must keep near to power stations. The storage battery is too heavy.'

In 1903 Henry Ford was running a small workshop with skilled workers in an assembly operation similar to that which was common in Europe. By 1914 he was a mass employer of unskilled labour, practising a revolutionary manufacturing technique. He had achieved what he set out to do: the construction of a light, utilitarian car that was simple enough to be controlled by anyone able to ride a horse and was sold at a price which most families could afford. It was

The Model T Ford of 1912, which, selling for £135, for the first time brought motoring by car within reach of the less well-to-do.

a triumph of standardization, of mass production. 'The way to make automobiles,' Ford declared, 'is to make one automobile like another automobile, to make them all alike, to make them come through the factory just alike; just as one pin is like another pin when it comes from a pin factory, or one match is like another match when it comes from a match factory.'

The car was the Model T Ford. It had a maximum speed of 40mph and sold, in Britain, for £135. In its original form it was extremely simple: it was doorless and provided with a single lever, the hand-brake and three pedals — for the clutch to shift between a low gear and a high gear, for reverse and for the footbrake. The throttle was fixed to the steering wheel and there were no instruments at all. It came in a single colour — black. Its chassis was suitable for car, truck or bus.

The Model T was itself a revolution; it was the 'people's car'. Its influence on the motor industry and on those who used motor vehicles was of immense importance. But of even more significance to the economic and social life of the twentieth century was the technical process by which it was brought into existence. Ford defined mass production in the 1926 edition of the *Encylopaedia Britannica* as follows:

Mass production is not merely quantity production, for this may be had with none of the requisites of mass production. Nor is it merely machine production, which also may exist without any resemblance to mass production. Mass production is the focussing upon a manufacturing project of the principles of power, accuracy, economy, system, continuity, and speed.

It is a striking but necessarily general description which needs amplification.

There were three stages to the production process in a motor-vehicle plant. In the first components such as cylinder heads, gears, engine blocks and body parts were machined; in the second they were put together in units; in the third they were incorporated in a vehicle. The fundamental development in technique promoted by Ford is best illustrated as it applied in the final, assembly, stage. Originally a car and its assemblers remained in one place; next, from 1907, the car remained stationary, while assemblers moved about between cars; finally the assembler remained in one place and the car moved. From early 1914, with manufacture now based at a new factory at Dearborn outside Detroit, the assembly line was mechanized, with the chassis hooked to a continuously moving conveyor passing from one worker to another. No human time was wasted in moving about, no labour involved in pushing the vehicle along the line. The increase in productivity was extraordinary. The overall time to produce each car was reduced from something like 140 hours to thirty-nine.

The Model T was a stunning success, in Britain as elsewhere. The fame it brought its creator was unprecedented and boundless. It has been reckoned that during the 1920s in the United States Henry Ford received more publicity than any other American apart from President Coolidge — far more than the runners-up, Charlie Chaplin and the homespun philosopher Will Rogers. He was nearly as well known elsewhere in the world. His reputation was protean; it meant different things to different people. He was, for instance, tremendously admired in the Soviet Union and later in Nazi Germany. For a reflection now of Ford's standing, it is easiest perhaps to look out Aldous Huxley's *Point Counter Point*. Or better still, his *Brave New World*, a satire and a warning of a materialistic future. In this world Ford was God. 'Our Ford', people say in the book, either as a

79

mild swearword or as a mark of veneration. (When speaking on psychological matters the expression 'for some inscrutable reason' becomes 'Our Freud'.) They make the sign of the 'T' and they date their era BF or AF, the dividing point being the year in which the Model T was introduced.

Ford was the poor farm boy from the Middle West made good; ill-educated, an ordinary guy with any amount of ordinary prejudices. He was rich but one of us. His achievement was astounding; he was a marvellous organizer and a man of great resolution. But he was no Edison, no original creative mind, and he owed much to what others, Ransom Olds of the Oldsmobile Company for one, had done before him. But in the 1920s, to a world shattered by war, his apparent ordinariness in terms of personality was appealing. Famously he declared the world to be

> living in books and history and tradition. We want to get away from that and take care of today. We've done too much looking back. What we want to do, and to do it quick, is to make just history right now. The men who are responsible for the present war in Europe knew all about history. Yet they brought on the worst war in the world's history.

Simple, but not unjustified. It was the sort of thing he liked saying, for there was a loquacious brand of homespun philosophy about Henry Ford. (And of course loquacity helped to sell his cars.) He played it all up, unleashing pronouncements on everything under the sun — pacifism, diet, folk-dancing, and Prohibition, which he supported vehemently.

The techniques of mass production — known as 'Fordism' — spread rapidly. In Britain, Ford's factory at Trafford Park, near Manchester, installed a moving assembly line less than a year after the introduction of the original in America. Understandably, given the engineering tradition which it challenged and the mediocre reputation in Britain of American cars, the reaction of the motor industry was unenthusiastic. But it signified an unstoppable revolution — a second industrial revolution — with implications for manufacturing industry of all types everywhere in the world. Well might Bill Ford, the present chairman of the company, remark, 'When your great-grandfather has changed the face of the world, it's pretty hard to know what to do for an encore.'

For good or ill. And of course it was with the ill, or the possible ill, that Aldous Huxley was concerned: the emergence of a world become totally materialistic, with its human beings deprived of independence, even of personality. This was the theme also of René Clair's film *A Nous la Liberté* and of Chaplin's *Modern Times* of 1936. In Chaplin's film, in the opening shots, the workers, flocking into a factory — what it makes is unclear — are juxtaposed with sheep. 'Charlie' is one of them, a worker on a moving assembly line. Suddenly the conveyor goes mad, pelting by, faster and faster. The workers, robot-like, attempt desperately to keep up. The machinery squirts them with oil and in a later sequence sucks them into its entrails, from which, as in a Disney cartoon, they emerge unharmed. Charlie tries to escape for a cigarette in the washroom, only to find himself confronted by a huge TV-type screen on which the magnified face of the factory boss appears. He is briskly ordered back to work. With mass production it is the machine which sets the pace of work. And the system is one that requires a tight discipline. Indeed, it has been said that mass production is not fundamentally a mechanical principle but a principle of social organization.

While the immediate effects of Fordism led to an increase in unemployment, its 'good side' meant a steady rise in the standard of living. The benefits of increased productivity were shared with the shop floor; the discrepancy between prices and incomes, on cars and on everything else, would diminish. Henry Ford himself took the initiative. Much of the legend which surrounded him was based on his award in 1914 of an eight-hour day and a $5-a-day minimum wage. *Modern Times* mocks the tyranny of the production line, with its setting, in Chaplin's own words of explanation: a world of automatons in which his own character and the 'gamine' played by Paulette Goddard are the only live spirits. It is a parody but it is not quite a savage indictment of 'Fordism'. The effect of this second industrial revolution inaugurated by Henry Ford was to lead to the consumer society, to higher incomes and to immensely greater social services and benefits. It was also to lead to the social revolution to which Osbert Sitwell referred when he remembered 'the motor ... [which] tinnily vibrated and steamed in the frost outside the door'.

4

The Rediscovery of Arcadia

When war broke out at the beginning of August 1914 Gertrude Stein was in England, and she did not return to her home in Paris until October. As soon as she got there she was struck by the change in atmosphere. It was partly that the foreigners were gone and that the streets were empty, but it was more than that; it was the smell, the strange but familiar smell of the horse-drawn Paris of her childhood. For horses were back, the automobiles drafted into war service or decommissioned. In 1912 the *Mayfair Magazine* had pronounced that the horse was finished, and best disowned and forsaken even by its friends. Soon, it predicted, the 'forlorn animal will betake itself to the Zoological Gardens'. It would have been a premature forecast in any event, for while the horse was no longer the noble steed of days gone by, it would still have been needed, war or no war, in a humbler capacity, pulling wagons and drays. But the war restored the horse to the centre of the transport system. It was the horses that hauled the immense quantities from the railhead to the front. As John Keegan has pointed out, horse fodder constituted the largest category of cargo unloaded at French ports for the British army on the Western Front during the war.

That automobiles at the beginning of the war were no more than peripheral — their need for solid roads being one drawback — was demonstrated as the armies gathered. The huge armies — German, French, Austrian and even the Russian — were transported with unprecedented speed and efficiency to the front by rail. However, once in place they were hardly more mobile than the Roman legions. General von Kluck's wide enveloping movement through Belgium and northern France was planned to be decisive, but its success depended on speed. While his transport included light motor vehicles, there were none to carry troops. By the time his army reached the Marne, after a sixteen-day march from Liège, it was exhausted.

There was then, however, a moment of glory, famous in motoring history, the episode of the 600 Parisian taxis which ferried badly needed troops to fight in the crucial battle. Later on, as more and more motor vehicles appeared, the mammoth battle of Verdun was won by the French only because, the railways unusable, supplies could be brought up nightly on secondary roads by an endless line of trucks. (There is a parallel with the Berlin airlift just over thirty years later.) And of course there were the tanks. The final superiority in motor transport enjoyed by the Allies was an important factor in their victory. In 1919 Lord Curzon stated that the Allied cause 'floated to victory on a wave of oil'.

Inventors and governments had appreciated for years the potential for automobiles in war. A long time back, about 1769, a French engineer, Joseph Cugnot, had built a three-wheel steam prototype tractor to pull guns, of which a later version was tested by Napoleon. The Swiss engineer Isaac de Rivaz, an outstanding figure in motoring history, in 1813 constructed a huge truck powered not by steam but, using coal gas, through internal combustion. This vehicle, intended to carry freight, was commissioned by the haulage company Paschoud-Rosset and managed to cover a distance of eighty feet uphill at Vevey, with a heavy load and four people aboard. Rivaz suggested to the French minister of war that the French army might employ his machine for the transport of troops (though it would not have been of much use on the retreat from Moscow). In fact, Rivaz's invention came to nothing, partly through shortage of funds and, more fundamentally, because of the inadequacy of the materials available at the time.

The successful development of internal combustion was to be delayed for many years. The East India Company, however, fresh from its experience of the Indian Mutiny, tested a specially designed road steam locomotive at Woolwich Arsenal in 1858, with the distinguished military engineer in charge reporting that 'an establishment

The 'War Car', designed and manned by F. R. Simms, manufactured by Vickers, was fitted with armoured-steel plate, a Maxim and two pom-pom guns, 1902.

of such engines and carts would enable government to dispense with half of the ordinary military force in India'. By the end of the Boer War forty-six traction engines were employed on work up until then the province of light railways, and it is significant that the two largest firms involved in the newly born British motor industry were the armament manufacturers Vickers (which bought up the Wolseley Tool & Motor Company) and Armstrong Whitworth. Working with Vickers was Frederick Simms, one of the most inventive of British motoring pioneers. It was he who coined the description 'motor car' and was responsible for setting up the Automobile Association. In June 1899 he exhibited his own 'war quadricycle', equipped with a machine gun, at the Richmond Motor Show, and in 1902, at the Crystal Palace, produced a more sophisticated version with a revolving gun turret.

The army blew hot and cold over automobiles as weapons of war, but Lord Roberts at least was enthusiastic. The journalist Owen John (a pseudonym) joined the Motor Volunteer Corps (later the Motor Reserve) on its formation in 1904. It was, so he said, the first army motor unit in the world, without NCOs and with just as many officers as men. It was great fun, for he was in the company of fellow enthusiasts, but with the army blowing cold, it was disbanded just

before the war broke out. By then anyway John had become rather disillusioned, convinced that light military vehicles mainly served to save elderly generals from the more arduous exertions of riding horses. Foreseeing the future importance of heavy transport for military purposes, he joined the Army Service Corps Territorial Force.

Cars belonging to the Motor Volunteer Corps, formed by members of the Automobile Club in 1901–2. Those present in this photograph include Field Marshal Lord Roberts, who was well aware of the likely importance of motorized vehicles in war. Roberts is a passenger in the car on the far left, and Lord Kitchener a passenger in the car on the extreme right.

At the start of the First World War the government had no alternative but to look to private individuals for such motor transport as it could mobilize. Two weeks into the war, the Royal Automobile Club arranged for twenty-five owner-drivers and their cars to be transported to Le Havre to act as chauffeurs for senior officers. On 31 October *Country Life* reported that one of the most striking features of the campaign in France was the 'vast' use made of mechanical transport. The motor was 'omnipresent' at the front. The journal commented that most of the tales of personal adventure came from dispatch riders, the majority of whom were private motorists and the owners of powerful cars. *Country Life* also mentioned the increasing number of armoured cars. Here was an opportunity for the old motoring spirit, that enthusiastic blend of amateurism and professionalism, spiced with adventure. Few could incarnate it better than the immensely wealthy 'Bendor', Duke of Westminster, famous later on for the number of his wives and yachts and famous already for his fast cars and disregard of speed limits. In South Africa during the Boer War he had been struck by the mobility of the Boers and by the immobility of his own side,

A motor cycle dispatch rider and machine-gunner during the First World War.

with its ineffective use of road transport. The Duke appeared in France with his own armoured Rolls-Royce — a machine gun bolted to the chassis — driven by his chauffeur, which he took into action. Since the commander-in-chief, Sir John French, an old cavalryman, was not at all pleased with such an innovation, the Duke transferred to the Royal Naval Air Service. He then commissioned from Rolls (paying for them himself) six more advanced armoured cars, this time with revolving gun turrets, which he carried with him to Egypt. With his armoured cars covering 230 miles in twenty-four hours, he achieved a spectacular victory over a Turkish column.

Virtually no one was quicker off the mark than another rich amateur, the first President of the Ladies' Automobile Club, Millicent, Duchess of Sutherland. She crossed to France on 8 August 1914, four days after the British declaration of war, to join the French Red Cross. The circumstances, she reflected, could hardly have been more different from those of her last Channel crossing, which had been to Le Touquet for a honeymoon — her second, the Duke having died — just two weeks before. The Duchess was soon diverted to Namur, where she ran her 'ambulance', a mobile hospital staffed by a surgeon and eight trained nurses. There they were under continual shelling as the Germans attacked and captured the town. The Duchess was a spectacular example, but she was just one of the many women of all classes who came out to care for the wounded or to serve as drivers. One pompous commanding officer complained that when he telephoned for some women drivers he was asked, 'What sort do you want? Front row of the chorus or ladies of title? We stock them all — take your choice.' But then, most commanding officers of the time, pompous or not, would have considered that the home, not the dangerous and squalid conditions of the Western Front, was the proper place for women. Indeed, it was not until January 1916 that the British army officially accepted women as ambulance drivers.

Women drove motor ambulances, lorries, motor kitchens and even 'motor baths' which circulated behind the lines with the water in a cistern heated by the vehicle's engine. They had to be mechanics as well as drivers. One member of FANY, the First Aid Nursing Yeomanry, Pat Beauchamp, who ended the war with one of her legs blown off by a shell, remembered that she had spent her second leave at home mostly in a garage, getting herself prepared. 'I positively dreamt of carburettors, magnetos, and how to change tyres,' she said. She also recalled how in France she and her colleagues came across an article in a leading daily newspaper entitled 'Women Motor Drivers — Is it a suitable occupation?' Individual paragraphs were headed 'The lure of the Wheel', 'Is it necessary?', 'The after effects'. 'We lapped it up with joy,' she said, adding that they were especially pleased by such statements as, 'The uncongenial atmosphere of the garage, yard, and workshops, the alien companionship of mechanics and chauffeurs will isolate her mental standing.'

Clearly the article was as concerned about the effect on women drivers anywhere, in France or elsewhere abroad, or, for that matter, at home. With so many men dead, in hospital or at the front, women were required to take over jobs of all sorts. Many gained an experience of motoring in Britain itself which they would never have expected to come their way. One was a Suffolk girl, Olive Turney, from a well-off family, who kept a diary of her time in Ipswich. In the mornings she drove a lorry carrying aircraft parts and in the afternoon a Model T taxi. There were, it seems, few problems, although on one occasion she had to take home a 'very drunk officer'. That was not too difficult, since also in the taxi was an impeccable sergeant-major who had been guarding the officer. The problem was that the taxi stalled. So tricky was it to restart by cranking that the sergeant-major maintained there ought to be a self-starter fitted to any car a woman drove, as 'no female ought to do much of that kind of work'. In contrast to the drunk officer, there was an elderly couple who hired Olive on Saturdays to drive their Wolseley. It made a welcome change, for while she admired her Ford, she did find it in many ways undeniably a 'rattle trap'. The couple amused her too, since there they were in 1917, dressed for motoring in a style fourteen or fifteen years out of date:

> There is a good deal of motor veil and on cold days the man wears a fur cap of the peculiar breed with flaps which always reminds one of a polar bear. He is a good-sized man, and with a very benevolent manner, but he looks the last word in fierceness when in motor costume.

What is especially interesting is her general reaction to a job she had taken on as her contribution to the war effort:

> I wouldn't have believed it possible that I could have so much enjoyed a life so totally different from what I had been accustomed to. But it was great fun — the freedom and unconventionality of it all, sitting in a taxi on a rank waiting for jobs, and all day long running about somewhere.'

As a result of the war, women like Pat Beauchamp and Olive Turney were unlikely to defer to men in the traditional way. As we shall see in the next chapter, the car would come to symbolize something of women's new ambitions and independence. What it meant in more practical form was that they were able to participate more fully in the expansion of motoring that followed in the 1920s.

During the First World War, wasteful use of petrol was frowned on and private motoring restrained. Moreover, the motor manufacturers were engaged in war production. The number of private cars licensed in 1914 was 132,000; by 1918 it was down to 78,000. Then, with the peace, numbers surged: in 1919 there were 110,000 private cars on the road, and the next year 187,000. By 1922 the figure was 315,000; in 1925 it was 580,000 and by 1930 it had swelled to over a million. Guidebooks and books on travel proliferated. The exploration of Britain, the rediscovery of the countryside by town dwellers, so enthusiastically embarked upon before the war, resumed, this time with many more people involved. The 1920s became the heroic age of touring. People set out to discover the delights of the countryside, to absorb a sense of Britain's heritage. It was in this spirit that Rudyard Kipling wrote, 'the chief end of my car, so far as I am concerned, is the discovery of England ... the car is a time-machine on which one can slip from one century to another'. And equally of course the discovery of Scotland and Wales. In fact, the 1925 edition of a guidebook, *Scotland for the Motorist*, written for the AA, was starry-eyed: 'We think of [the car] as a magic carpet by which we are raised above the everyday and the commonplace and wafted, gently and swiftly, to "fairy lands forlorn".'

But it was not that easy. A magic carpet could presumably be counted upon to lift the voyager clear of windstorm, rain and snow. Not so the car of the early 1920s, which was usually open, and, granted that it would be equipped with a hood, was nevertheless a very long way from weatherproof. It might lack windscreen wipers but it would certainly not lack draughts. There was plenty of advice for the prospective tourist. The motorist must remember that it was a good idea in cold weather to save the starter by turning over the engine a few times by using the dreaded crank; the car should be carefully checked over in advance by the local garageman. There was the matter too of luggage on a tour. It was best to have proper motor trunks and suitcases fitted to a grid at the back of the car, and it was sensible to buy special narrow trunks designed to fit along the running board. Should there still be a shortage of luggage space, you could send ahead changes of clothes to places along your route and anything found not to be needed after all could be sent home by parcel.

Nevertheless, hundreds of thousands of people — counting the motor coaches, millions of people — were to find the fuss and discomfort worthwhile. The motorist and family left behind the congested, noisy, industrialized, dirty city and the stresses of urban and suburban life to enter a pre-industrial world. They did so with an excitement and naïvety which were encouraged by the travel books. The artless enthusiasm was by no means just a British phenomenon. A German writer of 1929, recounting his joy in a motor tour, wrote of the poetry of the journey, the fairy tale world of streets and distant places and their miracles and adventures ... The idylls into which one is suddenly transported: a quiet country path over whose banks corn flowers and red poppies send their greetings from rolling fields, playing children in twisting village lanes ...

From the point of view of the modern reader, the gush of words characteristic of the travel books can easily obscure those features of the time which are most interesting. Happily, for the 1920s there exists a documentary film, a series of travelogues, made between 1924 and 1926 by Claude Friese-Greene, with the title *The Open Road* and the subtitle *A Pictorial Record of a Motor Tour from Land's End to John o'Groats*. The film is silent, with captions, and photographed, most unusually for the time, in colour. Films too are selective, but the viewer is less completely in the hands of the creator. For instance, while in *The Open Road* the camera lingers on some village cottages, of the sort still to be seen all over England, there shoots across the screen the bizarre form of an early open charabanc, to be found now, if at all, only in a museum. As it happens, Friese-Greene does not gush, but even so it is such incidentals which are at least as important to the modern viewer as the subject selected by the film's director.

It is striking how empty the countryside is; so empty in fact that for a good deal of the time Friese-Greene drives happily on the wrong side of the road. At the castles and other tourist sites there is seldom anyone else. At the same time, while children laugh and stare at the camera, no one, adult or child, seems surprised by the sudden appearance of the car. The tour starts in summer in the West Country. The beaches are crowded, with swimmers and everyone else by our standards dressed up to the nines. At Torquay, 'the Queen of the West', people relax in deck chairs in rows, but they are not sunbathing — far from it, the women usually shelter under para-sols. In fact, one of the most curious things about the film is how overdressed everyone seems: it must be the coldest summer on record, for there they are, in hats and gloves and often overcoats, whether playing bowls on Plymouth Hoe, admiring gardens or on the switchback at Blackpool. All the women, except the very old, wear cloche hats and virtually all the men are smoking pipes or ci-garettes. If the traffic is light on the country roads, it appears to be choking the towns. That is less true in Cardiff, where there are huge crowds of pedestrians, than in Edinburgh, where Princes Street is packed with an unending line of double-decker trams and open buses. The last programme in the series, on London, is amazing. Friese-Greene drives from the South Bank into the City via London Bridge. Tiny cars rush in and out, manoeuvring through the buses and monstrous lorries. A policeman on point duty — there are as yet no traffic lights — stands firm, restraining an army of juggernauts.

Guidebooks such as Baedeker, the Blue Guide, the AA and RAC, Dunlop, Burrows, Newnes and Black's give the bare bones of what to see and where to go. The travel books, so popular with a public avid for information, were more generally informative and more subjective, not to say idiosyncratic. To take an example: John Prioleau's *Car and Country: Week-End Signposts to the Open Road*. So ravished is the author by almost everything he sees that all sense of proportion evaporates. He is altogether too ardent a protagonist of motoring. Then there was the phenomenally successful H. V. Morton. He is a different matter. He loves hyperbole too, he is senti-mental, but he is funny. His books *In Search of England*, *In Search of Scotland* and *In Search of Wales* — based on articles for the *Daily Express* — are adventures, as a recent writer has put it, with a 'tone throughout which is bluff and optimistic, sentimental but not soppy'.

The public demanded romance and sentiment, a whiff of the AA's 'fairy lands forlorn'. (Friese-Greene supplied it too with lengthy shots of rural children.) When Morton sets off on the jour-ney described in his celebrated *In Search of England*, he opens up with some whimsy. The first person he comes across is a countryman who shows him a wooden bowl, the work, it appears, of 'the last bowl-turner in England', and made exactly as it would have been in the days of Alfred the Great. King Alfred turns up again — or rather might have turned up — when Morton, always on the lookout for ghosts, hopes to see him ride by his hotel window in Winchester. Lord Montagu ('an interesting type, a jolly man') shows Morton round Beaulieu, where again there is the possibility of a ghost. At Shrewsbury he suffers a nightmare in which Harry Hotspur appears, sitting on his bed; but Shrewsbury is a seductive place, with her lovely quiet streets that lie under a witching moon and 'take you back to Old England'. At Kenilworth an ancient actor tells him that 'our last real big sensation was in 1066'. So the story goes on, reaching perhaps its climax in York when, in the company of a sentimental American, Morton is overcome as he gazes on a procession from the Minster: 'First came the Chief Constable of York, booted and spurred, then came the Town Clerk in his robes, following him was a man wearing a fur-edged cap of the Richard II period, and holding aloft the great sword of the Emperor Sigismund.'

Wales, Morton finds more tricky to deal with because of the language. Still, he indulges in a riot of historical anecdote even if his conversations with the local people are restricted: in one bar he found the regulars unsure as to whether he was 'some kind of commercial traveller or the first swallow of the tourist season'. Happily he manages to waylay Lloyd George, out walking, and get into a conversation with him.

H. V. Morton makes plain in his introduction to *In Search of England* that it is the advent of the automobile which lies behind the craze for touring. Indeed, without it, this rediscovery of England would have been impossible. He writes:

> never before have so many people been searching for England. The remarkable system of motor-coach services which now penetrate every part of the country has thrown open to ordinary people regions which even after the coming of the railway were remote and inaccessible. The popularity of the cheap motor-car is also greatly responsible for this long-overdue interest in English history, antiquities, and topography. More people than in any previous generation are seeing the real country for the first time. Many hundreds of such explorers return home with a new enthusiasm, astonished that this wealth of historic, and other interest, any angle of which provides a man with an absorbing hobby for the rest of his life, should until now have been neglected at their very doors.

There were of course people who had acquired the 'absorbing hobby' long before motoring was dreamed of by more than a few enterprising eccentrics. They tended, though, to visit such areas as the Scottish Highlands, North Wales, Dartmoor and the New Forest. And the Lake District, where back in the 1880s Andrew Carnegie came across hotels and coaches flourishing the Stars and Stripes. Naturally, they were likely to be distressed at the idea that such country, by its nature wild and romantic, should be overrun by automobiles. George Abraham, in his 1913 book *Motor Ways in Lakeland*, was comforting, or perhaps only half-comforting. He describes the area as excellent for motor touring, his implication being that it was uncrowded. One of the troubles was that one man's definition was not another's. For six years before Abraham's book, at a time when there were many fewer cars on the road, a correspondent to *The Times* 'calls attention' to the fact that the car has taken possession of the Lake District and entirely altered its character. The descriptions 'spoilt countryside' or 'crowded roads' are highly subjective; the roads travelled by Friese-Greene, empty by our standards, were considered busy by contemporaries.

While we know the number of automobiles licensed each year, it is still difficult to measure the spread of tourism, how many visitors were going where. One indicator is the number of admissions to sites and buildings officially listed as ancient monuments. In 1931 quarrying close to Hadrian's Wall aroused considerable public disquiet and encouraged the government to introduce a bill in Parliament to strengthen the protection afforded to such places. These figures provided important data. Stonehenge (then under private ownership) had been visited by fewer than 4,000 people in 1901, very few of whom would have come by car. The figure for the year 1924—5 was 60,000 and for 1929—30, 100,000. The numbers of people visiting Whitby Abbey were 30,000 in 1924—5 and 40,000 in 1929—30. For Rievaulx Abbey the same comparison revealed 14,000 and 30,000, and for Melrose Abbey 40,000 and 55,000. In a memorandum to George Lansbury, the First Commissioner for Works, the Society for the Protection of Ancient Buildings wrote:

> In the course of the last 10 years public appreciation of our Ancient Buildings, which not so long ago was confined to a comparatively small part of the community, has recently become much more widespread, largely perhaps because of the increased facilities for touring the country by road.

The magazine *Nature* in January 1931, pointing out a consequence of the massive increase in tourism, was less cautious. The defect of the old 1913 act which protected ancient buildings, it stated, was that it made no attempt to safeguard their character in so far as it depended on their historical or natural setting. 'It was not foreseen that a vast extension of motor traffic was at hand which would bring in its train an increase in the number of excursionists for whose entertainment and refreshment provision would be made.'

What is clear, however, is that stately homes, to which people had flocked by train and horse in the nineteenth century, were comparatively neglected. Partly it was because country house owners no longer felt the same sense of *noblesse oblige*, partly that many were deterred by the expense of opening to the public. There was also turmoil in the property market. Baedeker, a very serious guidebook, sometimes comments in detail on the architecture of country houses, and sometimes goes on to mention opening hours. Longleat, it certifies to be open on Monday and Saturday afternoons; Chatsworth is open several days a week in summer; Blenheim and Knole are open too. But for tourists, even Knole was not old enough; they preferred the battlefield of Hastings. Again it is ancient history and legend that appealed. It is no wonder that H. V. Morton settles on Alfred the Great and Hotspur.

The quest for the countryside and its innocent delights may have been nothing new, but now in the 1920s it was different not only in the numbers of those who participated but in type. This was a people's version, less literary than it had been for the Romantics or for members of the Arts and Crafts movement. Its strength is reflected in countless books, newspaper articles and films of the inter-war years, and in this advertisement for Jowett cars:

Have you spied the purple iris blossoming along the river bank? Have you glimpsed a bit of heaven whilst 'picnicing' by the scented pinewood? The wind's on the heath, brother; the highway is calling; there's laughter and deep breath and zestful life over there on the hills. Freedom is waiting you at the bang of your front door.

And when, during the Second World War, people felt the need to crystallize their devotion to Britain they were more likely to envisage an ivy-clad cottage nestling under a hill than a smoky industrial city. Dream-like, mythic, unreal as it often was, the rural England or Scotland or Wales as seen by the motorist was of great imaginative and practical importance to a huge number of people. One trouble was that it had little to do with the realities of rural life, with cows and pigs (who would figure only daintily in the townsman's imagination) or with the bringing in of the harvest. It was not that country people who lived near the great cities were wholly unprepared for tourists, but that motoring introduced an unprecedented pressure. It is worth considering the reactions of two countrymen, neither of whom could remotely be described as a yokel.

The landowning family of Bray had lived at Shere near Dorking in Surrey for literally centuries. In the 1920s they were represented by Reginald Bray (1869—1950), a friend of Masterman and Trevelyan and Lutyens, a former elected member of the London County Council, and author of *The Town Child*, published in 1907 and based on his experience of social work in London. Bray's letters are revealing. The neighbourhood was changing fast as townspeople bought up what were once old labourers' cottages. The consequence, familiar indeed to us now, was a rise in prices which made it hard for Bray's employees and tenants to find a place to live. Cars allowed motorists to 'penetrate into the heart of the Common & light picnic fires out of sight'. Gangs of motor cyclists invaded the village on Sundays and made so tremendous a noise that they disturbed every-one, including the congregation in church. The effect of motoring could be double-edged. Someone, for instance, wants to establish a petrol station; Bray, with the environment in mind, is against the idea, but he is also aware that it could bring badly needed money into the village. After a particularly severe fire on common land, thought to be a result of carelessness by motorists, he writes to the AA asking them to use their influence, possibly through their jour-nal, to warn motorists of the fire danger. To do something about it himself, he provides space on his land. There is a proposal for a new road. Writing to the local council on behalf of the Tillingbourne Valley Defence Association, he argues that 'it would destroy the nature of the land through which it would pass'. He tries to maintain the right of pedestrians, who, he says, 'having been driven off the roads by cars, were being pursued on to footpaths'.

George Sturt lived some miles off to the west, still in Surrey, close to Farnham. Under the pseudonym George Bourne, he wrote a number of books on social change in Surrey, notably *Memoirs of a Surrey Labourer* (1907) and *Change in the Village* (1912). Arnold Ben-nett, a close friend, writing in 1909, maintained that 'Mr Bourne will owe his popularity in 2009 to the intrinsic excellence of his work'. In fact, from the look of it, Sturt is unlikely to be remembered at all in

2009. However, he was a magnificent and deeply pessimistic recorder of village life, particularly the old village life now fast disappearing. He loathes the tripper:

> Where the Tripper goes, he spoils everything for the native dweller, whether he goes for a day, or for years. He is loud (listen to the motor hootings), discordant, doesn't understand: has his silly romping jokes (listen again to the frivolity of the cultured, as you pass their gardens) rides roughshod over native people, yet hasn't the sense to know that they find him distasteful ... The essence of tripperhood is that it treats the 'peasantry' in a superior manner: it assumes that they are and expect to be servile.

Sturt sees the car as a symptom of the materialism which he detests, rather than its cause. Indeed, in his 1912 book he barely mentions the car at all. In his view the country village had been in decline for generations. What he really resents about the car is its part in the destruction of craftsmanship. Sturt was a partner in a firm of Farnham wheelwrights and descended from a family of wheelwrights. As far back as 1896 he had visited the 'autocar show' at the Imperial Institute in London, and had come away believing that he would either have to modernize his business or give way to commercial rivals. In fact he did neither, selling out only in 1920. In September 1912, well before Fordism had taken hold, he learns of the increasing mechanization in body makers' workshops, 'where the men may be seen scrambling new bodies of motor-cars together at top speed ... with no regard to fine finish of workmanship, and with little care taken in the choice of material'.

These villages — in the case of Bray's Shere thirty miles from the centre of London, in the case of Sturt still less than fifty — could no longer function in the old way. This is unmistakably Toad country, a region overshadowed by what Sturt called 'the immense restlessness' of London.

Yet, as the *Open Road* film makes clear, further from the cities there still existed endless acres of unspoilt country, vistas in which no urban taint touched the view. Ford Madox Ford, for instance, between long periods of busy and turbulent urban life, withdrew to country retreats of extreme simplicity. At the turn of the century he had lived in Kent, balancing life with, on the one hand, Henry James and Joseph Conrad, and, on the other, unquestionable rustics such

as Ragged Arse Wilson and Shaking Ben. After the war and prolonged service on the Western Front, he with his wife, Stella, retired
to the most remote part of Sussex. They settled first in a leaking, rat-
ridden, moribund labourer's cottage, then moving on to another
one which was slightly more comfortable but no less isolated. Ford's
mother declared it to be 'really the end of the world'. Here they
raised Sussex Large Black pigs, apparently the largest hogs in the
world, and as a result made the acquaintance of a neighbour, S. F.
Edge — 'irresistible when it comes to pigs,' said Ford — withdrawn
temporarily from the world of automobiles under the terms of a sev-
erance contract with Napiers. Of his neighbours more generally,
Ford could say, 'West Sussex to a Kent-minded man is as foreign in
speech and habits as is China.' How difficult local roads could be for
tourists was illustrated when Stella Ford, on horseback, overtook a
carload of 'busy-bodies' coming to peep at her husband in his new
retreat. The hill was too steep for them and they were gently rolling
down it backwards.

The deep country remained isolated. Some of it, as we have seen
in earlier chapters, more isolated than it had been before the railway.
The railways concentrated settlement and prosperity: in Ford's
country they had converted villages like Haslemere, Woking,
Sevenoaks, Croydon, Haywards Heath and Burgess Hill into towns.
As the Sussex estate agent questioned by J. J. Hissey had said, in the
old days closeness to a railway station was for his clients an 'almost
imperative condition'. The villages in between stations or removed
altogether from the railway system were left to decay. The automobile — car, bus, charabanc, motorcycle — was to change all that, but
not yet, not in the early 1920s. The main roads might be packed with
traffic at weekends and on Bank Holidays, but the hurrying drivers
seldom wandered far from the beaten track. They liked to stick
together, to follow each other down the well-marked routes. Moreover, it was there they could be sure of petrol, and anyway, as Ford's
busybodies had found, local roads were usually too rough for comfortable driving.

What is surprising is how easily in some villages sophistication
and simplicity could cohabit. Before he bought Batemans, Rudyard
Kipling lived at Rottingdean, a village by the sea near the ultra-
sophisticated Brighton. (Kipling too had his busybodies; while he
worked in his garden, horse buses would draw up to allow passengers

a glimpse of the famous man.) Here in Rottingdean, North End House had been occupied by Sir Edward Burne-Jones and his wife, who was Kipling's aunt. They were succeeded by another famous painter, Sir William Nicholson. Stanley Baldwin was about. Nor were prominent motorists absent: at Tallboy Cottage was Charlie Thomas, co-driver with S. F. Edge on a motor tour around the world. And at one time another large house in the village was occupied by Sir Edward Carson, the 'instigator of all the trouble in Ireland'. The words in inverted commas are those of Margaret Ward, born and bred in Rottingdean, who writes of the more sophisticated side of the village, tracing its development after the First World War, the encroachment of Brighton, the building of flats and the conversion of an old farm, Tudor Close, into a luxury hotel frequented 'by stage and film personalities'.

Margaret Ward's childhood friend Bob Copper also published his memories of the village. The two accounts read as if they were written of different places. Bob Copper's world is slow and unchanging. At the start of the twentieth century, he says, the speed of life was obviously dictated by the speed of horse-drawn traffic. 'But there was something in that steady pace that entered a man's heart and made for a leisurely frame of mind and a general lack of haste in decision and action.' The outside world 'was regarded in a vague and uninterested way by the locals as being somewhere over the hills to the north. Any town from London to Leeds, from Oxford to Edinburgh, was referred to as being "somewhere up the back o' Lewes".' (What they made of Kipling and India, heaven knows.) When around 1920, aged four or five, Bob was taken on a trip to Lewes, some ten miles away, he and his companions in adventure were given a send-off by his mother and other villagers 'worthy of a departure to Australia'. Even in the 1920s, the 'villagers were often bred, baptised, book-taught, betrothed, bedded, boarded, and buried all within hailing distance of the cottage which had seen their birth and many would never have occasion to travel beyond the perimeter of land that could be seen from the top of a haystack'.

Rottingdean is unusual not only for the mix of its inhabitants but in being the subject of at least four books. But other villages around England, mainly in the south, have had their historians too. These villages were largely self-supporting until at least the First World War and they might well have had their own barber, butcher, post office, cobbler, carpenter, policeman, blacksmith, and sometimes tailor and fire brigade. Villagers grew their own vegetables and raised chickens and killed their own animals. At Swanbrooke Down in East Anglia, up until 1914, it was unusual to marry anyone who lived more than three miles away. There were visitors, perhaps gypsies and tinkers, and labourers from outside who came to help with the harvest. Until the motoring age, population was often in steady decline. At Woughton-on-the-Green, now a suburb of Milton Keynes, the population had been falling since the middle of the nineteenth century — in 1911 it was 209; in 1921, 182; and by 1931, 167. As one would expect, there was little new building, at Swanbrooke Down virtually none until the 1930s.

Elmdon in Essex, fourteen miles south of Cambridge, was not on a direct route to anywhere. It too suffered from depopulation, to the extent that even in 1964 it contained fewer households than it had done 100 years before. The bicycle improved communications, as it did everywhere, but originally it proved too expensive for village women, although it did make commuting to work outside the village easier. Like village people all over England, the inhabitants of Elmdon habitually walked long distances. One farm labourer would leave his cottage at four in the morning and walk by the light of a lantern five miles to his farm to feed the animals, returning on foot in the evening. Women would walk to and fro to Saffron Walden, over six miles away, to do their weekly shopping. No wonder in later days there existed at Elmdon and elsewhere too in the countryside a marked aversion to walking.

There was of course the railway. However, even in populous counties such as Kent and Leicestershire only one village in every eight or nine possessed its own railway station, which meant more walking unless you managed to pick up a lift from the local carrier with his horse and wagon. The railway, though, could be less important than might be expected. In one Hampshire village, where the station was only a mile away, villagers seldom used it for travel to local towns. Not that the railway company would have minded much; its concern would have been for inter-urban routes, not short distance travellers. Nor was commuter traffic important. A mainline station had been established five miles away from Elmdon in 1861 and provided a direct connection with the City of London. But the first commuter arrived in the village only during the 1920s, and he hardly counted as a fully fledged representative of the modern world. He travelled to and from the station by pony and trap.

The most evocative, indeed moving, description of a village as it passes from one age to another appears in *Cider with Rosie*, an autobiography by the poet Laurie Lee. The village is Slad in Gloucestershire, where the Lee family arrived in the summer of 1918 when the writer was aged three. There were eight of them: Laurie, his mother and six siblings. The father had made off for the suburbs. Slad was a scattering of from twenty to thirty houses running down the slope of a valley, a village 'like a deep-running cave still linked to its antic past' where traces of the old stage roads lay still imprinted on the grass. And along the line of these roads, so villagers said, raced still the ghost of a midnight coach, drawn by flaring horses. There was a squire, the centre of the village and, like it, ancient. With watery eyes he performed his duties, opening his garden for a fête, delivering prizes at the village school and making speeches on special occasions. As for the outside world, it was most evident in the hooters which each morning summoned the younger inhabitants — walking or bicycling — to the textile mills of Stroud, a few miles over the valley. But the village itself lay in a time warp, its horizon of woods 'the limit of our world'.

It was a world where, in Laurie Lee's words, the horse was king and almost everything grew around him. Fodder, smithies, stables, paddocks, distances and the rhythm of the days. The horse's eight miles an hour was the limit of movement, as it had been since the days of the Romans. Nostalgically, Lee recalled a June day, sitting in the village schoolroom and listening to the sounds from outside: 'the creaking of wagons going past the school, harness-jingle and the cries of the carters, the calling of cows ... gunshots from the warren'. But it was a world that was coming to an end.

> The last days of my childhood were also the last days of the village. I belonged to that generation which saw, by chance, the end of a thousand years' life. The change came late to our Cotswold valley, didn't really show itself till the late 1920s, I was twelve by then, but during that handful of years I witnessed the whole thing happen ... The brass-lamped motor-car came coughing up the road, followed by the clamorous charabanc; the solid-tyred bus climbed the dusty hills and more people came and went. Chickens and dogs were early sacrifices, falling demented beneath the

wheels. The old folk, too, had strokes and seizures, faced by speeds beyond comprehension. Then scarlet motor-bikes, the size of five-barred gates, began to appear in the village, on which our youths roared like rockets up the two-minute hills ...

L. T. C. Rolt, engineer, writer and passionate motorist, spent part of his childhood on the northern slopes of the Cotswolds, near Winchcombe. In his words, 'Rural life in this part of Gloucestershire changed more profoundly in my lifetime than at any other period since this [his parents'] ancient house was built, the enclosures not excepted.'

Into these once-isolated villages came newcomers, some to build houses in a modern style, some to take over old ones as secondary homes. Out of the villages went the young, seeking jobs further afield, perhaps to leave the village for ever. Social ties with neighbours were loosened. Village shops were to close as the inhabitants found the local market towns more convenient, and probably cheaper. The towns were affected too. They might gain extra business, but on the other hand they might find themselves bypassed as motor transport swept its passengers on to other places which previously had been too far away. In Laurie Lee's words, 'The sun and moon, which once arose from our hill, rose from London now in the East.' It was not only transport but life itself which picked up speed.

It was less the car than the bus and Lee's 'clamorous charabanc' which made the difference to these country villages. Nationally as well, for cars were still well beyond the financial reach of most people and motor cycles were suited mainly to the young. The bus was a serious competitor at last. It was not of course just Thomas Tilling that suffered so badly at the beginning from problems of bus reliability. The pioneering company which, in May 1898, started up the first (petrol-driven) motor bus service, running a mile and a half along Princes Street in Edinburgh, closed down at the end of 1901, having lost £14,000. Other casualties included Harry Lawson's London Steam Omnibus Company. Later on the Birmingham Bus Company regretted conversion and reverted to horses. The historians of London Transport go so far as to say that had the reliability of motor buses been achieved more quickly the whole history of transport in London in the twentieth century would almost certainly have taken a different course. For one thing, some tube lines would probably have never been built. (Early taxis failed too. In December 1898 there were seventy-one electric taxis on the London streets; by June 1900 there were none. The hansom cabs were to enjoy another four years' monopoly.)

The Locomotives on Highways Act set free cars (and thus taxis too) but not heavier transport, which had to wait on the Heavy Motor-Car Order in 1904 for their emancipation. Thus there was ground to make up and new technology to be developed. As J. M. Birch of Birch Brothers said, 'The roads were very bad, the machines very unreliable, the drivers very inexperienced, and the maintenance staff very ignorant.' *The Economist* in March and April of 1905 foretold a great future for the 'motor omnibus' but warned would-be investors that this was still a very speculative business. Progress was hampered too, not in this case by technical defects but by a traffic accident which received wide notoriety: in July 1906 at Handcross on the Brighton Road, ten passengers were swept off the (open) top deck of a bus by the branches of a tree and killed.

Time, better roads and, above all, the First World War, with the demand it generated for trucks and the experience it gave to drivers, enabled the bus to realize its potential. Distinct types of operator emerged. One was municipal authorities, another large private companies such as Tillings, BET and Scottish Motor Traction. The connection between electric power and the automobile was to be close, and it is significant that BET — its full name, the British Electric Traction Company — registered as a company in 1896 both for the carriage of passengers and goods, and for the generation and distribution of electricity. Gifted entrepreneurs played their part with buses too. George White of the Bristol Tramway and Carriage Company is an example; by 1914 his firm was the second-largest operator of motor buses in England. White had had little formal education, and his parents had been respectively a painter/decorator and a domestic servant. In later years he moved on to form the first viable aeroplane manufacturer in Britain — what became the Bristol Aeroplane Company.

Progress among bus companies in the 1920s was so rapid that an attempt by a journalist to produce a regular *Travel by Road Guide* with detailed bus timetables had to be dropped; there were too many

Right: A poster by F. C. Herrick, 1923, advertising motor-coach tours by charabanc. These tours were immensely popular, opening up the countryside in an unprecedented way.

changes going on. In 1925 there was introduced the first true long-distance coach service in Britain, which ran between London and Bristol. The firm of Ribbles organized travel from London to Blackpool and the north-west by Leyland Tiger buses, a direct journey that ignored towns on the way. Excursions were very popular. Coaches went out on tours of such stately homes as were open and to the battlefields of France. H. V. Morton wrote of seeing chara-bancs piling up at Wells. Excursions for shopping attracted many customers. In 1927, for instance, Wright Brothers of Burnley in Lancashire pressed 'Shop Assistants and other Business People' to take tickets on their Pullman Saloon Service for shopping in Leeds, which they described as '*The acknowledged greatest and best shopping centre in the North of England*'. And when the shopping was done, the party went on to the Leeds pantomime. Many of these trips centred on sporting events, often football or horse racing, and, from 1926, greyhound racing.

Most of the trips of the type described above were organized by large firms, or at least by firms which operated a number of vehicles. In the smaller villages, though, small independents, maybe just one man and his vehicle, were the most likely to be found. It might be the traditional village carrier gone up to date. Take the example of Elmdon, the Essex village already referred to with its prodigious walkers. The carrier there had provided a somewhat irregular ser-vice, transporting goods and parcels and sometimes live chickens. He might also carry people — for instance, women shoppers who, to save money, might take a single fare only to Saffron Walden, or wherever else they were going, and then walk home. This carrier switched to motor in 1929. At Swanbrooke Down, before a bus ser-vice arrived — again in 1929 — there was no regular carrier. His place was taken, at least as far as people were concerned, by a vil-lager, usually the blacksmith or the boot maker, using pony and trap. Occasionally, though, you found enterprising individuals who switched well before the end of the 1920s. Ezra Laycock, the village postman at Cowling on Keighley Moor in Yorkshire, was one of them. His job entailed walking three miles every morning to collect the mail, so, to save time, he bought first a horse and cart and then, in order to carry passengers, a wagonette. In 1905 he took a further step forward and bought a motor omnibus. A successful business resulted.

Many of the independents of the 1920s were not country people at all. They were ex-servicemen, possessing a gratuity or able to borrow money, who took advantage of their driving experience and a knowledge of mechanics. These aspiring transport operators were fortunate, for while ordinary cars were in very short supply immediately after the war, there were on the market large numbers of now redundant army vehicles. Most of them were likely to start up with a single vehicle, often what was called a 'jitney', small, fast and cheap and bought on hire purchase. They took advantage of the run-down state of the railways, which were overcrowded and with fares set artificially at a high level. Queues for tickets were commonplace. Len Turnham, who ran a motor-taxi service and car-repair business, spotted his opportunity. He strolled along the queue for the booking office at Victoria Station selling cut-price tickets for a bus service to Brighton and back.

The switch from horse to motor in country towns and villages could be upsetting. While in the early days buses would often stop at once, wherever they were hailed, they were less cosy than the old horse carriers. For instance, Laurie Lee's mother — 'unpunctuality bred in her bones' — found it all but impossible to adapt to timetables. The horse world too was bred in her bones: her father had been a coachman and her five brothers had been intended to follow in his footsteps. One of them did, but another, a rip-roaring character, was taken on as a bus driver. Laurie Lee remembered him in charge of a double-decker, one of those 'solid-tyred, open-topped, passenger chariots ... the leviathans of the roads at that time — staggering siege-towers which often ran wild and got their top-decks caught under bridges', with Uncle Sid 'perched up high in his reeking cabin, his face sweating beer and effort, while he wrenched and wrestled at the steering wheel to hold the great bus on its course'.

But while buses in general offered new and desirable opportunities for shopping and recreation, it was the charabancs hired for outings which provided the real fun and that spirit of adventure and freedom lauded by H. V. Morton and indeed by writers on motoring since the very start. The 'sharrabang' (an Anglicization which did not stick), said Thomas Burke, 'has reopened the road to the poorest of us, and we can all catch the tang of open-air travel and the ecstasy of speed, which the railway cannot lend you'. He also noted with approval that the drivers were assuming something of the 'box-seat manner'.

Laurie Lee recalled how in the old days the choir outing to Gloucester in a farm wagon was considered a great excitement. Still it could not compare to a trip by charabanc; or rather by three charabancs to Clevedon with Uncle Sid out there in front with a crate of beer at his feet: '"Put her in top, Uncle Sid," we cried, as we roared through the summer country ... as we bounced and soared above the tops of hedges.' Clevedon, a small seaside town beyond Bristol, was something like four times as far from Slad as Gloucester, which a short time before the villagers had thought of as a 'foreign city'. On another occasion the expedition — this time with five charabancs — took the road to Weston-super-Mare, a larger seaside resort with a 'turgid pier'. Laurie recalled the long drive back by twilight with 'the small children sleeping, and the young girls gobbling shrimps. At sunset we stopped at a gaslit pub for the men to have one more drink. This lasted till all of them turned bright pink and started embracing their wives.'

Charabanc operators were often based at seaside resorts, where they could cater for outings from inland towns and villages and for the old and retired who frequently made up a significant part of the permanent seaside population. As early as 1910, an Eastbourne firm organized six-day tours to North Wales. The new opportunities for travel stimulated links between individual towns (or villages), one on the sea and the other inland. There was some brisk publicity. In Scotland, for instance, Rothesay, 'bustling and lively' was said to have 'earned many popular titles for itself — the "Brighton of the Clyde" and "the Madeira of Scotland"'. While the pier at Weston-super-Mare may have been 'turgid', many resorts along the coasts of Britain were spending money freely to make sure that their piers and promenades and all else which they had to offer were as attractive as possible.

But Rothesay and Weston-super-Mare and most of the others too were small fry in comparison to Blackpool and Southend. If Coventry represents the industrial impact of motoring and Brighton — as will be seen later — symbolizes its hedonistic spirit, Blackpool evokes the emancipation of the working class. As a recent book on this extraordinary town puts it, Blackpool, famous as Britain's largest, brashest, busiest and best-publicized popular resort, projects by reputation, enduringly, a permissive but unthreatening image of proletarians at play. With a resident population in 1930 of just over

100,000, it attracted 7 million visitors each year and was able, so it is estimated, to accommodate half a million in a single night. (The Southend figure was 5.5 million visitors.) H. V. Morton arrived in Blackpool in the late 1920s, just before the season started:

Blackpool Beach and the Tower in the 1920s. Road transport to Blackpool and other seaside resorts was making steady inroads into rail traffic.

> Four miles of boarding houses — waiting. Hotels, big and small — waiting. Furnished apartments, whose windows are like wide, eager eyes — waiting. Three piers, from whose extremities small boys catch dabs — waiting. Miles of yellow sand ... The largest and whitest open-air swimming pool in the world ... The Tower ... The Wheel, with its wide circle of empty cars ... cafés, restaurants, dance-halls, cinemas, theatres — all waiting for the Lancashire 'wakes', and for the deluge of free men and women who will soon descend on Blackpool like a riot migrating to the sea-coast.

Ten years later you could add an ice rink and a circus. 'Compared to Blackpool,' declared J. B. Priestley, 'places like Brighton and Margate and Yarmouth are merely playing at being popular seaside resorts.' The town was a capital of Show Business, a place with, so James Laver thought, more theatres than anywhere in the country outside of London. The great stars came — Charlie Chaplin before the war, when he was a champion clog dancer, Ivor Novello, Sybil Thorndike, Duke Ellington, Paul Robeson, Jack Buchanan, Cicely Courtneidge and Jack Hulbert — and above all the great favourites of the working-class north, Gracie Fields and George Formby. For Blackpool, while it drew visitors from all over the British Isles, was above all northern, above all Lancashire northern. On the beach or the promenade you might come across oddities like the Reverend Harold Davidson, the unfrocked rector of Stiffkey, sitting in a barrel, and next to him a cousin of Mahatma Gandhi who lay on a bed of nails. H. V. Morton declared Blackpool to be 'Lancashire's idea of the earthly paradise'. Don Haworth, born in 1924, remembered the soot and decay of east Lancashire and how in his native Burnley everything stopped for a week on the second weekend of July when half the population left town. Nearly everybody, he wrote, mill hand and boss, went to Blackpool. It was an unselfconscious place, and, after all, if you did not care for the noise and the brashness, you could take yourself off to Lytham St Annes, seven miles away down the coast.

Blackpool was not created by the automobile: it was a tumultuous resort well before a petrol-driven car had appeared on British roads. Indeed, even by 1939, more of its visitors arrived by train than by car, motor cycle and coach. Steadily, however, road transport had been gaining ground. The tonnage of traffic passing over the Preston to Blackpool road — the busiest holiday route in Britain — doubled between 1922 and 1925 and had more than doubled again by 1935. (Eight miles of the route was to form the first motorway in Britain.) In his *English Journey* of 1934, Priestley describes this road and the other approach roads too: they were

> very straight and wide [displaying] large, cheerfully vulgar advertisements. That is because they, like you, are going to Blackpool. Even if you did not intend to go to Blackpool, once you had got beyond Preston you would have to go there. The roads would suck you into Blackpool. That is what they are there for.

In a more stately tone, the British Association for the Advancement of Science, in the appendix to its 1936 annual report, observed that the existing parking facilities at Blackpool were insufficient for the motor cars which 'flow into the town every fine day in summer in embarrassing numbers'. But it is again Priestley who provides the most telling comment on how motoring was changing the face of Britain and how closely Blackpool had become associated with it. He is describing the system of arterial roads which he sees spreading over the country: 'Modern England', he says, 'is rapidly Blackpooling itself.'

The holiday resorts had their own influence on the development of the automobile — on the motor coach, on what started as the charabanc. In 1920 this vehicle was a simple affair. It was open, with a hood at the back which would be hauled down in bad weather. It seated up to thirty people in rows, each row with its own door and with the conductor obliged to cling to an outside running board as he collected fares. It was obviously unsatisfactory for long distances. By 1924 pneumatic tyres — a great improvement for all public passenger vehicles — provided increased comfort, and design became more elegant. The intense competition helped. The chassis became lower and 'parlour coaches', fully enclosed all-weather saloon coaches, were introduced. In 1927 the Greyhound fleet put into service four 'super de luxe buffet' coaches with lavatory and buffet. All seats were padded and equipped (as with an airplane now) with a fitment to hold lunch trays and a bell to ring the steward. These coaches were far removed from the old-type charabanc, though the old name lingered, employed disdainfully by those who did not use them. The old name stuck with the working class too. Richard Hoggart has described these coaches as the

> super-cinemas of the highways. They are, and particularly if they belong to a small firm specialising in day-trips for working people, plushily over-upholstered, ostentatiously-styled inside and out; they have lots of little chrome bits, little flags on top, fine names and loud radios. Every day in summer the arterial roads out of the big towns are thick with them humming towards the sea.

Ostentatious indeed, but then Mr Toad and many private motorists of his time and later had nothing at all against ostentatious styling or noise. Nevertheless, there was a notable difference in the approach to motoring. The private motorist revelled in his or her deliverance from the mass travel of the railways. It meant that you could drive alone or with spouse or lover or friends; the choice was yours. The coach passenger was still travelling in the mass — but, far from being a disadvantage, it was an essential part of the fun. The spirit was collective: coach passengers wanted to see others, they wanted to be with others. Moreover, unlike a train, a coach could be stopped by its passengers — often a group of like-minded people — should they hit on an enticing pub or a new place for lunch. You could take your own crate of beer and be as noisy as you wanted. (Well, not altogether, since some pubs objected to charabanc manners.) The holiday started when you got on the coach, not when you piled out of a railway carriage. The first child aboard to catch sight of the sea or to spot the Blackpool Tower earned a prize, a sweet or piece of chocolate. Coach trips took on their own rules, songs and customs.

The motor bus and the motor coach enabled the working class to participate in the motoring age, to enjoy for themselves its economic and social benefits. This was of the greatest importance. Few thinking people had been unaware of the political danger of a society split — and so conspicuously split — between haves and have-nots, those who could afford a car and those who could not. The philosopher and critic Rémy de Gourmont had called attention to the paradox: in a democratic epoch there had emerged an innovation which, in contrast to the railway, was by its nature individualistic and aristocratic. The population as a whole tolerated what was happening only because they believed that they would come to share in the benefits of automobilism. The *New Statesman* in 1926 insisted that there would be no need to call for a new spirit in industry when wages went high enough to allow workers to escape into the country at weekends. And the editor of the *Autocar* put it well when he wrote, 'The half of our industrial troubles would vanish if every worker had a motor vehicle, could see for himself the beauties of our own land, and by intercourse with strangers learn more of the actual truth of conditions in places hitherto strange to him.' Workers in the 1920s might not have had their own motor vehicles, but they did have the next best thing.

5

The Roaring Twenties

As the charabancs rolled home from Blackpool or Scarborough or Southend, they resounded with songs and music. But they were the songs of earlier times, not of Tin Pan Alley. It was 'Stop yer ticklin', Jock!', not even 'You can't Afford to Marry Me if you can't Afford a Ford'. Whatever the musical instruments aboard, they were more likely to be ukuleles than cornets or saxophones. And at the pubs, the charabanc parties did not request martinis or white ladies or manhattans. Maybe they knew from the cinema about flappers and sheikhs and shebas, but they would not be dancing the Charleston or yearning for the strains of Dixieland. And the women, while they might fancy Valentino, would not wear their hair bobbed, or crowned by a cloche hat. The Jazz Age was happening somewhere else.

If the motor cycle was familiar, the car still signified wealth and glamour. Its allure for the working-class young could be irresistible. In the novels of Patrick Hamilton, a world of pubs and Lyons Corner Houses, it is bait. There is Esther, aged eighteen, living in Brighton and working in a sweet shop, who has managed to save a nest egg. Motor cycles have come her way, but never has she stepped inside a car. Into her life steps a con man who takes her to the Metropole Hotel — a palace of luxury and grandeur — and shows her, parked outside, a 'slim, exquisite, beautiful, open car, painted bright red — a dream-car', which he claims to be his. By means of the car, the con man leads her to disaster.

In Hamilton's *The Siege of Pleasure* the scene is London and the victim Jenny Maple, exceptionally pretty and again eighteen. She has just landed a job as a cook/maid with a respectable household in Chiswick. Then, with a friend, she falls in with some men at a Hammersmith pub. One of them is Andy, aged about thirty and to Jenny, anyway fairly indifferent to men, distinctly unattractive. But then, lighting her cigarette with his 'beautiful cigarette lighter', Andy apologizes for the dirtiness of his hands:

> 'You get 'em covered all over with dirt — doing what I've been doing,' he added. She saw plainly enough that this was an invitation to ask him what he had been doing, but was not good-humoured enough to accept it.
>
> 'Muckin' about with one's car all the afternoon,' he explained, lighting a cigarette of his own.
>
> Jenny started: Had she heard correctly? Had he not said Car — 'one's car?' Car? The funny little man didn't have a car. Get away with him.
>
> 'Yes, it's a dirty job, I know', she said, as though she had frequently experienced nausea in the same task. (He probably worked in a garage, or it was his employer's car.)
>
> 'It is and all,' he replied. 'And it seems my car collects all the dirt there is in London.'
>
> 'Have you got a car, then?' It simply leaped out of her before she could stop herself.

Andy has indeed. '"Fond of Motoring?"' he asks her a minute or two later.

> 'Yes, I'm very fond of it, really', she replied. 'Specially in the summer months'. Jenny would have spoken more honestly had she said that she was fond of the prospect of Motoring in the summer months, for she had never been in a motor-car in her life. Hitherto an occasional pillion had formed the sum of her experience in this direction.

She gets drunk on port, agog at the sophisticated Andy, his car and a job he dangles in front of her. The party then piles into a car, there is a fatal accident involving a bicyclist and a disaster yet more calamitous than that which befell Esther.

Going up a step in the social scale and switching from fiction to real life, one encounters Mr Ryder, a senior bank clerk at Burnley, as described by Don Haworth. The time is the 1930s. We are still a long way from cocktails and jazz; certainly no one could perceive in Mr Ryder a former Bright Young Thing. He was not, however, run of the mill, a fact he signalled by wearing a bowler hat on weekdays, when most men wore cloth caps, and a cloth cap on Sundays, when they wore bowlers. In the street shared by the Haworths and the Ryders, transport was limited. There was a pony and trap driven by a man to whom nothing was more pleasurable than to pass motor vehicles broken down at the roadside. Then there were a couple of unreliable sports-type cars which 'both dripped oil and smelled heavily of petrol and were almost permanently under repair'. The Ryder household was the only one to possess an unimpeachably reliable and dignified car, and the ability to range freely into the far-flung countryside.

Only the colour of Mr Ryder's car — it was a pale daffodil yellow — was in any way exuberant. The car was not in daily use. In fact, it was only in use at all on Sundays during the summer months. The rest of the time (except when it was being cleaned), it stayed in a lock-up garage. 'No pleasure-motorist of normal prudence,' says Haworth, 'would think of using his car every day or leave it standing out in all weathers.' Mr Ryder, who came home to lunch, walked the mile between his house and the bank four times a day; when it rained he took the bus. For him to have parked all day in the street outside the bank where he worked would have seemed ostentatious, if not eccentric. And to expose the car (with its canvas hood) needlessly to the rain or wind would have been irresponsible. It was kept in an immaculate condition. On Saturday afternoons, Mr Ryder and his two sons washed and polished it so that it would be ready for its travels the next day. Even the engine compartment, 'which spaciously displayed all the separate organs, shone as though it had just been assembled'. Haworth remembered the 'wonderful smell' of petrol, polish and leather. When he took the wheel, Mr Ryder donned a tweed suit.

The same attention to the car, almost a reverence towards it, could be seen in America as well. In Sinclair Lewis's *Main Street*, the heroine's husband 'nursed his two-year-old Buick even in winter, when it was stored in the stable-garage behind the house. He filled the grease cups, varnished a fender, removed from behind the back seat the débris of gloves, copper washers, crumpled maps, dust and

A road hazard, London. In the 1930s *The Economist* was to speculate whether the prohibition of horses in central London would be followed by a ban on private cars.

greasy rags. Winter noons he wandered out and stared owlishly at the car.' It is true that cars then required more care than they do now. None the less, there was more to this than mere prudence. David Gartman, in his *Auto Opium*, describes his father in America after the Second World War. His father's identity, Gartman insists, depended on cars: '"I'm a Chevy man", he resolutely declared, and never bought anything else.' He worked in an oil refinery, where he found little to enjoy. However, his 'wounds were soon soothed by the comforting salve of automotive consumerism'.

The passion for their cars which characterized Mr Ryder and Mr Gartman was deeply felt but hardly lyrical — less even perhaps than that aroused in Patrick Hamilton's girls, and much less than that to be found among the affluent and upper class. Take this as an example:

> White, magnificent as a royal barge but earthbound and resting at ease on her powerful wheels, the Hispano absorbed the last flickers of daylight which, in the semblance of ivory and silver, descended on her coachwork. For three hours, with the force of a horizontal rocket, she had sped through the *Landes*. Now she was at rest. Children, come to worship, circled cautiously around.

The 6.5-litre Hispano-Suiza, half French, half Spanish, was hailed on its appearance in 1919 at the Paris motor show as the finest car in the world. In Pierre Frondaie's book *L'Homme à l'Hispano* of 1925 (from which the quotation comes), it is no mere piece of machinery; it is a projectile storming its way through the vast pine forest of south-west France, terrifying, as it goes, the wild boar and other denizens of the woods. Later in the book, as the Hispano descends on Biarritz, it takes the form of a beast of prey.

This is a fictional world of fast cars and sophistication in which the machines themselves become characters. In *The Island of Sheep*, John Buchan sets against each other two of the star performers in motor sport during the late 1920s and early 1930s: the British Bentley, 'a steady bulldog of a car', superbly adaptable, and the American Stutz, relentless and sinister, and slightly faster. There is a chase up through England into Scotland, with the Stutz ('a wasp-like thing'), carrying would-be kidnappers, pursuing the hero, Lombard, who escapes by means of luck and guile.

As we have already seen, there were plenty of novels about motoring. Indeed, one British husband and wife team named Williamson made a career of them: active from virtually the start, they were still going in the 1920s. But while the car is new, the plot can be quite old-fashioned. In the 1911 novel *Sylvia's Chauffeur*, you might expect in the chauffeur a petrol-scented version of Lady Chatterley's gamekeeper; you would, though, find only a conventional scenario with the chauffeur turning out to be a viscount in disguise.

The British writer most closely linked to cars was Dornford Yates, author of innumerable adventure stories, who made his name with the immensely popular Berry series, nine books of which were published between 1914 and 1952. (Three of them, *Berry and Co.*, *Jonah and Co.*, *Adele and Co.*, were republished in 1976 and 1981.) The 'Co.' consists of six people, three men and three women married or related to each other, and their adventures. According to Yates's biographer, one of them, the eponymous Jonah, a skilled driver, is partly based on S. F. Edge. Berry himself, the principal character, does not wear well. With touches about him of Bulldog Drummond, he is given to unremitting facetiousness, which takes on an angry tone when he is confronted with foreigners, Jews or nouveaux riches. Here is an example:

'*For-rard!*' yelled Berry. '*For-r-a-r-d!* Out of the way, fat face, or we'll take the coat off your back.'

A portly Frenchman leaped into safety with a scream.

With the exception of Berry himself, the characters are not very interesting. It is the cars that give pace to the stories and a lift to the writing. Dornford Yates is informative on some of the problems faced by motorists in the early 1920s. For instance, Jonah owns a Rolls-Royce which, so it seems, is without any locks. It is removed by a neighbour who mistakes it for his own. In their turn, the friends, equally oblivious, drive off in the neighbour's Rolls. On another occasion they wonder whether it would be safe to leave the Rolls alone for a few minutes in a country lane, and when they attend the local dog show think it safer to park in the garage of a nearby brewery. So inconvenient is all this that for their next car they send off for a steering-wheel lock. Other old problems are still only partly resolved. Punctures are frequent and so they make it a practice to carry two spare wheels. Dust is still a menace. When the car in front maintains an average speed of 45mph in hot weather on untarred roads, it is inevitable that those in an (open) car behind will be covered in dust after something like twenty minutes.

In *Jonah and Co.* there occurs an exciting race against time. The friends discover that the youngest of their group, Jill, is to be kidnapped when the train she has just caught arrives in Paris. The only way to save her is to intercept the train when it stops at Bordeaux, 150 miles away from their house at Pau. They have three hours. Temporarily bereft of Rolls-Royces, they borrow a fast but unidentified limousine which takes on a human persona. It, or rather she, is 'the lady whose lap we sat in moving at eighty-four' ... 'She ate her way up the rise, snorting with indignation' ... 'She responded like the thoroughbred she was.' Then, like Frondaie's Hispano, they are in the Landes.

> Within this magic zone the throb of the engine, the hiss of the carburettor, the swift brush of the tires [*sic*] upon the road — three rousing tones, yielding a thunderous chord, were curiously staccato. The velvet veil of silence we rent in twain; but as we tore it, the folds fell back to hang like mighty curtains about our path, stifling all echo, striking reverberation dumb.

They press on, the speedometer touching 93mph. 'So, our narrowed eyes nailed to the straight grey ribbon streaming into the distance, the sea and the waves roaring in our ears, folded in the wings of the wind, we cheated Dusk of seven breathless miles and sent Nature packing with a fork in her breech.' They get to Bordeaux just in time. This may not be writing to win anyone the Booker Prize, but in its high colour and verve it illustrates something of the romance and excitement that gripped motoring in the 1920s.

Berry and his friends could afford Rolls-Royces and fast coupés — two of them, called Ping and Pong. They were *rentiers*, able to spend the winter in the sunshine of Pau in the Pyrenees. To put it mildly, when not involved in an adventure, they had few responsibilities. They had, of course, been affected by the war — the men had fought in it — but they would still have been quite at home in the Edwardian decade. How far generally had people changed since the war? It is a question with a bearing on attitudes to motoring. Winston Churchill, unveiling at Oxford a memorial to T. E. Lawrence (killed in a motor-cycle accident), stated that, after the war, 'Mankind returned with indescribable relief to its long-interrupted, fondly cherished ordinary life.' Lawrence was an exception, 'left once more moving alone on a different plane and at a different speed'. Lawrence's reaction was indeed esoteric, but numerous people would have disagreed with Churchill's view that they were happy to return to the old way of life. Ford Madox Ford implied that for many it was impossible: 'You may say that everyone who had taken physical part in the war was then mad. No one could have come through that shattering experience and still view life and mankind with any normal vision.' Another writer, recalling the time, saw the world of the twenties as existing 'in a kind of historical parenthesis: a timeless St. Martin's Summer, in which the past was forgotten, and the future, as far as possible, ignored'.

And even if older people could settle down as before, the young could not. After the slaughter on the battlefields, the shattering of so many ideals, the disillusion with those elders who, for all their pomp and complacency, had so lamentably failed, it was not surprising. George Orwell was to write that at this time there existed among the young a curious hatred of old men, that the 'dominance of "old men"' was held responsible for every evil known to humanity'. All young minds, wrote V. S. Pritchett, were permeated by a basic belief that until you are free you do not know who you are. J. B. Priestley considered that a fundamental change had taken place. To Mr Smeeth, a senior clerk in the City who figures in Priestley's *Angel Pavement* of 1930, his children were foreigners,

> not simply because they belonged to a younger generation but because they belonged to a younger generation that existed in a different world ... They had grown up to the sound of the Ford car rattling down the street, and that Ford car had gone rattling away, to the communal rubbish heap, with a whole load of ideas that seemed still of supreme importance to Mr Smeeth. They were the children of the Woolworth stores and the moving pictures ... Their world was at once larger and shallower than that of their parents. They were less English, more cosmopolitan.

The imagery of the Ford car fits the time. For it was in the 1920s that the motoring age reached its full expression, its flowering, or, to use a better metaphor, its full pitch. Motoring was a blessing that was still unblemished. It gripped the young. As Tom Wolfe has put it, 'To the young, for whom fantasy often looms larger and more important than life, the car is the perfect receptacle for self-expression and escape from reality.' The motoring writer Cyril Posthumus recalled his excitement as boy living in the suburbs of London at Sunbury-on-Thames. From the age of seven, he and his elder brother eagerly scanned the village street for the next car that came along. More often than not it was a Bullnose Morris Cowley, with its high exhaust note and squealing brakes. Others he recalled were more recondite: an Angus Sanderson owned by the local electrician, Calcotts, Clynos, an ugly black Hands, a Rhode. A car every five minutes signified what they considered 'busy conditions'. Races at Kempton Park made for good days, with a stream of cars which were often rerouted through the road where they lived. Then it would be chauffeur-driven Daimlers, Rolls-Royces, Sunbeams and Packards, as well as lesser makes. In the London suburbs, according to James Kenward, the toy car was a familiar object on the pavements at least ten years before the children's parents became car owners. Vivian Ogilvy, a young adult, and his friends laughed at old buffers as they scrambled into their old-fashioned crocks. They too could recognize the make of car by the sound of its engine, but they were interested only in sleek new models. Sometimes the passion for cars took a different form, as with the French writer Pierre Benoit, author of the 1929 *L'Auto*, who as a boy dreamed of a huge car with emerald-green bodywork and a chauffeur to match, and its interior amply furnished with enamel flasks.

The young were beginning to have money to spend, to carry more weight economically. In poorer families the period between starting work and marriage was the time when a person was likely to be best off. Magazines directed at the teenage market appeared, among them (from 1927) the *Motor Cycle Book for Boys*. If boys could not aspire to cars, they could perhaps afford motor cycles. Sales soared. In 1919 there were around 115,000 motor cycles on the road; in 1930, 724,000 — an increase of between six and seven times. The girls too were enthusiastic, even if they were much more likely to be riding pillion — on the 'flapper bracket' — than actually driving.

These were the veritably young; there were also many others who were 'young at heart', and who acted young. It is a distinguishing feature of the time. Patrick Balfour, journalist and peer, asked rhetorically in the 1930s, 'In the twenties did not every man, however rich, feel richer; however young, feel younger ... ?' And they bought cars at an astonishing rate. If motor-cycle registrations in the decade increased between six and seven times, car registrations went up by half as much again.

Patrick Balfour was writing not of the habitués of Patrick Hamilton's sad saloon bars or of the Mr Ryders of Burnley but of the sophisticated and frivolous world of London and the Riviera, the world of the Bright Young Things, of Huxley and Waugh. The world too of Scott Fitzgerald, the exemplar, the paradigm, of the decade. Fitzgerald's books are soaked in connotations of motoring. Cars themselves abound. In *Tender is the Night* the central character, Dick Diver, owns an Isotta Fraschini, which for glamour rivalled the Hispano-Suiza itself. When late in the book his wife reflects on the staleness of her marriage and her resolution to leave Dick for another man, the description goes: 'Nicole had been designed for change, for flight, with money as fins and wings. The new state of things would be no more than if a racing chassis, concealed for years under the body of a family limousine, should be stripped to its original self.'

In *The Great Gatsby* the cars from New York pull up night after night in front of Jay Gatsby's enormous Long Island mansion, to park five deep on the drive, while 'men and girls came and went like moths among the whisperings and the champagne and the stars'. Gatsby's character is elusive, but, thinks his friend and neighbour Nick Carraway, there is something gorgeous about him, 'some heightened sensitivity to the promises of life'. His Roll-Royce 'was a rich cream colour, bright with nickel, swollen here and there in its monstrous length with triumphant hat-boxes and supper-boxes and tool-boxes, and terraced with a labyrinth of wind-shields that mirrored a dozen suns. Sitting down behind many layers of glass in a sort of green leather conservatory, we started to town.'

Gatsby's Rolls is a Death Car, like the Hispano-Suiza in Michael Arlen's *The Green Hat* and the car in Elizabeth Bowen's *To the North*. The association is obvious: cars are dangerous. And in real life some of the most significant deaths of the twentieth century involved cars: for instance, the assassinations of the Archduke Franz Ferdinand in 1914 and of President Kennedy. Some of the most glamorous individuals of their time have died in motoring accidents: Lawrence of Arabia, the film stars James Dean and Grace Kelly, and Princess Diana. Sometimes the associations were macabre. The dancer Isadora Duncan had witnessed her children drown when their car plunged off a bridge into the Seine. She herself was strangled, throttled to death, when the heavily fringed scarf round her neck was caught in a wheel of a Bugatti racer. The 1934 Ford in which the gangsters Bonnie and Clyde were killed in a police ambush was bought, riddled with 169 bullet holes, by a man who earned from it over thirty-nine years more than $2 million in exhibition fees.

The last chapter was concerned with the automobile as a functional entity, as an instrument which allowed people, however romantically they dressed up the experience, to make new discoveries, to follow the message and the footsteps of Lord Montagu and Rudyard Kipling. This chapter sees it as a cultural icon. No medium — not books, not newspapers, not radio — did so much to cast it in that role as the cinema. It would be difficult, to take just one example, to think of inter-war Chicago without calling up a mental picture of gangsters, tommy guns and cars. It is an impression that is based on fact, but, for anyone, the image would owe far more to film than to newspaper reports, let alone history books. Cecil B. De Mille declared that automobiles and movies were so to speak twins, rising to popularity together, both reflecting 'the love of motion and speed, the restless urge towards improvement and expansion, the kinetic energy of a young, vigorous nation'. (Indeed in De Mille's *Sunset Boulevard*, a melodramatic rendering of movie history, the Isotta Fraschini in which Erich von Stroheim drives Gloria Swanson to the Paramount studios is almost as much a character as the stars themselves.) Cars, usually chasing or being chased, had provided standard fare for films from the beginning. They feature in classics such as Griffith's *Intolerance*; in slapstick comedy, as with the Keystone Cops, and in crime thrillers with stars such as James Cagney, and Jean Gabin in a Citroën '*traction avant*'. The pre-1939 British cinema made road movies such as Hitchcock's *Young and Innocent* and Arthur Wood's *They Drive by Night*. Even George Formby was brought in to star as a motor-cycle contestant in the Isle of Man TT races in *No Limit* (1935), in which he has been described as being 'as funny as a serious accident'. In a later film, Spielberg's *Duel* of 1971, a travelling salesman is pursued across the country by a murderous automobile, an enormous truck which, with its driver never more than glimpsed, becomes a sort of robotic killer from a nightmare. The same theme turns up in *The Car* of 1977. As an example of how films can influence car manufacturers, it is worth referring to a recent report in the *Financial Times* (26–27 January 2002, weekend edition) entitled 'Aston Martin chiefs told to change out of bondage gear'. Apparently inflamed by the association between their marque and James Bond films, Aston Martin were proposing silver handcuff keyrings and 'leather underwear merchandise' to buyers of their car. Ford, the parent company, was not amused.

Film stars found an attachment to cars (whether genuine or assumed) helpful to their publicity. Rudolph Valentino, who was perpetually featured in publicity photographs getting in and out of cars, was at his death awaiting the delivery of an Isotta Fraschini. The cowboy actor Tom Mix attached a saddle to the roof of his car and had his initials painted all over the bodywork. Gary Cooper, evidently not the restrained character he usually played, sported the figure of a running girl as a mascot on his pale green Duesenberg. Robert Taylor was photographed polishing his Packard. It was good public relations to be concerned with the mechanics: Ann Miller, it seems, took great interest in the inner workings of her cars and was to be seen peering with a delighted smile at the engine of her Ford V8. More plausible motoring heroes were racing champions, car and motor cycle. Malcolm Campbell, whose initial racing career

One of W. O. Bentley's cars racing in 1929. The 'Bentley Boys' won at Le Mans five times in eight years.

achieved little success, discovered a Darracq — a very fast marque — in a junk yard, overhauled it ('her' would have been the correct description) and won a classic race at Brooklands. After the First World War he turned to spectacular attempts on the land speed record, becoming the first person to travel on land at more than 150mph. Public interest in his career was stimulated by his rivalry with Henry Segrave, winner of the French Grand Prix in 1923, with each of them attempting to beat successive speeds of first 150mph and then 200mph. In 1932, at Salt Lake City, Campbell achieved 300mph. He and Segrave competed too for water speed records. Segrave was killed in an attempt on Lake Windermere; the same fate was to befall Campbell's son Donald after the Second World War.

Other motoring celebrities were the 'Bentley Boys', a group of wealthy young sportsmen. With the financial backing of Wolf Barnato, son of the randlord Barney, they achieved huge racing successes in the 1920s, and great publicity as well, mainly of course as a result of their prowess but also because of a certain apparent amateurism and insouciance which was much appreciated by the British public. They filled the gossip columns. At one of Barnato's parties the waiters wore racing kit, including crash helmets, and the table was set up as a miniature Brooklands. After the Bentley company was taken over by Rolls-Royce, W. O. Bentley went on to join Lagonda, a British firm founded by a mechanically minded American opera singer, for whom he designed a 12-cylinder super-sports car.

Motoring was closely associated in people's minds with other sports and activities: with football and cricket, with horse racing, and with greyhound racing, which flourished in the inter-war years. No sporting tie, however, was more immediate than that with golf. Partly it was, as in the case of motoring and the cinema, that the two had grown up together. J. J. Hissey, in his 1913 book, recorded a conversation he had had, or rather tried to have, with a taciturn gentleman he met in an hotel dining room. His usual conversational gambits having got him nowhere and thinking to himself that everybody played golf nowadays, Hissey opened up on that subject. It was a complete failure. His companion replied 'briefly and sarcastically' that he was no golfer; in fact, he said, 'I think, as a game, it's inferior to marbles.' Hissey fled the room in disgust. Probably most motorists would have done the same. One attraction to them lay in the exercise golf provided, exercise held to be necessary if you spent time in a car. The *Gentlewoman* magazine in 1912 recommended it for that reason. The alternatives were uninspiring: 'When one has a car, walking becomes tame and uninteresting, cycling has no fascination.' Advertisements for early motor cars often treated their products as a natural conveyance for golfers or polo players. The association carried on, with one writer on motor touring declaring that nowadays golf clubs seemed almost necessary accessories to a touring car. The Automobile Golfing Society received a trophy presented by the *Autocar*. It does come as something of a surprise to see that in March 1922, Lord Montagu's old journal, the *Car Illustrated*, went so far as to change its name to *Car and Golf*. Readers wrote in enthusiastically. 'Why has [sic] motoring and golf not been combined before, it is an innovation overdue by ten years,' one demanded. Yet however well the two might fit together in principle, the mix was less satisfactory on paper. *Car and Golf* was usually divided into two distinct sections. They did, though, merge with articles on touring: for instance, one on touring in Scotland and another on the Severn Valley. Most interesting now perhaps is a piece in January 1923 on 'Riviera holidays'. (January was a suitable month for its appearance since the Riviera was still a winter and not a summer resort.) The atmosphere was lively — 'a perfect kaleidoscope of colour, carnival, laughing Amazons and jazz music'.

> Every year, as soon as the Christmas festivities are past, fashionable society turns its golden lorgnettes to this happy Utopia, where the sun rarely plays hide-and-seek and the damp chill of our English winter is unknown ... The advent of the motor car, together with the spread of its contemporary, the Ancient Game, has undoubtedly added vastly to the charm and luxury of the Riviera. Splendid roads and varying scenery, together with the presence of many picturesque golf courses of all-round excellence, supply the golfing motorist with a never-ending source of delight.

It was not only the 'damp chill' of England and the plentiful golf courses which made motoring holidays on the Continent, particularly in France, popular with those who could afford to travel. The roads abroad were empty and straight by comparison with home, although not always well paved. The crowds at seaside resorts were smaller and there were fewer charabanc drivers (so often guilty of 'hoggish behaviour', complained *Car and Golf*), and anyway the Continent was not that expensive given the depreciation of local currencies against the pound. It was just more fun to drive on the Continent. However, what Western Europe no longer provided was that sense of adventure which had been so dear to pre-war motorists. You had to go further afield. Two experienced travellers, one of them the director of the touring department of the AA, undertook a 6,300-mile trip in 1928 which carried them among other places to Romania, a country where the tourist with a car was virtually unknown and where they were received rather as if they were explorers. At one place, the villagers enthusiastically led them to the inn. The travellers wanted food, but the language problem seemed insoluble. They made what they imagined to be appropriate noises to show what they needed. The villagers, though, did not catch their meaning and, thinking that their guests were just being funny, laughed heartily and dug each other in the ribs. The two Englishmen tried imitating the boiling of an egg and the sound of soup, until finally it got across that they were just hungry travellers and not public entertainers.

Car Illustrated was not the only magazine to change its name in the

1920s. The *Gentlewoman*, a magazine with a strong interest in motoring, renamed itself in 1926 the *Gentlewoman and Modern Life*, a title which was not quite yet an oxymoron. It started off with a provocative double-page cartoon showing a dining room — dinner is over — with only women left at table. The men can be seen peering out impatiently from the drawing room, as the hostess commands, 'Come along, girls, no more stories. It's time to join the gentlemen.' How far the cartoon actually reflected women's emancipation, or at least an approach to social equality with men, is a moot point, certainly as it affected motoring. That the war had made a great difference is undoubted. Moreover, from a woman's point of view, cars were more user-friendly than they had been. You did not have to clamber over the thing to get aboard, there was (hopefully) no more cranking to be done to get the engine started and no longer did the wind blow directly into face and hair. What is more, with visual design so improved, cars looked beautiful. On the other hand, as a recent writer has pointed out, an official survey (albeit one on a small scale) conducted by the Ministry of Transport in 1933 suggested that only 12 per cent of driving licences in Britain were held by women. The person you would expect to find behind the wheel was the husband not the wife. There is plenty of evidence to show that old prejudice lingered. The term 'woman driver' was pejorative: it implied the woman dithered and crawled along the road, making uncertain hand signals. (That was despite the evidence from statistics which revealed the woman to be a better insurance risk than the man.) Women were still expected, metaphorically at any rate, to stick to the hearth, to care for the home. 'How can the present-day flapper exist for a 100 miles on the storm-tossed seat of her "boy's" motor cycle, apparently enjoying the experience to the full, and still apply the word "gentler" to her sex ...?' demanded an editorial in *Car and Golf* in December 1922. Women in the war had shown themselves capable of dealing with most, anyway, of the mechanical demands still entailed by driving. But they were a minority. Could women generally cope with punctures and breakdowns? Would they find even double-declutching straightforward — synchromesh gears being uncommon before the 1930s?

Yet there is no doubt that women were regarded by manufacturers as very important when it came to choosing the family car. Their status and influence varied with social class. It is to the point that

Models, their clothes designed by Sonia Delaunay, pose in front of her Talbot in the Bois de Boulogne, 1925. The car seems unusually restrained, for Delaunay was apt to paint her cars in vivid geometric and abstract designs.
© L & M Services BV Amsterdam
20030409

one of the most striking images of the time, perhaps the most striking of all, is Tamara de Lempicka's self-portrait of 1929, sometimes called *Tamara in Her Green Bugatti*. The painter, aloof and the ultimate in chic, sits at the wheel, an icon, the very spirit of women's emancipation and modernity, her car an instrument of pleasure and excitement. In the words of the *New York Times*, looking back from 1978, she is 'the steely-eyed goddess of the automobile age'. It is pure 1920s, pre-Depression, pre-disillusion, a world of high fashion, of Frondaie's Hispano-Suiza and of Biarritz, where 'from far off, up towards the Hotel du Palais, one heard the great lithe automobiles take wing'. By the late 1920s you could no longer, so it was said, appear at Biarritz or Deauville in last year's Hispano, any more than you could wear last year's fur coat or be accompanied by last year's breed of dog. True, Mibsy Bowles, Countess Porcheri, the American diamond queen who glittered 'like a Christmas Tree' on the Riviera, remained faithful to Rolls-Royces, but only until they were outpriced by a Duesenberg with a special body and then by the 18-cylinder Cadillac. Her friend Sir Francis Rose (Hispano and Rolls) described his grandmother's exacting taste when it came to ordering a car body:

They [the body builders] sent at least six carefully-painted water-colours. She had ordered a brougham-like design with large silver carriage-lanterns and basketwork sides with patent-leather mud-guards. The interior fittings were to be of tortoise-shell, mother-of-pearl, and gold marquetry. The inside door handles were copies of eighteenth-century sphinx walking-stick handles. Every detail was carefully discussed, even to whether buttons or tufts of fringe should be used for the *capitonnage* of the blue cloth upholstery.

Car interiors glowed with colour. They were furnished to match the lizard and snake skin that made up shoes and handbags. Said Lempicka, clothed by Hermès, 'I was always dressed like the car and the car like me.' Sonia Delaunay devised fabrics for the car to match clothes for the owner, and her own cars were painted in vivid geo-metric and abstract designs. Gabriel Voisin, a leading car manufac-turer favoured by Josephine Baker, devised his own tartan to decorate the coachwork of his 1922 saloon car. (Men could hardly compete with all this, but they did buy bulky raccoon coats; Paul Whiteman obliged by recording his 'Doing the Raccoon'.)

The British on the whole were less adventurous, although Lord Lonsdale attended the marriage in 1922 of Princess Mary and Lord Lascelles in a 'spanking primrose yellow and black Daimler'. But in Britain too fashion in cars was very important. Roll-Royce found that success could bring its own problems. Their cars sold so well to war profiteers and nouveaux riches that the car became for a period associated with them and was therefore less attractive to more tradi-tional buyers. The Earl of Cottenham, in his 1928 book *Motoring To-day and To-morrow*, stated that the red Rolls, with its highly polished aluminium and nickel plate, 'usually announces a City magnate from afar'. He also remarked on sports cars 'in trappings of won-drous hue' which proclaimed the flamboyant types of man or woman to whom they belonged. Cottenham was writing at a time when saloon cars were coming to dominate the market, but in the early 1920s, with open cars everywhere, the most timorous and elderly of drivers might find himself behind the wheel of what at any rate resembled a sports car. Royalty avoided risks of that sort. For reasons of dignity, and of convenience, given the top hats and mili-tary plumage he frequently wore, George V stuck to Daimlers spe-cially designed for him by Hooper. Indeed, much of the pleasure, for anyone, of owning an expensive car was that, having decided on a

chassis, you could still fit to it the type of coachwork, upholstery and
fittings which suited you. Body builders like Hooper and Mulliner
and Thrupp and Maberley were still very much in business, even
providing special bodies for cheap cars such as the Austin Seven and
Wolseley Hornet. For then as now, but with more opportunity then,
buyers saw in their car a means of expressing their own personality.

In 1928 Robert and Helen Lynd published *Middletown* (actually
Muncie, Indiana), a study of life and culture in a town in the American Middle West. It was not uncommon in Middletown to mortgage
your home in order to buy an automobile. 'We'd rather do without
clothes than give up the car,' said one mother of nine children. 'I'd
go without food before I'll see us give up the car,' declared another
woman. The United States, it was agreed, had reached saturation in
the automobile market. In 1930 the number of registrations was 26.5
million, as compared with 1.5 million in Britain and 1.46 million in
France, the two countries next in line. In Britain, for economic reasons, the craze to own an automobile did not afflict all classes as it
did in America. Nevertheless, the reaction of car owners was the
same. A character in Shaw's *The Apple Cart* of 1930 asks, 'What Englishman will give his mind to politics as long as he can afford to keep
a motor car?' And Mrs Peel, in her *Life's Enchanted Cup* of 1933,
comments on the effect of the by then cheap cars: 'Faced with the
choice of a solid house, a nursery and children to put in it, or the
possession of a car, the car wins the day.' The car represented your
personality and your financial standing, and, more than that, it represented the future, the machine age.

In 1925 Colonel Sir Alan Burgoyne, MP, addressed the Royal
Society of Arts on the future of the motor car. He started by reminding his audience that 'twenty-five years ago the motor-car was an
eccentricity; just before the war it had become an established fact,
but was still a luxury; to-day it is a necessity, and in the near future
no artisan's cottage will be built without its garage as part of the
design'.

The car was basic equipment for the modern person. A year or
two earlier the German *Automobil-Revue* had made the same point.
In fact, it went further: not only would the garage be taken for
granted, but the car itself might come with the house, with its cost
included in the rent. It would be considered in the same way as
water, gas, electricity, bathrooms and central heating. In 1931, some-

one quoted by the *Motoring Encyclopedia* — apparently a survivor from Edwardian times — suggested that the garage should be a part of a house almost as much as a billiard room!

Alan Burgoyne, in his lecture, also dealt with the psychology of buying. Motorists, he said, always want to upgrade their car. Someone who starts with a 10hp light car soon becomes discontented with its performance. If he can possibly afford it, his next car will be 12hp or more. 'He or she gladly pledges the future for a car in a way that would be unthinkable for any other commodity.' Aldous Huxley gave a witty and elegant description of the motorist's psychology in his book *Along the Road* of 1925. Huxley himself owned, so he said, a 10hp Citroën. Though whether it could really be called a car was debatable; owners of Napiers, Vauxhalls, Delages and Voisins would certainly say no. How envious one becomes, he muses, what bitter discontentment fills the mind of the 10hp man as 40hp shoots silently past him. How fiercely he loathes the owner of the larger machine!

> the temptation of talking about cars, when one has a car, is quite irresistible. Before I bought a Citroën no subject had less interest for me; none, now, has more. I can talk for hours about motors with other car-owners. And I am ruthlessly prepared to bore the non-motorist by talking interminably of this delightful subject even to him. I waste much precious time reading the motoring papers, study passionately the news from the racing tracks, gravely peruse technical lucubrations which I do not understand. It is a madness, but a delightful one.

Automania is evident in advertisements. The first advertisement for a car was issued by Benz in their 1888 prospectus. It is naturally restrained, showing two very respectable men on a horseless carriage, and merely announces, 'New! Practical! Motor-Car, powered by petroleum, benzine, naptha etc. ... patented in all industrial countries ... entirely supersedes the horse and wagon'. By the 1920s advertisements were less concerned about the car's usefulness than about lifestyle and self-expression and snob appeal. The Armstrong Siddeley, for example, very much a stolid, middle-of-the-road affair, is placed in 'settings of magnificence only matched by the Hollywood musical at the height of its extravagance'. The advertisements for the 1934 Nash represented huge cars far out of proportion to their owners. In one of them, a young girl questions her father as he drives his new Nash: 'Daddy, are we richer than we used to be?' For the very fast and very luxurious Duesenberg, advertising design and copy go over the top. Writer Michael Frostick gives a happy description of the setting: a distinguished man in a dinner jacket is seen in 'what can only be described as a house of cathedral proportions, while way above him in the dim recesses is his wife, or for all we know his mistress, playing the organ'.

Naturally the shift in advertising and public relations reflected (as well as induced) a fresh approach on the part of car buyers. So much about the car — its reliability, its comfort, its performance — could by the 1920s, be more or less taken for granted. The case of the American Auburn car provides an indication of what was happening. In 1923 the manufacturers were in trouble and management was handed over to E. L. Cord of Chicago. Having inherited 700 unsold cars, he touched up the bodywork and painted them in bold colours ... and they sold at once. There was the experience of Rolls-Royce, which in the early 1920s set up a factory in the United States. The venture was a failure. The car was sold in Britain as a high-powered, exceptionally well-built luxury vehicle with a long life. But in America there were many high-powered cars to compete with, available at a lower price. In 1930, for instance, the Rolls was priced at £3,500, the Cadillac at £1,500 and the Packard at £1,100. The fact that the superbly crafted Rolls would last longer was of little importance, for buyers did not care about long-lasting cars; they wanted new versions, often. Biarritz or Palm Springs, you went there in this year's model.

Henry Ford's attitude had not been at all like this. Originally, it is true, even the Model T possessed romantic, non-functional associations, for you gained prestige simply by the fact of owning a car, even if it was a mundane version. But by the middle of the 1920s in the United States there existed a car for every six and a half people — as compared to every forty-seven in Britain — which meant that mere car ownership was commonplace. Ford's repeated price reductions were of little help, for they acted to devalue the product: existing owners were continually being joined by people from lower down the social scale. The very nickname of the Model T, the 'Tin Lizzie', however affectionately bestowed, was a reminder of its modest pretensions. The name derived from the familiar domestic servant, the maid of all work, popularly known as 'Liz' or 'Lizzie'. The Model T was cheap but boring, and while some improvements were made, it was obsolescent technically, too rough and ready, too much what the wartime chauffeur Olive Turney had called a 'rattle trap'. An unkind joke took hold: 'Why is a Model T like a mistress? ... Because you hate to be seen in the streets with one.'

The Model T was a phenomenally successful car, with 15 million sold between 1908 and its demise in 1927. But the decline in its last few years was rapid, with sales plunging from 55 per cent of the American market in 1921 to 30 per cent in 1926. The victor was General Motors, led by Alfred Sloan, a very different sort of man from Henry Ford. Sloan's first premise was that the motor industry could no longer grow at its old pace, that, as things were, it was stabilizing. An instinctive salesman, he understood the attractions to the public of the emotional side of car buying and the snob appeal. He and his colleagues revolutionized marketing. Far from offering, as did Ford, a single model, General Motors presented buyers with a garage-full. To start with, the customer bought a Chevrolet (incidentally, a popular marque in Britain as well as America). When you could, you traded up to a Pontiac, and from there to an Oldsmobile and onwards, if you could afford it, up to a Cadillac. You were encouraged to keep going. Your individuality and your social status were made manifest in your car. Every year General Motors introduced a change in appearance and gave you an enormous choice of colours. Appropriately, the man in charge of styling, Harley Earl, was lifted from Hollywood, where he had designed custom-made cars for movie stars.

Henry Ford fell into line. The Model T was replaced by the Model A, which was launched with great publicity and success in 1927. The styling revolution took off, to reach its climax in the bizarre shapes of American automobiles of the 1950s and 1960s. The effect, visually at any rate, was less extreme in Britain and Europe generally. Customers were less blasé, industries were more fragmented, mass-production techniques were less advanced. Nevertheless, American influence was highly important, because the United States seemed to incarnate the future and, above all, because of the dominance of American films. Enough so to persuade Sir Herbert Austin publicly to deplore what was happening, and to insist that to produce new model after new model was uneconomic and led to an unnecessary depreciation of used cars.

The most serious consequence of the shift of influence in automobile manufacture from engineer to designer was the lost opportunity. Lewis Mumford, a vociferous and informed critic of developments in motoring, was to write that at this point, 'the automotive engineer took his orders from beauty specialists ... [It was] a secret collaboration between the beautician and the mortician.'

6
The Open Road to Brighton

There are many subjects with affinities to motoring. Fantasy is an important one. A famous children's story, *Chitty-Chitty-Bang-Bang* (sometimes without hyphens, sometimes minus a 'Chitty'), comes to mind, its name derived from three racing cars of the 1920s owned and driven by Count Louis Zborowski. The story enacted in book, film and play has as its eponymous hero a magical, amphibious and airborne car. Salvador Dalí used the car as a symbol of ruined civilization in his *Apparition de la ville de Delft*. And on a different note, one can add that while Tamara de Lempicka in her self-portrait imagined herself in a green Bugatti, in real life she drove only a modest Renault. To Marcel Proust, motoring supplied an unexpected association with music. He is visiting his parents, and to notify his arrival, to bring them to the park gate, his chauffeur plays two notes repeatedly on the car's horn. To Proust the sound brings to mind a theme from *Tristan and Isolde*.

But of all the associations that attached themselves to the motor car, none was more powerful than sex. From the start the car challenged carefully nurtured conventions. Osbert Sitwell put it well:

mine was the first generation in which young men were allowed to take their sweethearts for drives ... They would sit together, the two of them, the man at the wheel, the girl beside him, their hair blown back from their temples, their features sculptured by the wind, their bodies and limbs shaped and carved by it continually under their clothes, so they enjoyed a new physical sensation, comparable to swimming; except that here the element was speed, not water.

Boy and girl now had a place to be together which was both private and exhilarating. According to another commentator, motoring was so potent an aphrodisiac that it was no longer the sound of her lover's footsteps which made a girl's heart beat faster: 'Only the hum of a six cylinder motor will rouse her enthusiasm.'

There were songs for sex as well: Cleo Gibson's 1929 'I've got Ford Engine Movements in My Hips' and Robert Johnson's 'Terraplane Blues',

> I'm gonna hoist your hood, mama
> I'm bound to check your oil ...

In more homely style, Tin Pan Alley came up with songs like 'Fifteen Kisses on a Gallon of Gas', 'I'm Going to Park Myself in Your Arms' and 'When He Wanted to Love Her He'd Put up the Cover'.

At motor shows, caressing and coaxing girls clung amorously to the cars on display. Advertising copy emphasized technical features which hinted at erotic possibilities. A famous 1920's advertisement for the Jordan Playboy — quite a name in itself — showed an indistinct picture of a cowboy galloping alongside a girl in a sports car. The text, rich in its associations, starts:

> Somewhere west of Laramie there's a broncho-busting, steer-romping girl who knows what I'm talking about. She can tell what a sassy pony, that's a cross between greased lightning and the place where it hits, can do with eleven hundred pounds of steel and action when he's going high, wide and handsome.

If Noël Coward's contribution, an ode to the Kingston By-pass, was hardly one of the master's best, the English were not generally behindhand. The writer Odette Keun, one-time lover of H. G. Wells, published her *I Discover the English* in 1934. After what is an interesting and reasonably complimentary discussion of the English character, she reports that, nevertheless, we are not by nature at all amorous. Our lovemaking she considers to be 'primitive, morose, hasty and reduced to bare essentials'. But not necessarily, it seems, was it unenterprising; and certainly the approach was self-assured. Miss Keun relates her experience of a London park, where she has gone to sit quietly in a chair with a book. An Englishman arrives, bows and squats down on the grass by her side. (She interrupts herself to stress that she is not a young woman and that it must be habit not real attraction which has brought him.) 'He talks to me about the weather — so politely that it is impossible to reply only by a grunt. After two minutes, though, it is "won't you come for a drive with me in my car?"' Oh, she says, what a preponderant role the owner-driven car plays in the sexual relationships of the English!

No one was going to say the same thing about the charabanc — vehicles which lacked privacy and where the men drank too much. The motor cycle, though, was another matter. The MP Sir Arnold Wilson recorded in his diary how he had watched an endless line of traffic passing by at speed. The really cheerful people were not in the cars, they were the girls riding pillion on the motor cycles: for them 'life at the moment had a "kick in it"', as for their sakes 'the young men strove to outdistance each successive car'. For the young motor cyclists and their girls, there were the capacious beaches of Blackpool; in the south the nearest equivalent was Southend, the resort, as it has been put, 'for the London that rides in trams, and stands behind counters and hawks from bleak suburban door to door'. But had Odette Keun accepted one of those advances in the park and the initial venture proved satisfactory, the motoring Englishman would probably have suggested a weekend at Brighton. For, after all, what 'all men learned, south of the Thames and east of the Solent: [was] that Brighton meant sex'. No doubt at all. A. P. Herbert's hero in his book *Holy Deadlock* reflects that he must be careful not to mention even the word 'Brighton', for he is sure that, should he do so, his secretary 'would indignantly leave the building.'

The correlation of Brighton and sex was a venerable one. The town had been made popular, indeed had been made the most fashionable resort in Europe, by the Prince of Wales, later the Prince Regent, and his fun-loving friends. The traveller John Byng, in Brighton at the end of the 1780s, wrote that he encountered 'such a harpy set of painted harlots, as to appear to me as bad as Bond St in the spring'. There was an association with speed as well, moving fast along the road to London, horse racing on the Downs. The Prince himself set the pace, making the journey by horse to London and back — over fifty miles each way — in a single day. While at this period the one-way journey for coaches and carriages took two days, demand and improved conditions brought the time down by the 1820s to between five and five and a half hours. (On the public coaches the horses were changed at ten-mile intervals with the transfer effected in not more than a minute and a half.) By 1834 the Criterion coach cut the journey to one of three hours and forty minutes, an achievement to be compared with Léon Bollée's winning time in the 1896 motor run of just short of three hours.

By the start of the motoring age Brighton was no longer the superbly fashionable resort of earlier years. But if there was about it a touch of Blackpool, it possessed none the less some of the attractions of Nice and Deauville. It helped that it was situated at a convenient distance from London, with which it had excellent rail communication. Also it was blessed with a particularly energetic and talented hotel owner and impresario in the person of Harry Preston, a small man who 'moved in a haze of cigar smoke and to the popping of a thousand champagne corks'. Preston was a keen motorist who acquired his first car in 1902, sponsored motor rallies and even planned a motor-racing track of over a mile along the sea front, running east from the Palace Pier. A year later, the president of the Civil Engineers, doing some counting at the roadside, calculated that some 1,200 motor vehicles an hour — cars, motor cycles and motor tricycles — were travelling along the Brighton Road. It must have been a worrying sight to the blacksmiths at their forges. Taking one section of the road, the twelve or thirteen miles from Charlwood Park to Bolney, running through Crawley and what is now Gatwick Airport, the Ordnance Survey map of 1903 shows a 'smithy' on or just off the road about every two miles.

Brighton was a startling mixture. Arnold Bennett noted in his journal that while his first stroll along the front had impressed him very favourably, he was struck by the 'comfort, luxury, ostentation, snobbishness and correctness' and the contrast with the living conditions of the artisan class. And Brighton was still raffish, as Thomas Burke emphasized in 1922. There were similarities with London — its nickname was not for nothing 'London by the Sea'. In each, said Burke, you found 'the rough stuff of the London stage' and 'blazing kerb-stone stockbrokers', and motors, cigars and prostitutes. But London had much else to weigh in the balance, while

Brighton existed by and for these things. Burke had no doubt but that the Prince Regent, as

> George IV, most vulgar of many vulgar kings ... would be delighted with [Brighton] to-day. The 'fat adonis of forty' would find much congenial company, for the parade on Sunday morning is a parade of Fatties and their kept women. This parade is rehearsed on Saturdays, when life on the Brighton Road is made unbearable for ordinary people by a whirlwind of limousines, fatness, Corona Coronas and patchouli. The sharrabang may be noisy, but spontaneous noise is not always so vulgar as certain demonstrative attitudes in a Rolls-Royce.

Burke goes on to say that 'when the obscure merchant had made money, his first thought is an automobile; his second — a "fixture" at Brighton'.

Yet there was more verve about the town than that. Here, for instance, is a description from Graham Greene's brilliant *Brighton Rock* where Pinkie waits to negotiate with the gangster Colleoni under the domed lights of the Cosmopolitan Hotel. He watches the

> young men [who] kept on arriving in huge motoring coats accompanied by small tinted creatures, who rang like expensive glass when they were touched but who conveyed an impression of being as sharp and tough as tin. They looked at nobody, sweeping through the lounge as they had swept in racing models down the Brighton Road, ending on high stools in the American bar.

Greene's Cosmopolitan was in real life the Bedford. The most famous hotel, though, was the Metropole, opened in 1890 as the largest in the country outside London, and celebrated in T. S. Eliot's *The Waste Land*, where Mr Eugenides, the Smyrna merchant,

> Asked me in demotic French
> To luncheon at the Cannon Street Hotel
> Followed by a weekend at the Metropole.

It was there, it may be remembered, that Patrick Hamilton's conman had taken the eighteen-year-old Esther to sweep her off her feet.

Still, the motorist looking for entertainment did not have to go as far as Brighton. From the late 1920s, often on roads leading out of the great cities, he or she could enjoy one of the most characteristic phenomena of the period: the roadhouse. Characteristic but transient, although to many it seemed then that roadhouses had come to stay. Take this piece from the introduction to the book *Roadhouses and Clubs of the Home Counties*, published in 1934:

> When from the watch-towers of the future some horn-rimmed historian surveys the early Nineteen-thirties, he will scarcely fail to observe that amongst this period's otherwise undistinguished contributions to our social welfare there is one item that stands out in agreeable relief. We may fancy him turning away with a smile from his dreary contemplation of depressions, dictatorships and disturbances, selecting a clean white sheet of paper, and addressing himself to the pleasant task of recording the BIRTH OF THE ENGLISH ROADHOUSE.

The roadhouse (sometimes road house, sometimes road-house) in Britain was born of the pub and the petrol-filling station. It seems that the proprietors of the latter discovered that 'passing drivers would accept replenishment no less gratefully than their mounts'. There was also an American lineage with prohibition, or, strictly speaking, anti-prohibition connections. Country hotel- and innkeepers were not as closely involved as might be expected; they were, said the writer Ivor Brown, too sleepy, and failed to establish themselves on the new bypass roads. In the play *Road House*, produced at the Whitehall Theatre, London, in October 1932, the setting, at the start, is a pub, The Angel Inn, just off the Portsmouth Road. Apparently it has done no business for the last six months, that is, since the opening nearby of a new arterial road. So the proprietors decide to turn it into a roadhouse, renaming it the Angel Face Road House. They convert the duck pond into a swimming pool, install a dance floor and bring in a band, add a putting green, and turn the bar over to cocktails. (After that, the story peters out, relying on some implausible jewel thieves and contrasts between old and new.)

To start with anyway, the democratic origins of the roadhouse were stressed. In one wing of the Berkeley Arms Hotel at Cranford there was a public bar 'where one may play darts in the company of the local lads', while in the other 'there is the delicate sophistication of a Mayfair restaurant, complete with jazz band, skilful chef, and noiseless long-tailed waiters'. However, the democratic balance was

A roadhouse in the style of a French château: the Berkeley Arms Hotel at Cranford, Middlesex. In the public bar you could play darts with 'the local lads' but elsewhere on the premises you could encounter 'the delicate sophistication of a Mayfair restaurant complete with jazz band'.

not universal. The Comet at Hatfield, for instance, set aside a room for waiting chauffeurs. Décor generally in roadhouses was 'art deco'; traditional fittings of brass and elaborate glass were out. Sporting facilities were important. Swimming pools, indoor, outdoor or both, and ballrooms were virtually essential, as was some form of golf course, and you might also find tennis, squash and badminton courts. 'Even aerodromes', pronounces one guide, although in practice that seems to have meant that flights could be arranged at a nearby airfield. Bowling alleys could be an attraction. In the American film *Road House* (Jean Negulesco, 1948), the largest space on the premises is occupied by a bowling alley. Some roadhouses, like the Clock at Welwyn on the Great North Road, were organized along the lines of motels. A 1935 writer, probably with these in mind, states firmly that while he has sensed a feeling 'in some quarters that the very words "road house" meant something naughty', it was not true. They are perfectly respectable places, he maintains stoutly.

Perhaps, but more probably not. With the less than fastidious reputation of the motor trade, it would be unsurprising to find that many of the roadhouses were on the seedy side. To quote Patrick Hamilton, 'Just as certain people look unmistakably "horsey", bear the stamp of Newmarket, he bore the stamp of Great Portland Street. He made you think of Road Houses.' And there is Graham Greene's *The Confidential Agent*. The agent in question, who has been out of Britain for some time, is given a lift from Dover by a girl in her 'little scarlet cad car''. They stop on the road at a 'house ... hotel ... whatever it was. This sort thing was new since his day.' It was a roadhouse grafted on to a genuine Tudor building. But there is something, the agent thinks, distinctly ungenuine about the manager, Captain Currie. He is well entrenched in the trade: his first roadhouse had been the Spanish Galleon, near Maidenhead, a lively Thames Valley town offering the same sort of amenities as Brighton.

Roadhouses were quite often established in old buildings and made much of the fact. Unusual artefacts were an advantage. The Bridge House on Reigate Hill boasted the chair used by Charles Dickens when he lived in Doughty Street, Holborn; M.G.'s on the Stratford—Birmingham road contained oak panelling originally, so it was claimed, belonging to Simon de Montfort. At the Wagon Shed at Horley on the Brighton Road 'celebrated residents [were] the famous trio of monkeys, Jacko, Jill and the Old Man'. Roadhouses varied in size, cost and what they offered. Those on the outskirts of London were particularly lavish. The Spider's Web, for instance, set in lovely grounds on the Watford By-pass, provided parking for 2,000 cars. The most famous of all, the Ace of Spades on the Kingston By-pass, was also one of the most venerable, having opened in 1927. (It had a twin of the same name on the Great West Road.) The restaurant was open twenty-four hours a day all the year round, and could accommodate 700—800 people at a time; the ballroom could hold 350 people. Extras at the Ace of Spades included a polo ground and a riding school.

The roadhouses did not really survive the Second World War, even in America, where petrol rationing quickly lapsed. They were likely to revert, turning once more into ordinary pubs or hotels, sometimes under the same management. For instance, with its monkeys presumably gone, the Wagon Shed remained under Mrs Harrison, the original proprietor, for years. In 1944 she was still advertising it as a roadhouse and she continued in residence until the 1950s. By 2002, it had become a hotel, the Skylane, no longer with swimming pool and with the grounds much reduced. The memory of the Ace of Spades on the Kingston By-pass survives only in fragments on top of a flyover. The old sculptured metal sign of a spade is still in place, perched above the Ace Golf Superstore and its neighbour the Virtual Showroom, which advertised — past tense, since it is now closed down — what it called 'the coolest cars in the flyover'. Still, some of the old fame sticks, for, on the site opposite, across the flyover, are the Ace Pharmacy and an Ace Bakery.

If the introduction to *Roadhouses and Clubs of the Home Counties* is overblown, and gives a significance to roadhouses which was valid for a few years only, it supplies a reminder of how the world had changed since the carefree twenties. The 1930s opened against a background of economic and political desolation brought about by the Wall Street crash, the Depression and, for Britain, the enforced abandonment of the gold standard. In any event, though, it seems unlikely that attitudes to motoring would have stayed as they were, that its romantic appeal could have remained so refulgent. For one thing, motoring would inevitably have been taken more for granted, with its purely functional attributes coming to the fore. In *Eyeless in Gaza* (1933), Aldous Huxley, once so passionate a motorist, could write that 'men don't spend their lives thanking God for cars; they only curse when the carburettor is choked'. There is a character in Elizabeth Bowen's *To the North* of 1932 who muses, 'Modern life becomes increasingly complicated. It seems a short while since motoring was in itself a pleasure ... But nowadays the whole incentive to motoring seems an anxiety to be elsewhere.' It was not just that people had grown blasé; it was that the disadvantages which motoring brought in its train were more widely perceived. The number of road accidents was one of them, another the consequences to the environment, above all to the countryside. Reflective people suddenly woke up to what was happening, astonished that they had not done so before. Here, for example, is an excerpt from *England, Ugliness and Noise* of 1930:

> Why has the preservation of rural England so recently become a leading topic? A few years ago interest was confined to the quiet efforts of the National Trust ... Have we become suddenly sensitive to ugliness and vandalism? — or have they made such strides that we have woken in alarm to see the rural beauty of England being filched from us.

And a leading planner, Thomas Sharp, could say that the 'present ruin seems to have developed overnight'. It almost was overnight, or at least it was over a very short time. There had, though, been warnings in the 1920s, voiced most clearly by Patrick Abercrombie in the complacent days of 1926 in his *The Preservation of Rural England*:

> It is only since the war that the normal method of approach to the country has been changed from the railway, by which it is accessible at fixed spots and at fixed times, to the motor car and bus, by which it is accessible by main, secondary and local roads in all directions and almost continuously. The sudden outburst of the motor bus has caused a revolution in locomotion quite as remarkable as and indefinitely more swift than the railways. The immediate physical assault upon the landscape by motoring can indeed in no wise be compared with the scars inflicted by the railways: but the complete permeation of the country is more thorough.

One of the most vivid and influential books of the time about the danger to the countryside was C. E. M. Joad's *The Horrors of the Countryside* of 1931. The villains in the book are the motorists, people who at first sight have little resemblance to the questing souls presented by H. V. Morton. Joad has spent a day walking peacefully across country. Presently he tops a rise in the ground to come in full view of a main road. The road is covered with cars. Bonnet to tail they stretch continuously, in an unending line:

> The procession moves, now faster now slower, and every now and then two cars in it change places; but always it goes on. The faces of the motorists are strained and angry; upon them there is an air of tense expectancy, and in the intervals between their spasmodic bursts of activity they glower at one another. From the country they are completely cut off; they cannot see its sights, hear its sounds, or enjoy its silence.

But these unhappy people, crazed by the discomforts and monotony of driving as they may be, are not quite divorced from their predecessors (or themselves) of the 1920s. They are spurred on, whether they know it or not, by a need to escape from modern civilization. They are in search of a retreat, 'a retreat bathed in an atmosphere, the fragrance that is distilled by old and traditional things'. Their own tragedy is that as soon as they find what they seek, it disappears: 'The motorist is in fact the modern "Midas"; whatever he touches turns to tin and brass.'

1. De Dion Bouton. An early
advertisement for a well-
known make with strong
period flavour.

II. The interior of a Rolls-Royce Phantom 1, Coupé de Ville, 1927, with bodywork by Clark of Wolverhampton. The inspiration is an Edwardian drawing room. The seat cover, a tapestry, was specially woven at Aubusson.

III. Armstrong Siddeley, 1930 advertisement. The Armstrong Siddeley, stolid and very much middle of the road, is placed in a setting of magnificence 'only matched by the Hollywood musical at the height of its extravagance'.

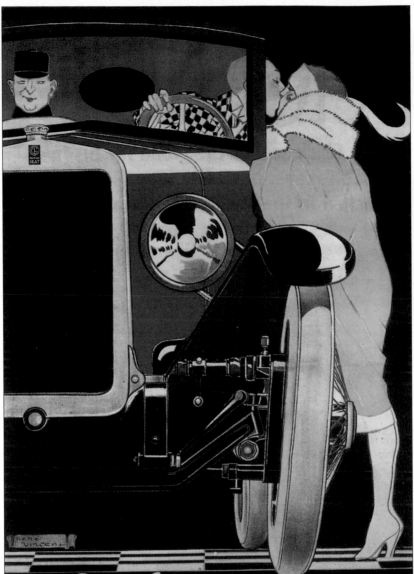

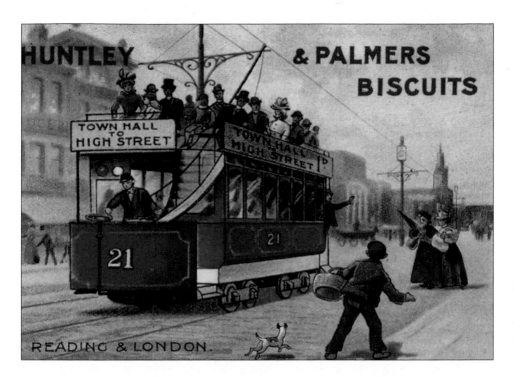

V. A Victorian tram used in an advertisement for the Reading firm of Huntley & Palmer Biscuits.

Left: IV. René Vincent's poster for Georges Irat Cars.

VI. Poster by André Edouard
Marty for the 1933 Motor
Show at Olympia.

Right: VII. Poster by L. B. Black
entitled 'Tour London's
Country by General Coach'.

TOUR LONDON'S COUNTRY
BY GENERAL COACH

FOR ILLUSTRATED BOOKLET APPLY:—
PRIVATE HIRE DEPARTMENT (L.G.O.C.). 31. BROADWAY. WESTMINSTER. S.W.1.

VIII. Salvador Dalí,
*Apparition de la ville de
Delft*, 1935–6. The car as a
symbol of civilization in
decay.

In Joad's view, the England of his time was to be seen as two countries which existed side by side. One was the old peaceful, traditional, to an extent still hierarchic England:

Buses at Box Hill, Surrey, on a bank holiday, 1924.

> It is possible to find, even in counties bordering on London, villagers who know no more of the metropolis than did their ancestors in the days when packhorses performed the office of railways and motor lorries. When it is invaded, this county does not change; it disappears, often with startling rapidity ...

The second country is that which surrounds the towns and adjoins the main roads:

> Its characteristic features are petrol pumps and garages, tea places, usually 'Old English', shanties, bungalows and innumerable notice boards. It has few native inhabitants, but it is a dormitory for town workers and a corridor for motorists ... Those of the original working folk who remain in it abandon their traditional occupations and become parasites on the motorists and suburbanites; they keep wireless sets, buy gramophones and tea cakes in frilled papers, batten on the Sunday press and grow basely rich.

Country number one, says Joad, had a life of its own; country number two derives its life from towns: 'it is, indeed, a most pathetic thing to see how the exodus of those who find life in the modern town no longer tolerable destroys the very rural amenities which they go forth to seek'.

A most important and early ally for the conservationists was the BBC. In February 1929 an editorial in its weekly journal, the *Listener*, referring to a radio talk given a few days earlier by the town planner and architect C. R. Ashbee, recommended its readers to visit the 'Ugliness Exhibition', which originated in Leicester and was now touring England. In London it was to be seen at the premises of the Royal Institute of British Architects. The exhibition's theme was that something must be done quickly to save the countryside from wanton destruction. The objectives were comprehensive: to stop the damage to scenery, the destruction of parks and beautiful buildings — sometimes whole villages — and to prevent the building of roads in unsuitable places. The organizers of the exhibition urged that a 'belt of green' be introduced round every city. By January 1930 the *Listener* felt able to declare that broadcasting had played an active part in the campaign being waged to save England's beauty, and announced the start of a series of fortnightly talks to be given by eminent conservationists.

The BBC was to maintain its support for the campaign over the next few years. Its commitment to the cause was undoubted, but it was concerned that its campaign should not be too closely associated with the pure romantics, in the words of its director of talks, 'people who were out of touch and out of sympathy with all modern life'. (This was the more important since it was being advocated by some at the time that its broadcasts be restricted solely to entertainment.) Additional issues emerged, as, for instance, the need to exert pressure on Members of Parliament and on local authorities. The *Listener* also pointed out how essential it was to think regionally and nationally: for example, while warning of the dangers threatening Hadrian's Wall through quarrying nearby, it stressed that it would be a mistake to concentrate attention exclusively on individual beauty spots or historical monuments.

The campaigners were anxious to explain their objectives most carefully to town dwellers, the people, after all, mainly responsible for the depredations to the countryside. They had to be educated on what constituted beauty, and imbued with 'a definite standard' of beauty. A note of condescension creeps in, which sounds clearly in a broadcast on 20 February 1932 made by the Minister of Health, Sir Edward Hilton Young, on the subject of his Town and Country Planning Bill then on its course through the House of Commons. The minister, a personal supporter of the campaigners' aims, stressed that 'planning' was not a matter of building Utopias. His bill was what he called a 'firm business proposition'. It was perhaps a reasonable if disingenuous argument for him to make, but that he did so implied that the country as a whole was unconvinced of the aesthetic arguments for conservation. He went on to a statement which cannot have reassured those listeners who were hoping for stronger legislation in the near future. 'You may wonder,' pronounced Sir Edward, 'why a Minister of the National Government is concerned with a small affair like town and country planning when there are such much bigger affairs to be looked after ... There are unemployment and the pound sterling.' (How the Minister of Health was supposed to help with these is another question.)

Hilton Young's bill became an act of Parliament and was intended to deal with an urgent problem, that of 'ribbon development'. Patrick Abercrombie had used the phrase 'the ribbon unrolling along the roadside' when describing how new houses were distributed one by one along the motor-bus routes. Miles of road frontage were built up, one house deep. Professor Joad had given his own description of how it looked when he was driving along the new arterial road from London to Southend:

> For the greater part of the way [the road] was flanked by houses, so that one had the sensation of motoring through a continuous loosely strung out town. A few of the houses were semi-detached, but the great majority were separated by nicely calculated intervals of half a dozen or a dozen yards. At the back of each house was a narrow strip of garden, at the far end of which there were cabbages; a barbed wire fence separated the cabbages from the flat Essex country, which, inflamed by occasional blobs of angry pink, stretched mournfully away into the distance.

While Joad would have approved of the act's intention, he must have been infuriated by the minister's disparaging reference to 'a small affair like town and country planning'! Not least because *The*

Horrors of the Countryside had been published by the Hogarth Press as one of four 'pamphlets' dealing with fundamental contemporary issues. Another of the pamphlets had been concerned with unemployment and carried a foreword by Maynard Keynes.

To the campaigners generally, town and country planning was far from being a small affair. To them, the issue went to the heart of civilized life — the saving of the radiant and gentle countryside of England, with its unique villages and its age-old churches and manor houses, was a matter of fundamental importance.

To Thomas Sharp, now, with the car [and bus], 'all land could be regarded as building land'. There was a ready market, along the arterial roads and deep in the countryside. The old landlords, demoralized by high taxes and low returns from agriculture, sold off land on an unprecedented scale. Farmers were only too pleased to cut their losses; local councils provided smallholdings. The people looking for somewhere in the country were seldom well off; while they might visualize cottages, they frequently had to make do with more modest substitutes, which might well be prefabricated stuctures of timber, concrete or asbestos commissioned by Hilton Young's own ministry. Such building, objectionable in itself to the wealthier classes and traditional country lovers, was frequently shoddy and ugly ... and single storey. The word 'bungalow', like 'charabanc', descended the social scale and was used contemptuously by those more happily placed financially. 'Bungalow' spawned variations: 'bungaloafer' for those who lived in them, and 'bungaloid'. The vociferous churchman Dean Inge of St Paul's wrote in the *Evening Standard* in 1927, 'The whole face of the country will be spotted with bungaloid growths within which childless couples will sleep after racing about the country in little motor cars.'

Along with the bungalows and shacks went gimcrack roadside cafés and filling stations. Gimcrack since their proprietors — in the latter case often redundant blacksmiths — were also short of funds. Cheap and monotonous building defaced the countryside within reach of the larger cities and along the coasts. For mile after mile the shoreline of Lincolnshire and Norfolk was built over, and that of Cornwall under serious threat. But it was the south coast at its eastern end which attracted the most attention. With good reason, for this coast and the land behind it included some of the most beautiful scenery in the country. The climate was relatively mild and sunny,

London was within a reasonable distance, and it was fashionable, with a large resident population. The 1911 census showed that 40 per cent of the residential population of seaside resorts was concentrated along the coastline of Sussex, Kent and Hampshire, the majority in Sussex. What is more, possible desecration was trumpeted loud and clear by the multitude of writers who inhabited the region. A recent author has put it that, 'In the inter-war years not a country lane in favoured parts of Surrey, Sussex and West Kent but resounded with the click of typewriters.'

The literary associations long predated typewriters. Jane Austen, for one, started a novel on the development of the Sussex coast. (She died before she could complete it.) Her subject was 'Sanditon' — also the name of the book — a village she placed on the coast between Hastings and Eastbourne. A Mr and Mrs Parker are on their way there, travelling from Tunbridge. Obliged to leave the high road and risk the perils of a very rough lane, their coach is overturned. A gentleman who lives nearby comes to the rescue. Mr Parker, slightly injured, explains their journey and waxes enthusiastic: '"Everybody has heard of Sanditon", he pronounces; "for a young and rising bathing place — certainly the favourite spot of all that are to be found along the coast of Sussex."' His new friend is polite but not exactly thrilled: '"Yes, I have heard of Sanditon", he replies. "Every five years, one hears of some new place or other starting up by the sea and growing the fashion."'

This was 1817. These resorts were to go from strength to strength, boosted by the railways, which enabled them to compete more easily with towns such as Gravesend on the Thames estuary and Broadstairs and Margate on the north Kent coast. The roads continued to be hazardous, even the Brighton Road, with all its reputation for fast travel. In the 1830s, in his *Sketches by Boz*, Charles Dickens imagined the Tuggs family, who, having come into some money, are deciding to which seaside town they will move. They shortlisted Gravesend, Margate, Brighton and Ramsgate. Brighton, the only one on the south coast, they rejected on the grounds that the road was too dangerous: 'All the coaches had been upset, in turn, within the last three weeks; each coach had averaged two passengers killed, and six wounded.'

The pressure on the roads to the coast was relieved by the railways, but it was, of course, a temporary respite. By the early twentieth century the roads were in no state to cope with the demands of motoring. By the 1920s the motor traffic was prodigious. While it is not possible to measure with any precision its extent during the inter-war years, there do exist some highly indicative figures, formulated by Dr H. C. Brookfield in his 1950 thesis, *A Regional Study of Urban Development in Coastal Sussex*, which apply to years immediately after the Second World War. They show around 1.74 million individual journeys annually by train between the London area and the main Sussex resorts (some 70 per cent of the total), as against an estimated 10 million travelling by bus and coach. In addition, perhaps another million made the journey by car, motor cycle and bicycle. Overall figures for 1938, the nearest comparable year, would have been markedly lower, but there is no reason to believe that the proportions would have been much different.

The Brighton Road, which carried the heaviest traffic, became a byword for traffic jams. The motoring writer John Prioleau related his experience of a summer evening in 1924:

> One day last summer, it was my extraordinary ill-luck to drive up from Brighton to London in the evening between 6 o'clock and 9 o'clock, and as a result of those three appalling hours, I decided that nothing but 'life and death' shall drag me, either in my own or someone else's car, to Brighton during the summer. From the Brighton Aquarium to St James's Street I was not for one moment out of what can only be described as a queue of private cars, and motor bikes of every sort and size, and more chars-a-bancs than I believed existed. Quite apart from the dust, the crowd, and above all the intolerable noise, the danger to everyone concerned was considerable.

Prioleau's indignation is the more credible since normally he is resolutely cheerful, a great man for the open road and its delights.

Brighton was not Blackpool. First of all, as we have seen, right up until 1939 the number of people coming by road to Blackpool, swiftly as it had grown, never exceeded the number arriving by rail. No doubt the passengers by coach for Brighton — almost all of them day-trippers (a favourite word of the time) — were just a southern version of their Blackpool opposite numbers. However, the two groups were coming to a different sort of town. For instance, the 1931 census

Right: The seaside.

148

showed Blackpool to have nearly 4,000 lodging-house keepers and 240 hotel keepers, whereas Brighton, with a larger population, contained less than a third of Blackpool's lodging-houses but more than double its hotel keepers. For generations Blackpool had been working class, the Sussex resorts, upper and middle class. This was true of the residents, many of them *rentiers* for whom 'dividends kept their mystic origin', of the commuters and of the visitors who came by car and train. What is more, residents and many of the visitors were elderly, less noisy, less likely to drop litter, less ostentatiously convivial than the newcomers. And they were distinctly snobbish. On the south coast, the automobile in the form of the charabanc, the excursion coach, introduced a cultural clash on a scale much more acute than elsewhere.

Yet it was difficult to insulate a town and to keep out the importunate crowds, who after all brought money with them. Professor Joad claimed that he saw no difference between any of the larger seaside resorts; to him, they were all awful. One July day he went to Worthing, next in importance on the Sussex coast to Brighton and Eastbourne. He described it as 'totally abominable'. He was offended by its 'purulent beastliness, its utter horror'. Everything that he saw on sale was fake and tawdry, 'over everything was the careless, squalid disorder of trivial profit-making'. He despised the crowds on the beach, composed, as he saw it, of people without initiative or individuality. In order to bathe in the sea, he started to undress on the beach. An official stopped him; Joad was outraged.

But whatever Joad said, resorts did try to discriminate in favour of certain types of visitor. Frinton in Essex, for example, banned excursion coaches altogether. Tenby in South Wales, 'the British Madeira', also tried to guard its traditional clientele against unwelcome newcomers. Resorts were often divided in two, attracting trippers to one part and leaving the staider residents to the other. Brighton and Hove, though technically separate towns, provide a classic example. Southend and Westcliffe and Hastings and St Leonards are others. Eastbourne, a town which prided itself on its respectability and superior social tone, was especially challenged by mass tourism. The Edwardian journalist T. H. S. Escott wrote, 'No earthly spot could perhaps be so virtuous as Eastbourne looks,' and the *Eastbourne Pictorial*, making no bones about it, pronounced, 'Brighton is democratic; Hastings is salubrious (and, it must be con-

fessed, a trifle dull); but Eastbourne ... is distinctly and decidedly elegant.' It carried residential segregation to extremes. At the start of
the century the town faced two tests of its resolve. In 1901 the
London, Brighton & South Coast Railway wanted to build an
engine works there. The working class were in favour but — shades
of Oxford — the project was turned down. Then there was a furore
about electric trams, for which there were strong economic arguments. As trams were considered a working-class form of transport,
the proposal was rejected, with its opponents arguing that should
they be introduced, Eastbourne could 'say goodbye to the better
class of visitor'. So motor buses were ordered instead and proved in
the early years as unreliable in Eastbourne as they did elsewhere.
Still, the trams were kept out.

It was easy for a resort to lose its reputation or to be lumbered with
one which was unwanted. Bognor, for instance, between the wars
was considered boring because it became identified with nursing
homes and clinics. And Brighton (incidentally a tram town) did not
want to be thought of only as a place you went with your girlfriend in
a scarlet 'cad's car'. It was anxious to give a more balanced picture of
itself. The trouble was that its indecorous reputation was firmly
fixed in the minds of the newspapers and the public. Councillor
Clarke of Tonbridge, popularly known as the anti-mixed bathing
champion, criticized Brighton beach, denouncing its 'rather chilly
diversions' as a sinful orgy. The papers worked up the problem of
the racecourse gangs, adjusting the town's claim to be the 'Queen of
the Watering Places' to 'Queen of the Slaughtering Places'. That was
misrepresenting Brighton as Britain's Chicago; its murder rate was in
fact nothing extraordinary. The authorities were usually quick to
respond to these attacks. In a court case in which a woman was
acquitted of the charge of running a brothel, a lady magistrate, Mrs
Smith, alleged that the police allowed hundreds of brothels to keep
in business. The chief constable protested indignantly that this was
a horrible accusation to make against the police force. (Mrs Smith
refused to be intimidated, as she put it, but she did concede that perhaps 'hundreds' was an exaggeration.) There was the Methodist
minister at a church conference in Brighton who declared the town
to be the 'fastest' in the world, 'that it was full of slaves of sensual-
ism'. 'Babes,' he went on, 'are being nursed in the cradle of immoral-
ity and vice.' Here the mayor took up the challenge and rather

limply called attention to the great number of churches in the town.

If the bus, the coach and the car provoked a cultural challenge, they also influenced the way people spent their holidays. The traditional seaside landladies found it necessary to adapt. In his best-selling novel of 1931, *The Fortnight in September*, R. C. Sherriff introduced the landlady of Seaview in Bognor, who was fighting a losing battle — she never complained, but 'return-day charabanc trips and bungalows were sapping the strength of Mrs Huggett's heart'. Longer-stay visitors altered their habits: instead of spending the whole holiday in one place, they were more footloose (or car-loose), staying only two or three nights in any one resort and then moving on. The towns were affected. As at Blackpool, the accommodation of motor traffic, on the street and for parking, meant upheaval at the centre of the town. In some places upheaval turned into destruction, as at St Ives in Cornwall, where the heart of the town was demolished to make room for a car park. The orientation of towns was altered. The railways had encouraged development from the centre, 'radiation from a central nucleus'. In seaside resorts the hotels were built near the station, and people favoured the most central beaches. Motor buses encouraged a quite different movement. They promoted circular development and movement towards the periphery. At Brighton, building now grew up in the hinterland, behind the town, and on the chalk plateau to the east of the Kemp Town district, where the cliffs and hills had prevented railway construction.

To preservationists, the evidence of the damage done by the railways was near the forefront of their minds ... as an object lesson in what happened if you just let material progress rip. Railway lines and yards and engine shops split communities, as at Paddington in London. At Edinburgh the lines had been driven right through the middle without thought of the visual effect on the outstandingly beautiful city. To them, our ancestors, dominated by the ideology of laissez-faire, of Adam Smith's 'invisible hand', had bequeathed a legacy of sordid and ugly towns. 'We cannot afford to wait for a similar emergence of economic beauty from a devastated countryside' wrote Patrick Abercrombie. G. M. Trevelyan took up the theme in a lecture he delivered in 1931. The Victorians, he thought, might perhaps have been proud had they been able to introduce ugly buildings and advertisements into the countryside at the pace we achieved. But he goes on more seriously.

The Victorians at least acted up to their own ideals like the moral, serious folk they were. They did the best they knew, even though in our eyes much of that best was bad. But we sin against our own light. We know that we are disfiguring England and murdering beauty, yet we continue to do so ... Or, to speak more precisely, those of us who care for preservation of natural beauty are still outnumbered and overborne by those who, though not all of them wholly indifferent to our cause, hold other considerations to be of greater importance.

The preservationists' arguments awakened many people to what was happening, and, as we shall see, helped to promote preventive legislation. Yet it was still hard to come up with safeguards which were fundamental rather than simply ameliorative; the problem faced by Lowes-Dickinson before the war was still unresolved. *Britain & the Beast*, a book edited by the architect Clough Williams-Ellis, a leading protester, and published in 1937, is revealing. A number of eminent people contributed but some of the chapters, notably those on Scotland and Wales, are remarkably weak. Usually the arguments are very forcefully expressed, and sometimes it seems as if everything in modern life obnoxious to the writer is attributable to the automobile.

There was a shrill and melodramatic tone to preservationist protests that may have been useful in waking people from their lethargy but risked being counterproductive. It must have been a relief to many to turn to gentler but nevertheless effective persuasion: for instance, satire, a fine example of which is Osbert Lancaster's *Progress at Pelvis Bay*. The theme is seaside development. We see the evolution of wayside inn into a 'great modern luxury hotel' and are shown the arrival of the first motor vehicle, 'a small charabanc' which made several trips along the coast until 'it finally exploded on the hill going up to Pelvis Magna one hot afternoon in the summer of 1909 — a laughable incident that was fortunately attended by small loss of life'. Lancaster mocks the Pelvis Bay roadhouse:

Many of the thousands who, during the summer, motor down to Pelvis Bay by way of the new Flushbrook By-pass must be familiar with the castellated tower of the 'Hearts are Trumps' roadhouse ... The Olde Englishe Grille and the Restaurant Fleurie catered for all tastes and supplied every species of fresh farm and dairy produce straight from the Argentine, expertly prepared by a large staff of skilled chefs. The American Bar provided light refreshment for those who could not tarry long, and finally in the beautiful new dance hall, with its modernistic sofas, lalique panels and cleverly concealed lighting Ed Sugarprong and his Twenty-Seven White-Hot Tubthumpers provided the hottest jazz to be heard between Hammersmith Broadway and Pelvis Bay. Last year the Pompeian Swimming Pool, complete with artificial waves and floodlit every night from seven till two, was opened with a pretty ceremony in which forty of the loveliest bathing belles in Britain took part.

Another witness of the times — his evidence presented years later — was Laurie Lee. One early July morning in the middle of the 1930s, aged nineteen, he set out on foot from his home in Gloucestershire to make his fortune. He carried with him a rolled-up tent, a change of clothes, a tin of treacle biscuits and — the wherewithal to earn his keep — a violin. He was on his way to London but, a heroic rambler indeed, he made a long detour along the Channel coast, in order to see the sea. Lee was fortunate, as he reflected later, that he could avoid the high road and travel by ancient country roads which still clung to their original tracks. It was before 'the landscape had been bulldozed for speed'. He arrived one day at Worthing, to him a very different place from that described by Professor Joad. He played his violin to 'the rich, pearl-chokered invalids' he encountered on the front, a generous audience, it seems, to itinerant musicians. What he also encountered was a new coastline, one which

> had begun to develop that shabby shoreline suburbia which was part of the whimsical rot of the Thirties. Here were the sea-shanty-towns, sprawled like a rubbishy tidemark, the scattered litter of land and ocean — miles of tea-shacks and bungalows, apparently built out of wreckage, and called 'Spindthrift' or 'Sprite O'The Waves'.

Worthing was placed on the coastline between Littlehampton and Newhaven which by the end of the 1930s had become almost continuously built up. In itself, this overbuilding was more shocking then than it would be now. We after all are used to it, be it with our home-grown examples or, on the Continent, with Spain, Greece and the South of France. There is, though, a difference. Ugly as they usually are, the buildings which nowadays disfigure the shore — homes, hotels, cafés, bars and shops — are for the most part solidly constructed. In the 1930s much of the building was ramshackle. This was particularly true of the shanty towns which intruded on to the beaches. Some of these settlements were professionally organized and developed, but many were not; they were homes for squatters and sometimes unhygienic as well as unsightly.

The coastal shanty towns in some cases preceded motoring. At Shoreham beach, a few miles west of Brighton and Hove, no car could have risked a drive over the shingle; the only hard surface was provided by planks. The settlement itself was simple, without pub or shops, initiated, it appears, by an enterprising individual who, finding the pebbles provided inadequate standing for his tent, bought a redundant railway carriage and pitched that instead. It was a breakthrough of a sort, for railway carriages, tram cars and vans became standing living quarters on these coastal plotlands. They had the advantage that anything on wheels escaped local authority rates. Other settlements were established on the Selsey peninsula, beyond Bognor, on the western edge of Sussex. An occupant of one of them described it in pre-motoring days as seeming 'a hundred miles from anywhere'. What the automobile did was to magnify and scatter these settlements. At Selsey, there was originally a railway station by the eastern beach, but it closed down when the western side of the peninsula grew more popular. Then it was replaced by a bus terminal. Mrs Stawell, in a book written in the 1920s, described how the once beautiful sands at Selsey had disappeared under rows of houses. Of the place now, she thought, it was 'difficult to speak except in terms of wonder ... To right and left a long line of cars stretches into the distance, with no gaps and apparently no end.' The car, though, reached its fullest recognition not on the south coast but at Jaywick Sands on the Essex coast, 'a motorist's Mecca by the Sea'. At Jaywick the main highway was named Brooklands and other roads included Chrysler-Crescent, Austin-Avenue, Singer-Street and Renault-Road.

At least at Selsey and Jaywick roads existed. At many of these settlements there were only unmade tracks. From a practical point of view, that was of the less importance in that residents and visitors were more likely to arrive by bus than car. Again the lack of facilities often mattered little, since, like their fellows inland, the migrants of those days were reasonably indifferent to urban amenities. The *Listener* in October 1936 observed that more and more people were

Peacehaven, c. 1935. The most notorious of the shanty towns, brought into being by motor transport, which littered the south-east coast of England in the 1930s. It was described authoritatively as a 'disgusting blot on the landscape' and 'a monstrous blot on the national conscience'.

finding ways of escaping the great seaside towns and acquiring bungalows or shacks in what was — at least until they came on the scene — open country. Or even 'open beaches'. For that was what it amounted to at 'Bohemia', a collection of corrugated-iron huts on top of the dunes near Sutton on Sea, a small resort in Lincolnshire, that was promoted as 'the very ideal of a Gipsy holiday life'. For some, a small community would have been attractive, since the closeness of neighbours could have made it easier to bear what, many years later, the *Guardian* called 'the Peacehaven syndrome'. The victims were couples from the Midlands and North who, on retirement, set off for the south coast in search of a 'twilight dream home'. The *Guardian* was quoting a doctor who described how difficult such people found adjustment. So difficult, claimed the doctor, that often the husband died prematurely, leaving his widow to struggle on in a place remote from old friends and relatives.

Peacehaven, close to Brighton, became the most notorious of these shoreline plotlands. In *Brighton Rock* Pinkie takes Rose to the country. Their bus passes through Rottingdean, by then absorbed by Brighton, the sand gone. '"It's lovely," said Rose, "being out here

— in the country with you." Then came Peacehaven itself.'

> Little tarred bungalows with tin roofs paraded backwards, gardens scratched in the chalk, dry flower beds like Saxon emblems carved on the downs. Notices read: 'Pull in Here', 'Mazawatee tea', 'Genuine Antiques', and hundreds of feet below the pale green sea washed into the scarred and shabby side of England. Peacehaven itself dwindled out against the downs: half-made streets turned into grass tracks.

Peacehaven came to embody what was wrong, the uncontrolled destruction brought about by the automobile of some of the most beautiful country in Britain. In the words of a recent book, Peacehaven 'stretched conspicuously over a vast acreage of some of England's most cherished landscape, the South Downs, at its dramatic meeting with the sea'. To Thomas Sharp at the time, it was a 'disgusting blot on the landscape'; to another commentator, it was 'a monstrous blot on the national conscience'.

To Laurie Lee, the shanty building, while it was not what he had expected, held a perverse charm. It looked, he wrote, 'as though everything about it had been thrown together by the winds, and might at any moment be blown away again'. That is more or less what did happen in some places. By the late 1940s much of the east shore of Selsey had disappeared under the sea. Jaywick suffered severely in the 1953 floods, which also wrecked many of the Canvey Island plotlands on the Thames estuary. The army was a help, despite E. M. Forster's warning in 1937 that the fighting services were bound to become serious enemies of what was left of England. While the army's gunnery and tank ranges did little actually to increase the national stock of beauty, the defensive strip established along the south coast shoreline during the Second World War finished off — 'blew away' — any number of shanty settlements. After the Second World War, the planning laws were stricter, and, more important still, the increased wealth of the population at large and a marked rise in the value of shore land led to the replacement of the sheds and huts and shabby bungalows by modern housing estates. (Not that nothing at all is left: in January 2002, for example, a 1934 wooden beach hut at West Bexington on the Dorset coast was sold for £120,000.) The automobile has endowed us with a built-up shoreline, but at least the shanties, like the roadhouses, proved to be transitory.

7
Road against Rail

"We thought the railway system would last for ever, and it is dying now and the whole movement of the population is being reversed."

J. B. Priestley

As people from the towns hastened to the country to take possession of cottages and bungalows and shacks, their paths crossed with countrymen going the other way. It all predated the car, or at least the car as a significant influence. After all, it was in 1896 that J. J. Hissey had described the depopulation of the countryside as becoming a serious question. The census of 1901 showed that in the ten years since its immediate predecessor the number of farm workers in the age group fifteen to twenty-four had dropped by more than half, a result of the protracted agricultural depression which started in the 1870s. Not that all of them took to metropolitan life. Since happily the depression did not stop people drinking, many redundant workers found jobs in local breweries. (In the case of one of the largest brewery companies, 37 per cent of their employees in 1901 were former farm workers.) The shedding of labour continued after the First World War. In Oxford displaced farm workers provided the largest single source of labour at Morris. Professor Joad noted sourly that, motoring, whatever else its effects, did provide country jobs. A German visitor in the 1930s observed

that the land was no longer worked by families: the sons were manning petrol pumps and the daughters were working as waitresses in roadside cafés. And the sons at least were paid good wages; by the time they were twenty-one they were earning more than their fathers did after thirty or forty years of work on the land.

An Emerson Farm Tractor, 1917. For years tractors cost more to use than horses, their advantages in Britain proving less than on the much larger farms of North America.

Nevertheless, the blight which gripped the countryside, the atmosphere of gloom and decay that it brought about, could not be disguised. It was indeed a skewed sort of Arcadia that the enthusiastic motorists discovered in the 1920s. Naturally, the writers who inspired their voyages of discovery wrote not of derelict farms and neglected fields but of medieval churches, romantic landscapes, craft shops and arcane rituals. Yet should the tourists' eyes happen to stray, and always provided that dirt — for decayed farms are filthy — was not rationalized as nature in her natural bloom, they must have gone home in a somewhat ambivalent mood.

Any motorist, though, sensitive or not, would have noticed how many horses were at work on the land. Even in the mid-1930s on farms in England and Wales there were fourteen horses to every tractor. It would have been easy to assume, sitting at the steering wheel, changing into a lower gear in order to cope with some muddy lane, that farming deserved its fate, that farmers were congenitally incapable of coming to terms with the modern age. Such a judgement would have been unfair. Long before, behind the horses (literally as well as metaphorically) stood an extensive range of steam machinery which was used for binding, hay making, threshing and grinding, in fact for all sorts of work around the farm. In Hardy's *Tess of the d'Urbervilles*, first published in 1891, there appears a prototype of the motor mechanic. The farm hands are in the fields working with a steam-driven threshing machine, an engine which in the author's words 'was to act as the *primum mobile* of this little world'.

> A little way off there was another indistinct figure; this one black ... By the engine stood a dark motionless being, a sooty and grimy embodiment of tallness, in a sort of trance, with a heap of coals by his side: it was the engineman. The isolation of his manner and colour lent him the appearance of a creature from Tophet, who had strayed into the pellucid smokelessness of this region of yellow grain and pale soil, with which he had nothing in common, to amaze and to discompose its aborigines.

And there could well be a traction locomotive as well. Farming gave continued employment to the horse certainly, but it had also sustained the road locomotive over decades of general neglect. But the question remains: if farms were so go-ahead, why did they not more rapidly exploit the possibilities of the automobile?

Introducing his bill into the House of Commons in 1896, Henry Chaplin — himself very much a representative of the farming interest — had pointed out, to ironic cheers, how motor vehicles would lower transport costs for farmers. Lord Montagu insisted on the same point in his contribution to the Badminton book on motors. In January 1902 *Country Life* published an article entitled 'Motors on the Farm' in which it recommended farmers to buy steam wagons. However, it also acknowledged that there was no demand for motors on the part of estate owners and farmers. The reason was clear: the depression had left them short of funds with which to invest. Farmers had to make do. One of them, the writer A. G. Street, observed of the car that 'its advent marked an epoch in rural affairs rather more definitely, I think, than in urban ones', but he also wrote that while personally he took easily to the car, he also hung on to his old steam engine until the time when the cost of its repair became prohibitive. Motor wagons brought undeniable advantages: for instance, by the

mid-1920s livestock no longer walked to market or to the railway but travelled in a stock lorry. Tractors, though, were not as universal as might be

A Leyland steam wagon, *c.* 1898.

imagined. In the United States and Canada a tractor could plough as much in a single day as a team of horses could accomplish in a week. British farms, however, were much smaller, and the cost benefits of a different order. In 1935 it was calculated that a new Fordson tractor (originally a derivation of the Model T) with strakes on its wheels cost much the same as a pair of good horses. But the working life of the horse was ten to twelve years, twice that of a tractor used for normal farm work. (And a Fordson with pneumatic tyres cost an extra £40.) An inter-war survey in East Anglia concluded that tractors did not generally lead to lower costs per acre, but that tractor farms did obtain higher output and thus greater profit. The future might be obvious but it was some time before it arrived.

Tractors get little attention in histories of the automobile. One reason is that they were barely road vehicles; they were more self-moving, very slow self-moving, farm machinery. Commercial vehicles too are neglected. We hear much about the Royal Automobile Club and the Automobile Association and very little about the Institution of Automobile Engineers or the Commercial Motor

Users' Association. Cars of course play a more important part in most people's lives, and, there is no denying it, are a good deal more glamorous than lorries and vans and buses. Yet of all the British automobile pioneers, none — not Lord Montagu or S. F. Edge or anyone else — enjoyed a career more extraordinary and picturesque or more significant than Rookes Crompton, a man whose life was closely tied up with commercial motor vehicles. To start with the extraordinary and picturesque: surely no one else ever arrived at his preparatory school the holder of a military campaign medal. Nor do you expect to find a British expert on road locomotives moving at ease at the court of the Emperor Franz Josef in Vienna, let alone at such ease that he was in a position to introduce the Emperor's heir, the Archduke Rudolf, to Baroness Vetsera and thus become a proximate cause of the most sensational and — in its effect, most important — scandal of the nineteenth century, the tragedy of Mayerling.

Born in 1845 near Thirsk to a well-to-do Yorkshire landowning family, Rookes Crompton was from the start fascinated by mechanics. At the age of six his mother took him to the Great Exhibition in Hyde Park. He at once dragged her to the Machinery Hall, where he stood transfixed by the gleaming steam locomotives on show. When the Crimean War broke out, his father, a former MP, joined his militia regiment and took the family to Gibraltar. The boy, eager to be nearer the action, persuaded his parents to let him join up as a cadet in a Crimea-bound warship commanded by a cousin of his mother's. When the ship arrived at its destination, Crompton managed to obtain a pass to visit an elder brother in the trenches in front of Sebastopol. (The visit entitled him to his medal, the Crimean Medal with Sebastopol clasp.) The war over, aged eleven, he set off for school, being, as he wrote in his reminiscences, 'older than my years'.

Crompton's engineering career began in earnest at Harrow, where he started on the construction of a full-size, steam-driven road engine. After gaining experience at a locomotive works in Doncaster, he joined the Rifle Brigade and was sent to India, where his evident talent induced his superiors to allow him to concentrate on road locomotives intended for the haulage of guns and supplies. The Great Trunk Road proved an ideal testing ground. There were difficulties: one was the need to adapt engines imported from Britain so that they burned wood rather than coal. And circumstances differed, for in India the engines were competing against elephants rather than horses. From a technical point of view, Crompton's main achievement was his experiments with rubber tyres. By 1870 he could declare with confidence that the traction engines used in agriculture in Britain would become obsolete and that rubber tyres would replace steel-rimmed wheels. He was later to write — and he was not a boastful man — that 'we already possessed a degree of knowledge and insight into the problems of motor transport such as was obtained by others thirty years later.'

The contrast between the attitudes to road locomotives in India and in Britain was striking. In India Crompton's experiments were supported by pretty well everyone from the viceroy down; in Britain neither business nor government was interested, although Crompton did manage to obtain some exemption from the red flag rules. He entered a competition with a road steamer hauling a two-deck omnibus capable of seating 130 people. Judges and dignitaries clambered aboard and Crompton treated them to a display of fast driving and manoeuvring. It was not a success, for his passengers succumbed to what his biographer, L. T. C. Rolt, described as 'the first acute case of car sickness in history'. Depressed by the lack of interest, Crompton set up his own electrical business, making dynamos and fitting electrical plant. He installed the first systems at Buckingham Palace, at Windsor Castle and at the Aldwych Law Courts. (It was while he was working on the Vienna Opera House that he made the ill-fated introduction.) With the Boer War, Crompton returned to the army to command the corps of traction engines, and in the First World War he was one of the designers of the tank. He died, aged ninety-three, during the Second World War, a man of outstanding ingenuity and breadth of achievement. Rolt goes so far as to write, 'It would not be claiming too much to call Crompton the father of the modern motor road.' With his long experience, he was also a leader in the development of freight transport.

In 1907 Colonel Crompton, as he had become, in his presidential address to members of the Institution of Automobile Engineers, took as his subject 'the future of automobilism'. As a theme it was not by then original. But Crompton's approach was unfamiliar: he was concerned with the motor transport of freight, not of passengers. The development of goods-carrying vehicles by motor manufacturers, he told his audience, would serve the public far better than their current preoccupation with private cars. Certainly in 1907 this form of motor transport was virtually restricted to light work. There were vans and small commercial vehicles on the roads (even, as we have seen, on the road to Brighton in 1896), but they were mostly converted cars, light enough to qualify for the 1896 relaxation of rules. They were quickly adapted to a variety of purposes, commercial and municipal, and served as fire engines and ambulances, as hearses and dust and water carts. Politicians made use of them and so did religious missions, who fitted them out as chapels. Since they could make deliveries and collections more speedily than horses, they were in demand by department stores. In London, for instance, Maples and Gamages both employed them, and Schoolbreds of Tottenham Court Road bought thirty-one vans as a replacement for 124 horses. Along with the bus, such vehicles helped to revolutionize life in the country, although it was to be years yet before they seem to have affected villages such as Laurie Lee's Slad. The advantages of light commercial vehicles were expounded with zest by Edwin Pratt in his *History of Inland Transport*, published in 1913. He describes how 'in the recesses of Wild Wales' they are worked as mobile shops travelling from village to village. It was, he writes, a partial return anyway to the days of the pedlar and packhorse.

That might be so, but it was, according to Pratt, the large firms which had most to gain. In the knowledge that stock could be replenished rapidly, they could afford to hold less of it, and they could also cut down on branches. He adds, 'The real competition today is no longer between large traders and small traders. It is a competition between commercial giants.'

For heavy commercial vehicles, for lorries, the situation was very different. Leyland Motors, to become the best-known manufacturer of heavy commercial vehicles, sprang from a family blacksmith's business in Leyland, a township near Liverpool, and produced a crude steam wagon back in 1884, following it up in the 1890s with more sophisticated vehicles, including a steam lawnmower. Another large manufacturer was Foden, with a background in traction engines and mechanical threshers. However, the difficulties were formidable. For one thing, until 1904 they were subjected to the old red flag rules; for another, these heavy machines were unreliable — like the early buses but more so. And they were very unwieldy. A series of road trials carried out between 1897 and 1901 which included Leyland, Thornycroft and Daimler machines showed how far there was to go before they could in any way provide competition with the railways. Or even with horses. Two large haulage firms, Carter Paterson and Pickfords, experimented by using petrol-driven wagons in Brighton to carry holiday luggage. Failing to make it pay, they reverted to horses. McNamara & Co., carriers since 1837 for Royal Mail, ran seventy-seven petrol-driven motors, mainly on Post Office work, a venture which sent them into receivership. In fact, during the decade 1901 to 1911 the number of horses engaged in the transport of goods actually increased, rising from 702,000 to 832,000. A 1913 traffic census of vehicles entering London showed that while by then practically none of the passenger vehicles was horse-drawn, the opposite was true of goods vehicles, of which no less than 88 per cent still depended on horses. What is more, lorries, even when reliable, tended to spend much time standing about unused. Even in the 1920s for distances up to around three miles it was cheaper to use horses. In many city streets the wide turning circle of the motor lorry made its use impracticable. Even where that was no problem, wear and tear and the high consumption of fuel which resulted from continuous stopping and starting militated against heavy motor vehicles, both lorries and buses.

The demands of war brought about a decisive change. Lorries were needed in great numbers to carry troops and supplies, and manufacturers perforce concentrated on them in the way Colonel Crompton had urged. As we have seen, Verdun showed how vital they could be. Yet the public generally was still unaware of their potential. And it was not just the public it seems, for a book published in 1919, *The History and Economics of Transport*, intended for students taking a degree in commerce, while describing how road transport had been replaced by the railway, omitted any mention of the internal-combustion engine and its consequences. It was the national railway strike that erupted at the end of September 1919 which demonstrated most clearly to the world at large the importance of commercial motor transport. When the strike started, it looked as if the bad old days of pre-war industrial conflict were back with a vengeance, and back at a time when the country was still in the early stages of post-war recovery and alarmed by the possible spread of revolution from Russia. The seriousness with which the strike was regarded led the Paris newspaper *Le Temps* to declare the crisis to be the most acute in the experience of the British Empire, and one which 'affects generally the whole of the civilized world'.

The government responded energetically, converting Hyde Park into a huge open-air clearing house for food supplies. An urgent plea was made to avoid using petrol for inessential purposes. Sporting events were curtailed and the stewards of the Jockey Club sharply criticized for failing to cancel a meeting at Newmarket until virtually ordered to do so. A quiet descended on the countryside; in some places it was as if pre-motoring times were back. In Canterbury, it was reported, Saturday was like an old-time market day, and 'Farmers drove in their carts and gigs, and many other country folk used antiquated vehicles long disused.' The motorist was seen as essential to keep the economy going. Volunteers thronged to carry food and commuters. Motor cyclists conveyed messages and letters. The strike lasted from 22 September to 5 October, but by 1 October *The Times* could head a column 'Triumph of the Lorry', announcing that in the last few days the motor lorry had come into its own. Two days later the paper went further:

> The triumph of the motor lorry, demonstrated so plainly in the prompt collection and distribution of milk and food during the strike, has done more to advertise the possibilities of motor transport to the people of this country than even the much greater success achieved by the motor lorry during the war.

Thus, when a potentially yet more damaging crisis occurred with the General Strike of 1926, the importance of the lorry and of motor transport generally was well established. And by then there were many more motor vehicles available. The number of goods vehicles was up from 62,000 in 1919 to around 250,000, while the number of private cars and motor cycles had risen from 225,000 to over 1.3 million.

One reason for this fourfold increase in commercial vehicles over seven years was the availability of the superfluous army vehicles. They were as eagerly snapped up by would-be goods carriers as by those wanting to transport passengers. John Jempson of Rye was an example of a small carrier of the time. He started off with a Model T light lorry, bought for £124, in which he set out in the early morning transporting fruit and vegetables to London, sixty miles away. He returned in the evening with a load of fertilizer, flour and cattle food from the London docks. Jempson charged the same as the railways but provided a quicker service. In a smaller way still was the Dearman family. The father, a carrier, found it impossible to cope with the motor; his son W. C. Dearman believed that 'he would never have been able to drive under any conditions without a pair of reins'. But the younger Dearman owned a car which he used to carry goods and sometimes people. He worked for himself and also for the Twickenham Gravel Company, employed, with a lorry, to collect manure from the stables at Paddington Station for sale to nursery gardens. Jempson was competing with the railways, Dearman with the horse. But a carrier, especially of the larger sort, had a wide choice and was not bound to one particular means of transport: it was a question of which form of haulage suited which job. The firm of Wordie of Aberdeen, for instance, railway agents who plunged early into motors, also used horses. In 1938 Wordie's fleet numbered 272 motor vehicles with 113 trailers, and 1,084 horses.

By the early 1920s, while steam was fast disappearing as the motive power for cars and buses, it was still quite usual for freight transport. Two-thirds of Pickfords' fleet in 1919 were steam vehicles. At one stage Pickfords advertised 'petrol for speed: steam for heavy haulage'. A steam lorry could tow a trailer as well as itself carry a load. (One recalls Colonel Crompton's prototype pulling a 130-seater bus.) And steam lorries had fewer moving parts to go wrong. However, they were demanding in other ways: a road built in 1928—9 in Lancashire — steam vehicles were much used by the textile industry — was provided with hydrants to supply water to the lorries every few miles.

In the end petrol won as improved power/weight ratios gave a decisive advantage. Petrol or steam, it was the large lorries that provided the most obvious challenge to the railways. For some time, though, their threat was underrated. *The Times*, in its comments on the motor lorry and its role in the 1919 strike, considered that lorries might actually prove a boon to the railways for they might 'afford some hope of relief to the railways from the congestion which has been so long a legitimate ground of complaint'. The general opinion was that road and rail transport were by nature complementary. Freight hauliers would continue to look to the railway for long distances and to use their own fleets of motor lorries (or possibly horses) for short ones. Experience with passenger transport provided evidence of benefits to

Motor cycle and sidecar, 1930s. These vehicles had sold in huge numbers in Britain during the 1920s.

both sides. The car allowed commuters to live further into the country and to drive to and from the railway station. The motor industry gained, and so, by selling tickets for the main journey, did the railway company. If anybody went in for poaching, it might well be the railways, not the road hauliers. Certainly as far as passenger traffic was concerned. It had, after all, been the railway companies in the 1900s which had taken the leading part in providing bus 'feeder services' to carry passengers to and from the station. Particularly active was the Great Western Railway, which assembled a fleet of motor buses — it owned eighty of them by 1908. They were used as feeders, and were intended otherwise not to compete with rail services but rather to supplement them in thinly populated areas where motor transport might prove a cheap alternative to extending rail lines.

So why should not such cooperation work with goods haulage? One reason against was that the relationship was out of equilibrium, for lorries were improving technically almost month by month, while trains were not. Another was railway complacency. In commenting on the 1919 strike, *The Times* complained of railway inadequacies, probably having in mind the problems caused by the war.

What it called a 'legitimate ground of complaint' went back further. In 1901 a book, *The Ruin of Rural England*, more or less blamed the railways for the continuing agricultural depression. One chapter was headed 'Government by Railway Company', another 'The Ruin of Essex by the Great Eastern Railway'. All the great arteries of commerce, the book charged, were in the hands of the railway companies. They fixed their rates between them. They cared little about their customers. The transport of perishable goods such as fruit — which in the harsh circumstances of the time the English farmer was advised that he should turn to — was subjected to such delays that the produce was often ruined by the time it reached its destination. The railways might be fast when they got going, but that was not much use if they took an age to go about it. When *The Ruin of Rural England* was published, while there were dangers in bad publicity, the railways could take risks with their customers. With road transport beginning to provide effective competition, it was another matter. In 1919 motorists flooded on to the roads in celebration of their first summer of peace. The demand for petrol soared and local suppliers needed constant replenishment of stock. One firm near Edinburgh found that it took from ten to twelve days for petrol dispatched by rail from London to reach them. So they did the obvious thing: they hired lorries. This was by no means an isolated example. S. Vere Pearson, writing in 1929, recalled the experience of a friend of his in the 1920s, the proprietor of two factories in the Greater London area, who found that heavy machinery sent from Manchester by rail regularly went astray. He too changed to road transport.

In Britain, the Trafford Park industrial estate just outside Manchester supplies what is perhaps the best illustration of the challenge posed by road transport to the railways over the carriage of long-distance freight. In the 1890s the land on which it was to be established came up for sale and a bid by the city council was bettered by Harry Lawson's associate, the speculator Ernest Hooley. His idea was to develop the land for expensive housing and a racecourse, and later on as a centre of the rubber and bicycle trades. However, his partner Marshall Stevens, one of the leading businessmen in Manchester, had other ideas. With the recent completion of the Manchester Ship Canal (of which he had been general manager), Stevens anticipated that Manchester's attraction to business would be greatly increased. He was interested not in the traditional textile

firms but in the likely high-flyers of the twentieth century. At Trafford Park — Hooley having moved on — he created the first and
largest industrial estate in Europe. Merely a mention of some of the
estate's tenants gives an idea of its importance. Ford established
their British factory there in 1911 and there were the big oil companies Shell Mex, Texas Oil and Anglo-American. There were Massey
Harris, manufacturers of agricultural machinery, Brooke Bond tea
and a Hovis flour mill. Pickfords were an early arrival.

Stevens attracted tenants to the park by supplying them with
basic services — with water and drainage, with electric power and, of
the greatest importance, with excellent transport facilities. That of
course meant roads, but also a gas-powered tramway (supplemented
later by an electric tramway) which ran across the park. Communications with the outside world consisted primarily of the ship canal,
with its direct link to the sea, and the railways. The estate constructed rail lines of its own to connect with the Dock Railways and
through them to the main lines to the south. Other connections
were established with the rail systems of the north-east and Midlands. But Stevens, a man with 'an unrivalled understanding of
transportation in all its aspects', had no intention of accepting railway dominance; in fact, it was partly to escape that dominance that
the Manchester Ship Canal had been built in the first place. He
resented the arrogance of the railways and their refusal to quote for
carriage alone, insisting as they did — like the old-established air-
lines in our day — on unwanted frills. He considered that they
abused their virtual monopoly: in the early 1880s, for instance, to
transport raw cotton between Liverpool and Manchester, a distance
of thirty-five miles, they charged the highest rate in the world outside
the Panama Canal. So Stevens turned to the possibilities of road
haulage, in 1912 proposing to the Canal Company the establishment of a Motor Transhipment Depot in the park for the inter-
change of traffic between the docks and their hinterland. By 1935,
while the railways still carried two-thirds of the traffic to and from
the estate, there were nevertheless 5,500 motor vehicles using Trafford Park every day, carrying an annual load of 1 million tons.

Stevens pungently expressed his hostility to the railway companies in Parliament, of which he was a Member. Soon after the
First World War, speaking in the House of Commons on behalf of
the Federation of British Industries, he declared that 'inland canals

had been paralysed by railway interests; road competition had been stunted by railway interests'. He accused the Minister of Transport, Sir Eric Geddes, of using his great power to assist the railway's attempt to dominate the carrying trade. Geddes was not acting with any vicious intent, said Stevens, but because 'he is so imbued with railway policy that, subconsciously, he can do nothing else'.

The fact that Geddes was the minister says much for the government's resolve to organize an efficient transport system. He was a star; in charge of the military railway directorate during the war, he had been notably successful in his handling of transport in France. In July 1917 he was appointed First Lord of the Admiralty, keeping his Cabinet rank when he moved to transport. Geddes, like Stevens, was a transport man — 'Transport is my religion,' he was quoted as saying. He was determined to make the system work on what he considered to be the right lines. But it is hard to believe that Stevens was unfair. Geddes had railways in the blood: he was descended from a railway family, and before the war had been heir apparent to the general manager of the North Eastern Railway. He had no intention of allowing a free-for-all between road and rail transport, declaring that it would be 'nothing short of criminal to permit a continuance of the old system of competition between light railways and roads, railways and canals'. It was not just Marshall Stevens and the Federation of British Industries who feared that road transport would be put at a disadvantage. Lord Montagu and most people connected with the motor industry were afraid of the same thing. They were not at all reassured by the presence of other old railway hands in positions of influence.

But things turned out differently. The Railways Act of 1921, besides tying up a lot of legislative loose ends, was intended to set the scene for a coordinated transport system, one based on the allegedly complementary nature of road and rail. What actually happened was that between 1924 and 1934 the railways lost something like a quarter of their goods traffic to road transport. There was no year after the First World War when the volume of freight which they carried reached the pre-war level. At the same time, the road hauliers were picking up local business previously carried by horse transport.

The loss to the railways of long-distance work had not been anticipated. With hindsight their loss is unsurprising. For one thing

motor hauliers were more flexible, and able more easily to meet customers' preferences for hours of collection and delivery. They were
free to accept or refuse the work on offer, while the railways as
'common carriers' were obliged to accept whatever was proposed to
them. Then there was transhipment, the loading and unloading on
the way, which (unless sidings existed) the railways could not avoid.
By contrast, road hauliers, who could simply load up at the start and
unload at the end, reduced their labour costs markedly. The insurance risks of damage and theft were reduced as a result and so therefore were premiums. (The risk of theft was reduced but not
abolished; after all, 'falling off the back of a lorry' remains a familiar
expression.) Pricing was easy: a motor haulier could go down to the
nearest railway station, discover the railway rates for a particular
journey and then undercut them.

Along with all this, the motor hauliers were blessed with minimal
restrictions, falling running costs and rising vehicle efficiency. For
instance, the coachbuilder Scammell introduced the articulated
lorry in 1919, and there was increasing use of pneumatic tyres. And,
at least as important as anything else, the motor hauliers demonstrated the energy and enterprise so often characteristic of a new
industry which the railways, mature and complacent, lacked.

In more general terms, the railways faced competition in the 1920s
— for freight and passenger transport — under two serious disadvantages. One was imposed upon them. That was their relationship
with the government, which regarded them with a mixture of benevolence and suspicion. The benevolence meant that the government
— as it was to show when the situation deteriorated — was there as a
protector of last resort. After all, the railway system was of vital
importance to the economy, and it employed a great many people. In
1935, for example, while the Post Office was the largest employer of
all, it was closely followed by the London Midland & Scottish Railway. Next, in third place, came the London & North Eastern Railway and in fourth the Great Western. While the London Passenger
Transport Board slotted in at fifth place, immediately afterwards was
the Southern Railway, with the industrial giants Unilever and Imperial Chemicals chasing along behind. Between them the four companies employed some 550,000 people. In addition, and not to be
ignored, were over a million (usually ill-rewarded) shareholders.

But there was the suspicion too, which went a long way back, its consequence a heavy constraint on the railway companies' freedom of action. They were seen as potential exploiters ready to abuse their power. An act of Parliament had laid down that as from 1893 any trader who complained of increased charges could appeal to a special commission and it was left to the railway company concerned to show that the increase was fair. This control of charges made it difficult to respond to a rise in costs and to negotiate with the unions. It was in fact responsible for a national railway strike in 1911. The war made life more difficult yet. Then the companies found themselves, with salaries, wages and fares all frozen, confronted with the sharp (if temporary) post-war inflation. That problem was half sorted out, but there remained another and expensive legacy of the war in the neglected track and rolling stock. What is more, the 1921 Railways Act, in putting together the four large groups, dissolved the hundred or more separate companies which had previously existed and with them the boardroom seats to which they had been able to appoint MPs. Lobbying power was much reduced.

The other disadvantage suffered by the railway companies was self-inflicted: their complacency. After all, they were used to being winners. In the years before the First World War they had enjoyed a consistent increase in traffic, both freight and passenger. Now, even where freedom of action existed, they found it difficult to adapt, to adjust their thinking and actions to road competition. They ignored the lessons of the conflict between rail and road in the United States and, ironically, like the British motor industry, they relied too much on a tradition of technical excellence. They showed no inclination to close down uneconomic lines. When the plight of the railway system fully revealed itself late in the 1920s, a royal commission (one of its members the octogenarian Colonel Crompton) was set up to report on the 'Co-ordination and Development of Transport'. It laid heavy blame on the railways, criticizing their failure to compete, even to try to compete, by reducing fares where it was necessary to do so. The committee commented that 'the truth of the doctrine that facilities create traffic appears to have been forgotten'. It also criticized the companies' lethargy: the right to run feeder bus services was not included in the comprehensive Railways Act of 1921 — they should have lobbied much sooner than they did to have this omission corrected. The committee did praise the electrification on suburban services and on the Southern Railway, and commended the excellent passenger service between important cities. At the same time it contrasted these services with the record on shorter journeys, where trains were slow and badly scheduled, and as a result lost business to road transport. The committee added acidly how remarkable it was that in eighty years there had been practically no improvement in locomotive speed in Britain.

Passenger transport tended to attract greater attention than freight. For one thing, it gripped the public imagination more strongly, for another it provided the battleground for the fiercest competition between road and rail. Again, much of the business falling to buses and coaches was new, entirely new — that is, it represented journeys which would not have occurred had automobiles not existed. Thus it could be claimed that the railways stagnated rather than declined, and it was true that in 1938 the railways still covered slightly more passenger miles than buses and coaches. However, by a more significant measure, that of revenue from ticket holders, the decline is very visible. The railways in 1938 earned only £56 million as opposed to their rival's £76 million. In 1920 the railways' figure had been twice that of their rivals. Since business expenditure was excluded from these estimates, the railways' overall share may be somewhat underestimated. On the other hand, cars and motor cycles are not included at all, and it has been calculated that by 1938 they accounted for half the amount applicable to all forms of public transport.

By the later 1920s the state of transport in Britain was widely regarded as chaotic. The plight of the railways was another anxiety to pile on top of the others — the dismay about the number of people killed and injured on the roads, the congestion in towns and the effect of motoring on the environment. H. G. Wells (who had foreseen what might happen) was harsh in a radio broadcast he made in November 1932. It was incredible, he said, how unprepared we had been for the motor car and for its effect on our society and on our lives. We did nothing to prepare for it, we left our roads as they were to become choked with traffic and 'we did nothing to adjust our railroads to fit in with this new element in life until they were overtaken and bankrupt'.

The railways were in fact making an attempt to adjust themselves, not indeed by closing down uneconomic lines but by shedding labour. Their labour force of 735,870 in 1921 was down by 1935 to

550,000. Other industries in decline, for instance cotton, were doing the same thing — hence of course the chronic unemployment problem. An attempt at a more constructive solution to the problems of struggling industries, much favoured at the time, was 'rationalization', sometimes called 'amalgamation', sometimes 'emergent evolution'. It meant compulsory mergers, the introduction of efficient management and the elimination of excess plant. As a result it was expected that costs would drop and (where applicable) exports resume. (The alternative, a devaluation of the pound, which in Britain meant the abandonment of the gold standard, was considered out of the question.) Official reports, newspapers and journals, and influential individuals gave rationalization their support; indeed they called out loudly in its favour. It was the remedy supported by the government and promoted by the Governor of the Bank of England, Montagu Norman, who established a special committee of experts to help with it. The Coal Mines Act of 1930 set in place a reorganization committee charged with putting the coal industry in order. With cotton the state intervened to create a compulsory cartel to raise prices, and to compel the destruction of surplus textile machinery. Shipbuilding and iron and steel were other examples of industries which submitted to rationalization.

The railways were a special case. The idea of rationalization at its most extreme, in the form of nationalization, had been floated for years. Back in 1901 the author of *The Ruin of Rural England* had seen it as the cure for their inefficiency and arrogance, and in 1908 Winston Churchill, not exactly a socialist even in his radical days, had written as President of the Board of Trade to Asquith, the Prime Minister, suggesting 'railway amalgamation with state control'. Anyway, they were half rationalized already, with the small companies pushed into the large ones and with their charging structure regulated. They were also unusual in that though they were very large, they were nevertheless just a section of something very much bigger, the enormous transport industry, the other part of which, motoring, was, with electrical engineering, the British economy's star turn. Never could rationalization look to have a better chance of working. The Railways Act, it had been hoped, would achieve what was necessary in a natural, unforced way. It had failed, so more stringent legislation was needed.

By the late 1920s Sir Eric Geddes had long departed the scene, ironically to become chairman of Dunlop. The most influential figure on transport matters was Sir Josiah Stamp, from 1927 president of the executive of the London, Midland & Scottish Railway. He was self-made, his father the manager of a bookshop in Wigan, who had left school aged fifteen to enter the Inland Revenue. During his life — ended by a bomb during the Blitz — he was an internationally recognized expert on reparations, a director of the Bank of England, governor of the London School of Economics, president of the British Association and a peer. In January 1940 he was to turn down an offer of the chancellorship of the exchequer. Unlike Geddes, a chain cigar smoker, prodigious eater and enthusiastic consumer of brandy and ginger ale, Stamp was a non-smoking teetotaller and a pillar of the Wesleyan ministry. His personal austerity was in harmony with his belief in a rigorous discipline for 'depressed and distressed industries'. He supported the view that rationalization was the most humane and economic way out of their troubles, dismissing the argument that monopolies meant a raw deal for consumers in the form of higher prices and/or shoddy goods on the grounds — later to appear unduly complacent — that widespread share-ownership would check company directors' ability to exploit their power.

As chairman of the Railway Companies Association, Stamp was the official leader of the railways, and carried much of the responsibility for making the several 'rationalizing' transport acts of Parliament work. While he was to declare that 'we have every desire that road transport should take the place for which it is economically suited', his concern was to rescue the railways. These acts were intended to help the railways meet road competition on fairer terms and to check 'wasteful competition'. The first of them took effect from 1928 and empowered the railways to operate road transport services of their own. Then followed the Road Traffic Act of 1930, which regulated passenger services, and the Road and Rail Traffic Act of 1933, which dealt with the carriage of freight. The Finance Act of 1933 increased the duties on goods vehicles.

The acts of 1930 and 1933 worked through systems of licensing. Both bus operators and road hauliers were granted licences only if they could prove their proposed area of operation to be in need of their services. Speed was regulated, vehicles rigorously inspected and conditions of employment laid down. The old free-for-all was over;

the railways could, and did, object to applications for a road licence. The motor firms, passenger and goods, acquiesced, doing so partly because the tide favouring 'rationalization' was flowing so strongly that they had little choice, and partly because the larger companies among them were disturbed by the erratic record of smaller operators, whose vehicles were frequently in a wretched state and undependable. For one thing, such a state of affairs was bad for public relations; for another, the planning of bus routes, to take an example, was made difficult with the cowboys barging in and out. Moreover, when it came down to it, bus companies were accustomed to restraint of trade; they already exercised it between themselves by carving up the market into exclusive territories — 'zoning', as it was called. Zoning was the more natural in that many of the bus companies were owned by municipal authorities concerned only with their own districts. Customers too were happy enough. Fares and other charges went on falling, buses continued to improve in comfort and the compulsory inspection of vehicles undoubtedly promoted greater safety and reliability.

The apportionment of territory by bus companies reflected their industry's structure — its dominance by large firms. For example, British Electric Traction, Thomas Tilling and Scottish Motor Traction owned more than fifty bus companies and ultimately came to control fleets that carried over half the bus passengers in the country. This concentration made it easy for the railway companies to diversify. Rather than develop their own motor fleets, they bought into existing bus firms. (They had given an undertaking not to buy control, so they made do with 49 or 50 per cent.) So rapidly did they move that the Royal Commission on Transport observed sardonically that 'the chief method adopted by the railway companies to protect themselves against road competition appears to be to get on the road themselves'.

The haulage industry was a different matter altogether. In 1938, for example, of the half-million freight vehicles on the roads, 70 per cent were owned by traders who used them solely for the carriage of their own goods. (For them a licence was automatic.) Ownership of the rest was split between 60,000 firms, so many that the railway companies could not hope to gain the level of control that they achieved with the buses. They contented themselves by buying up, through joint purchase, the two largest hauliers, Carter Paterson and Pickfords, by then a subsidiary of Hay's Wharf, and taking 50 per cent of Wordie and holdings in other firms. Nevertheless, the total assets accumulated by the railway companies amounted to no more than a modest proportion of the whole.

In such circumstances the differences in attitude within the road-transport industry showed up quickly. The hauliers were, for one thing, less amenable to control. In May 1938 the chief executive of a large haulage company spoke on the BBC about the 'Troubles of the Road Carrier'. While, unsurprisingly, he welcomed the disappearance of 'weaker operators', he claimed that the railways' rights to regulate the grant of road licences meant that 'the road operator is fighting with hands tied behind him'. What he did not tell his audience was that — even without hands — road-haulage firms had, since 1930, doubled the amount of tonnage they carried. What is more, it was to turn out that in the bumper year of 1939 growth would increase by no less than 35 per cent.

The story should, briefly, be carried forward. Consolidation and regulation established order in place of chaos. So far, so good. But the sense of partnership proved far from seamless. The cherished view that, with the right background, road and rail would naturally complement each other, was proved too optimistic. Certainly there were advantages to cooperation: Pickfords, for instance, obtained more favourable rates at railway depositories and advertising space at stations. On the other hand, when it came down to it, how far were railway representatives on boards and committees likely to support strategies, beneficial as they might be for road profits, which took business away from the railways? It was more often a case of once a rail-man, always a rail-man. And the same with road-men. Mutual intolerance, amounting on occasion to mutual antipathy, was commonplace. What is more, for all the fine talk, eliminating 'wasteful competition' must in practice on occasion have discouraged constructive competition. Existing operators were favoured over new ones, under a policy which got the nickname of 'grandfather's rights'.

Rationalization in the 1930s was followed in the 1940s by nationalization — tighter control yet. The virtues of such control were to be debated for most of the rest of the twentieth century, the pros and cons argued out, a staple of politics. What is clear, though, is that the system failed to protect public transport, and in particular failed to achieve that longed-for balance between road and rail.

8
Coming to Terms

FATHER OF ELIGIBLE DAUGHTER TO MEDICAL STUDENT: *'Well, sir, and what are your prospects?'*
SUITOR: *'I thought I had already mentioned that my practice is at the cross roads just outside Brighton.'*

> The Best Motoring Stories *(1931)*

The difference between the Britain of Friese-Greene's *The Open Road* of 1924—6 and Cavalcanti's *Roadways*, a film documentary produced hardly more than ten years later, is startling. In 1937 the countryside is buzzing with automobiles; to drive now on the wrong side of the road would be suicidal. Anyway, the narrator (for of course there is a sound track) makes it seem as if the least infringement of the Highway Code would be dealt with severely. In headmasterly tones he reassures us that the old, happy-go-lucky, free-for-all has been sorted out, and that now it is up to us as we venture on the fine new roads of Britain.

Yet, in spite of the patronizing, *Roadways*, twenty minutes long, is a model of conciseness in its description of the revolution in road transport. It is lively too. We listen to the conversation of lorry drivers as they drink tea in a roadside café and prepare to pass the night in a dormitory. The camera takes in the factories, a petrol station, a roadhouse, as they flash by. There are campers with a roadside tent, youths resting by the road with their motor cycles, an AA man saluting. There are jokes: a woman in a Baby Austin brakes too sharply as she tries to start off from traffic lights; a trainee lorry driver has a problem changing gear; an ancient car is overtaken by bicyclists. There is more light relief as a red flag man is shown out in front of a horseless carriage; they have all gone now, observes the narrator, 'some say they were all run over!'

There is a very marked difference in how cars look, 1920s to 1930s. In the days of *The Open Road* the great majority were open, or partly open. The 'three-quarter landaulet town carriage', for instance, provided a rigid hood over the chauffeur but an open top (with canvas hood stowed away) in the back for the passengers. With a 'limousine landaulet' you were more closed and less open, while the plain 'limousine' left the chauffeur in the open with the passengers covered. With the 'Pullman-limousine' the whole car was closed. Old hands deplored the move in the mid-1920s to closed cars. The veteran motoring journalist and author Leonard Henslowe sniffily described them as a 'drawing room on wheels'. Such cars might be 'in the ascendant' but so, he added, are 'artificial foods and artificial sunlight'. By 1930, though, Henslowe had accepted the inevitable; he considered the ideal to be the saloon with a sun-roof — so long as the roof was always kept open except at times of rain or fog or snow.

Whatever one's views about open and closed bodies, there was no doubt that the newer cars were an improvement. Certainly the models exhibited at the 1925 Motor Show at Olympia made previous cars look old-fashioned. And it was more than just a question of looks, for technically the new cars were better. They were more comfortable and equipped with a wider array of accessories. Henslowe could say in 1926 that 'this year's cars are more complete, cheaper and better than those of any year since the inception of motoring'. In *Buying a Car? The Car Buyers Annual* for 1930 he recalled other improvements that had come about since he first started to write on motoring before the war. Road surfaces were much improved and punctures were rare. What, he wonders, would a motorist have thought of an automatic screen-wiper even fifteen years before? With the magneto superseded, ignition now was simpler. What is more, it had become possible to look forward to 'perfect springing, perfect steering, finger-tip gear changing and four wheel drive'. Four-speed gearboxes, already used extensively in sports cars, were to be found in saloon cars, although that would not, thought Henslowe, suit those drivers who expected to go everywhere in top gear.

In 1930, despite warning signs of the approaching Depression, cars were still selling well. In the luxury market, Rolls-Royce had absorbed Bentley, and Daimler belonged to BSA. A newcomer, the SS Jaguar, was about to make its name with excellent performance at much less than top price. There was a choice of sports cars, with Alvis and Rover, Lagonda and Jensen. Among expensive cars, a cruising speed of 90mph was not unusual. As for prices, a Daimler in 1930 was selling at £2,400 (£90,000 today), a Bentley at £1,575 (£60,000). A large Renault was even more expensive, but that was as a result of import duty. Owners of cars like these continued to patronize their own body builders and some affected still a truly Edwardian magnificence. The Duke of Bedford, for instance, up until the Second World War maintained two large and fully staffed houses in Belgrave Square, where he kept four cars and eight chauffeurs. Since he himself rarely left the country, their purpose was mainly to ferry guests invited to the Duke's country palace at Woburn in Bedfordshire. For the first part of the journey only. These town cars went no further than Hendon, on the London outskirts, where guests were transferred to cars sent up to meet them. Since suitcases travelled separately, what with chauffeurs and footmen, eight people might be involved in carrying one person from London to Woburn.

The Duke was averse to change, holding naturally to pre-war formalities. Others took a plainly nostalgic, even reverential view of old motors. Enthusiasts kept them in working order. Old cars were allocated categories: those manufactured before 1905 were 'veterans', those before 1931 'vintage'. Once more the veterans took the Brighton Road in annual revivals of the 1896 run. L. T. C. Rolt described preparations for the 1932 run in words close to those used by Charles Jarrott, writing of the occasion thirty-eight years before:

> In my recollection of that November morning, the garage was half-dark and filled with choking exhaust fumes. In this smudge-filled gloom there was feverish activity as heavily muffled figures busied themselves about their strange vehicles which emitted desperate panting, tuffing and wheezing noises.

Yet it would be misleading to give the impression of effortless change. In the background was a highly competitive market that was instrumental in bringing about the failure — whether in terms of actual bankruptcy or forced withdrawal — of manufacturer after manufacturer. Partly it was the effect of the war; it took time for established firms to reconvert to peacetime work. Demand outstripped supply; almost anything could be sold. According to a writer in *The Economist*, new firms appeared, acquired empty premises, issued prospectuses with photographs of cars and generous predictions of profits, but lacked any experience at all of making cars. Forty new makes of car were introduced between 1919 and 1920, and then another forty-six between 1920 and 1925. One was the Speedy Car, which enjoyed a very short life. In their advertisements its proprietors proclaimed a registered address on the Holborn Viaduct, a centre of the car trade, and works in London at White City, Peckham and Putney. The car was priced at 110 guineas [£115.50] and a ten-guinea deposit was to be sent with the order. It looked cheap, but it was not. The advertisement excited the suspicion of the editorial staff of the *Motor*, who investigated, to find that the only factory actually in existence was little more than a shack and contained a mere two cars in the process of assembly. You would have got neither of them with your deposit.

The bubble burst, and while some specialists survived, for many firms the aftermath of the boom was savage. They had no way of competing with the economies of mass production now adopted by companies such as Morris. In 1930 two-thirds of British cars were produced by Morris and Austin. By 1938 their share had fallen somewhat, but even so Morris, Austin and a revived Ford accounted for just over 60 per cent of production, with Vauxhall (part of General Motors), Standard and Rootes holding around 10 per cent each. Motor manufacture throughout the world was concentrated; in the United States 90 per cent of cars were produced by General Motors, Ford and Chrysler, while in France (where by 1932 only twenty-three car factories survived from something like 350 a few years earlier) Citroën, Renault and Peugeot took a 75 per cent share. In Italy in the 1930s, Fiat typically produced between 80 and 90 per cent of the national output.

Once-famous names disappeared. Crossley, of Gorton near Manchester, was one of the very best, the first firm in Britain to manufacture the internal-combustion engine. Crossleys sold excellent and expensive cars, and their customers included the King and the Prince of Wales. During the First World War they produced thousands of vehicles for use as lorries, staff cars, tenders and ambulances. The slump was their undoing; to adjust to an altered market, they switched to smaller cars, which failed to catch on. Crossleys dropped car manufacture in 1937, though they continued to make commercial vehicles. Another manufacturer that attempted the same strategy by going downmarket and failed was Invicta, makers of Invicta and Railton, very powerful but complex cars highly thought of for racing. The Scottish Argyll Motors company had counted in 1906 as one of the biggest automobile manufacturers in the world, with a production of seventy vehicles a week. They were too ambitious, over-extending themselves with a giant factory, and collapsing before the First World War. (They were not quite down and out, and produced some cars after the war.) Clyno of Wolverhampton enjoyed a meteoric career in the 1920s, during which it pressed hard on Morris and Austin. Its problem was to compete on both price and quality; finding itself unable to do so, it chose the first and sacrificed the second — a policy that failed. The firm went out of business in 1929 after a life of seven years.

The casualty list carries on. The Sheffield Simplex was another excellent make; it dated back to 1904 and came to an end in 1927. There was the Trojan, a car that has been compared to the Model T and the Volkswagen but never attained their sort of sales. A more familiar name is Talbot, originally Clément-Talbot, first assembled and then manufactured at a factory in Barlby Road, North Kensington, from the early 1900s. It took its name from the Talbot family, earls of Shrewsbury, with the twentieth earl the principal investor. (Lord Shrewbury is interesting; in the 1880s he was a cab proprietor, the first to replace iron-hooped wheels with solid rubber tyres.) Talbot was sold to Rootes in 1935.

Yet for all the difficulties along the way, the small car represented the future. There was a large market waiting to be tapped, one that was only partly satisfied by the ageing Model T and its successor. It was possible of course to buy second-hand, like Terence Horsley, who in 1932 published *Round England in an Eight Pound Car* (say £300 today). He was, he said, a 'tramp-motorist'. Still, as he pointed out, his car cost less than a new overcoat. But the disadvantages were formidable and, after all, had second-hand cars possessed a better reputation, his book would never have found a publisher. So he set off along with a companion, Bill, aged ten. The sound of the engine carried him back, Horsley said, to his childhood, to memories of narrow roads between green hedges coated with soft grey dust, to 'begoggled eyes' and 'resigned postures in hedge bottoms while a perspiring chauffeur toiled at wired-on rims'. Nostalgic it may have been, but the engine, as they started off, emitted a 'sequence of explosions'. In second, the gearbox gave a kind of hysterical shriek. The car in favourable conditions could make 34mph, but against 'half a gale' and rain 20mph was maximum, with the canvas hood blown vertically upwards. There were punctures, which Horsley unwisely had not reckoned on, and were the car to be left unused for more than a day or two, starting became a difficult business. One reason for traffic jams, claimed another writer, was the number of decrepit, sometimes twenty-year-old cars jogging home from the seaside.

Or you could buy a motor cycle — a lot of people did. In 1910 there were 36,000 motor cycles on the road in Britain as against 53,000 private cars; in 1914 it was 124,000 to 132,000 cars. During the war, in terms of numbers, motor cycles outsold cars, and they continued to do so until 1925. In terms of speed and general performance, the average British motor cycle could hold its own, sometimes more than hold its own, with the average car. What is more, it took up much less space to garage. The chairman of Raleigh in 1926 added his voice to those who championed motors as valuable in combating class hostility. He wrote in the *Daily Mail*, 'Give a man a motor cycle to ride and to tend and mend in his spare time and you take from him one of the chief causes of disgruntlement.' And a year or two earlier a visiting American automobile engineer had observed that the class of people who in the United States possessed Fords in Britain had motor cycles. However, even with sidecar, they were uncomfortable, and anyone riding pillion was apt to feel disagreeably isolated. And of course there was the snobbery tied to motoring, the pervasive resolve to upstage the Joneses. The motor cycle rated low on the social scale: as one early and enthusiastic motor cyclist said, having toured all over Europe on his machine, 'you may be a freak riding it, but no one mistakes you for a millionaire'. Moreover, from 1930, with third-party insurance compulsory, running costs were higher. By then the motor-cycle industry was firmly in decline.

There was another alternative, for a time anyway — a hybrid, the cyclecar, a machine which cost less than a motor cycle but more than

the cheapest four-wheel motor car. The cyclecar, a French invention, arrived on the market shortly before the First World War, and
sold in Britain at a typical price of around £70, a good deal less than
the Model T's £135. It was defined as a small motor car of narrow
wheel gauge and light construction, probably a three-wheeler, quite
likely to be air-cooled, and sometimes with the passenger sitting in
tandem behind the driver. In Britain, the best known was probably
the Morgan, which was built originally in the workshops of Malvern
College. Another was the GN, the most successful, made in the
stables of the Frazer-Nash family at Hendon. Then there was the
more expensive and better-constructed Humberette, which sold at a
basic £120. Soon there were sixty makes on the market, and the
Cyclecar Magazine in 1912 could claim a sales figure of 100,000. The
shortage of cars immediately after the First World War produced
another boom; it was, though, brief. *Car and Golf* could find nothing
pleasant to say of cyclecar makers: they had 'sprung up like mushrooms and launched their miserable, ill-designed vehicles on an all-
too-ready market'. Another description portrayed the cyclecar as
combining the comfort of a cement mixer, the noise of a pneumatic
drill and the directional ability of a chicken with its head cut off.
Cyclecars faded away in Britain, although they continued to be sold
into the 1930s in Germany, where the effects of the war and inflation
limited demand for more orthodox vehicles.

How rich did you have to be to run a car? In 1926 the Society of
Motor Manufacturers and Traders estimated that to run two cars an
income of over £2,000 (say £75,000 today) was required, while for a
single car £450 was the minimum. C. T. Brunner, writing in 1928 —
when there were 885,000 private cars on the road — put the minimum income at a higher figure, and made some calculations: if costs
fell to the extent that the minimum income necessary went down
from £700 to £600, the potential market would increase by 88,000; a
further reduction to £500 would mean another 128,000 possible
buyers; a drop to £400 brought in another 214,000. In 1934 *The Economist*, on the basis of Inland Revenue returns and the rise in
incomes, considered that the minimum figure was now below £400
and, indeed, was rapidly approaching £300. What is particularly significant is that a small increase in income could produce a dispro-
portionately high increase in the amount spent on travel. The
economist Colin Clark calculated that an overall increase of a third

in the average wage would mean that while people would increase expenditure on food by 10 per cent and on clothing by 25 per cent, the amount they would spend on travel would rise by no less than 50 per cent.

William Morris was eloquent on the effect of price reductions:

> Is it sufficiently realised in this country that every time you make a reduction, you drop down on what I may call the pyramid of consumption power to a wider base? Even a ten pound reduction drops you into an entirely new market. If a man cannot pay the last £10 ... he cannot buy the car. The one object in life of many makers seems to be to make the thing the public *cannot* buy. The one object in my life has been to make the thing they *can* buy.

Morris was as good as his word. The price of his two-seater Morris Cowley, originally £465, was steadily reduced, dropping to £375 in early 1921, then to 285 guineas (£299.25) in the autumn. At the 1922 Motor Show it was going for £225. Morris was amply rewarded for his policy. Taking only the first few years into account, his share of car output jumped from 5 per cent in 1920 to 28 per cent in 1923.

In 1919 the number of cars licensed in Britain was 110,000; in 1938 it was almost 2 million. Manufacturers were steadily reducing prices (as well as improving the cars technically), able to do so through increased productivity, much of it due to economies of scale. In the period from 1924 to 1935 output per man-year doubled. The index of car prices, adjusted to the cost of living (which was going down) taken at 100 in 1924 stood at 75.4 in 1930 and at 54.3 in 1938. At the same time potential buyers were getting richer as wages rose. In 1899 the net income per head in Great Britain, taken at 1900 money values, amounted to £44.10; in 1925 it was £45.90 and in 1938 £57.40. Cars came down in price and the money available to buy them went up.

There were other factors at work as well to explain the extraordinary growth in motoring, particularly in respect of coach travel. Wage earners had more time for leisure as the working week was steadily reduced, coming down from an average fifty-four hours before the war to forty-eight hours. In the 1930s paid holidays were more common, making it practicable for people to travel further afield. Then there was the wider availability of hire purchase for cars. The beginnings, after the First World War, were inauspicious.

The immediate burst of car buying attracted at least thirty finance houses into the market. Discount houses and insurers became involved, and Lloyd's underwriters were hit hard by fraudulent claims. Nevertheless, hire purchase, following the American pattern, became increasingly popular, and it has been estimated that by the end of the 1920s 50—60 per cent of new cars and a large proportion of motor cycles were bought by instalments. However, as Sean O'Connell has pointed out, motor manufacturers' advertisements and trade-press comment were very restrained on the subject, and hire purchase, except in terms of house mortgages, for many people remained suspect and unbecoming. It is notable that the United Dominions Trust, the largest company in the market and very respectable, emphasized that its interest was above all in motor vehicles used on business, delivery vans and doctors' cars, for example.

Nevertheless, it is to the point that in 1930, when Montagu Norman as Governor of the Bank of England was anxious to stimulate the shaky economy, one method he used — and one much at odds with the Bank's customary policy — was support for the United Dominions Trust. The Bank actually doubled the UDT's paid-up capital by buying its ordinary shares. Apart from anything else, its action was further evidence of the importance of the motor industry. Whereas in 1922 in Britain only one person in every seventy-eight was a car owner, in 1938 it was one in every fifteen. Automobiles had penetrated right through society, with cars for the middle class, buses and motor cycles for the working class. And there was the ineluctable increase in the quantity of goods carried by road. In 1939 it has been estimated that 7 per cent of the total labour force were employed in the manufacture and servicing of automobiles. In addition, there were professional drivers and those employed in the construction and maintenance of roads, and also those who manufactured components. Indeed, components bought in from outside accounted for almost 60 per cent of the production cost of a car. Dunlop, a most important supplier, their plant at Birmingham occupying 300 acres, ranked in 1935 as the seventeenth-largest employer of labour in the country, with Lucas, which supplied electrical components, coming in at twenty-six, ahead of Austin, the largest employer among motor manufacturers, ranked at twenty-eight. (Morris, though the largest in production terms, was still to an extent an assembler and employed many fewer workers.)

In fact, Austin too might buy in many of his components. For the original Austin Seven, the radiator was provided by Serck, the carburettor by Zenith, the magneto by Watford, the springs by Richard Berry and aluminium parts by Stirling Metals. Another major supplier was Smiths, who claimed to make 85 per cent of the clocks fitted in British cars. Triplex, manufacturers of safety glass, were entrenched in the motor industry. They deserved to be, if only for their sales pitch. When, in 1927, Henry Ford was involved in a car accident a lively spirit in their sales department sent him a telegram at his hospital in Detroit. It expressed regret at his misfortune and went on to say, 'Trust you have not been cut by broken glass. Fit Triplex and be safe.' They got the business, and set up a factory in New Jersey to supply Ford. (Henry Ford must have been used to cheeky messages. One letter he received was from the notorious bank robber John Dillinger, who had just stolen a Ford car. It was wonderful, wrote Dillinger, suggesting that the company's slogan should be: 'Drive a Ford and watch the other cars fall behind you.' He got a letter too from Clyde Barrow — of Bonnie and Clyde — complimenting him on the Ford V8.)

Many of these suppliers had been in business for years, with Dunlop's involvement dating back to the days of Harry Lawson. In addition to selling their tyres, they had on offer for early motorists sixty different designs of dust coat. Another enterprising firm in those days supplied 'motoring chocolate' with which to while away the time during roadside repairs. Lucas was originally a Birmingham manufacturer of metal goods such as shovels and oil cans, and had produced the 'King of the Road', a strong-selling bicycle lamp. Fisher Ludlow, makers of steel motor bodies, was descended from a firm making spouts for kettles which had made a good deal of money in the Boer War and the First World War supplying mess tins for the troops. A newcomer on the scene, a new firm altogether, was the Pressed Steel Company, which was set up in the mid-1920s alongside the Morris works at Cowley. It manufactured steel panels for Morris cars and William Morris personally was for some years a large shareholder.

By the end of the 1920s motoring was a dominant force in the economy, and directly and indirectly a very large employer. Politically, its influence was growing virtually by the minute, as more and more people became purchasers of cars and motor cyles. However, while the government intervened with legislation in the case of commercial transport, it had no clear ideas about private motoring. Some changes to the law were undoubtedly necessary, for as it stood it was based on the 1903 act, which had been drafted in completely different circumstances and which laid down a speed limit of 20mph, now so ludicrously out of date that the police were under instructions not to enforce it.

The government's detachment was inherited. Back in the 1890s it was the motorists themselves who had taken the initiative. Politicians and civil servants, being most of them quite uninformed about the new invention, were obliged to rely on the experts, even if few of them were in a position to do more than guess at the likely social and economic consequences of motoring. After all, Lord Winchilsea, chairman at the celebration dinner that followed the 1896 Brighton Run, had wondered publicly whether motoring would amount to anything. At any rate, the government and Whitehall had leaned heavily for advice first on Sir David Salomons and his Self-Propelled Traffic Association and then on the Automobile Club. To quote William Plowden, 'against the background of an industry which had grown up haphazardly from backyard workshops and bicycle repair firms, the Club long remained by far the most important force for defining and imposing standards'. So influential was it that at one and the same time the Automobile Club represented motor manufacturers in negotiations and advised its members on the merits of the cars these manufacturers produced.

One thing the government did especially care about was the state of the roads and the blinding clouds of dust kicked up by automobiles that travelled along them. Again a solution was largely left to the club, which in 1905 commissioned Rookes Crompton to discover what should be done. Was it a matter of making the roads fit for cars or the cars fit for roads? Crompton was keen; the advent of the automobile and internal combustion rekindled an old passion. To say he was familiar with the dust problem would be an understatement: he knew about it from his time in India, and from more recent times as well, since he had taken energetically to bicycling since his return from the war in South Africa. So energetically that, though he was in his fifties, he could bicycle 200 miles a day without getting tired. However, as Crompton was to recall in his memoirs, you needed no more than a few miles on the road to sample the dust in full measure. When he and his companions met at a pub for lunch

or tea, they could hardly recognize each other under the mask of dust which coated faces, clothes and hands.

Crompton's experiments were based on an elaborate system whereby cars were photographed as they were driven over prepared dusty surfaces at the Crystal Palace and, later, over selected roads. In the end, though, it was clear that it was not the cars but the roads themselves which would have to be altered, would, in fact, have to be reconstituted. That the great highways of the coaching era were neglected and sometimes encroached upon by landowners along their route did not make things easier. But even had they been in pristine state they would not have sufficed. Essentially they were pathways of stone held together with mortar, rubble and whatever miscellaneous material was to hand, and mixed with clay. The illustrious road engineer John McAdam had calculated that the heaviest load they would be forced to bear would be four to five tons carried on four wheels. To start with, it was the heavy traction engines with iron-shod wheels and the loaded wagons they hauled which caused the damage. In those days cars were light, relatively slow-moving and in some ways similar in design to the carriages on which they were based. However, when cars got faster and were fitted with pneumatic tyres, the effect was drastic. The suction action of the tyres drew out the binding medium in the roads, which then disintegrated. In the mean time, they produced quantities of dust. In 1909 Blackpool, with characteristic enterprise, organized an 'Aviation Week' and in preparation for it the entire road from Preston was put in what seemed to be good order. Yet by the following February it had become almost impassable.

Eventually the problem was to be solved by tar spraying, bituminous macadam and quick-drying concrete. But there was another difficulty which directly concerned the government and was to lead to increasing central control over local authority expenditure. Not only minor roads, but main highways as well were maintained and largely paid for by local authorities. Some of these authorities were efficient, others were not, and much depended on the powers allowed to the county surveyor. But a principal highway might involve a multitude of authorities. For instance, the Great North Road, usually considered the most important of them all, fell under the jurisdiction of no fewer than seventy-two authorities, of which forty-six were actually engaged in its maintenance. The plan to construct Western Avenue, a main road leading out of London, was complicated by the existence of twenty-three different local authorities along the projected route.

In 1910 the government was forced to take a firmer step towards active intervention. Impelled by public fury at the state of the roads, it established the Road Board, with Crompton as consulting engineer and W. Rees Jeffreys (responsible for founding the Commercial Motor Users' Association) as secretary. This board was empowered to help local authorities with money and advice, and did much to advance the development of satisfactory road surfaces. However, its position was ambiguous, for it reported to no one in particular, was not incorporated within the Civil Service but spent public money. It was what later came to be termed a 'quango'. The war in any event put a stop to its work, and afterwards it was abolished, with its functions absorbed by the newly formed Ministry of Transport under Sir Eric Geddes. The roads by then were in a worse state than ever, but all went well and money was poured out. In 1925 the *Spectator* could pronounce, 'The improvements which have been effected in British roads during the last few years are very great indeed ... ' Sir Alan Burgoyne could tell the Royal Society of Arts that British roads were the finest in the world. Satisfaction was the order of the day.

The reservoir which held and dispensed all this money was the Road Fund. Once more, the politicians had shied away from direct control. An arrangement had been made with Lloyd George in 1910, when he was Chancellor of the Exchequer, that money raised from vehicle licence fees and petrol tax should go into a special account, the Road Fund, and be spent exclusively on roads. So, the more cars the merrier, the more money to go on roads.

Everything was wonderful until Winston Churchill became Chancellor in 1924. He was determined to end the anomaly whereby one form of tax was compartmentalized, earmarked for a particular purpose. The argument that he was bound by what one chancellor had agreed — an agreement incidentally confirmed by Austen Chamberlain when he was chancellor — Churchill asserted to be untenable; he was determined to bring motor taxation into the main stream of revenue. Of a hostile Tory MP who objected to a raid on the Road Fund, he demanded, 'Would you ... propose to build joy roads to Brighton or Ascot at a time when you could not afford to build cruisers?' 'Joy roads' had a good ring from Churchill's point of view. He also referred to the new arterial roads as 'these great new race tracks', and to motoring as 'luxurious locomotion'. He worked up the old Edwardian theme that motoring was solely for pleasure, and rich man's pleasure at that. Having assured local authorities that they would not suffer, Churchill carried out his first raid — the word used by his opponents — on the Road Fund in 1926. The following year, ignoring a petition organized by the Automobile Association and signed by more than 350,000 people, he took £12 million, all that there was in the fund's accounts. Road improvement and road building were seriously set back.

To Whitehall the raids were the more attractive in that, by checking 'excessive' expenditure on roads, they brought some relief to the hard-pressed railways. But the fate of the Road Fund cast a long shadow. 'People remember what happened to road tax,' said a university vice-chancellor suspicious about the introduction of a graduate tax, who was quoted in the *Financial Times* on the 23—4 November 2002; 'if the money goes to the Treasury in a tax then politicians will end up spending it on something else'.

The approach to the general election of 1929 brought the relationship between government and automobilism into clearer relief. First, there was a reaction to a new proposal by Churchill, whereby a petrol tax — the original petrol tax had been abolished in 1920 — should be levied on top of the existing vehicle tax. There was, as could be anticipated, strong opposition from the public, but it was also expressed by three members of the Cabinet. Two of them, Joynson-Hicks (a past president of the AA) and Steel-Maitland withdrew their objections under pressure, but the Colonial Secretary, Leopold Amery, circulated a memorandum to his colleagues insisting on the immense importance of the motor industry, which, he said, 'is destined to be by far the most skilled industry in the world in our generation, as well as the predominant factor in defence'. Secondly, the place of the automobile in the economy figured as a central issue in the general election. The Liberals under Lloyd George fought on an expansionist platform, rejecting the orthodox arguments in favour of retrenchment and restraint. Their case had been set out in detail in what was known as the 'yellow book', *The Liberal Policy for Industry*:

> In the forefront of any development programme should be set the improvement of our road system. The growing importance of the road in commerce and industry today is even yet not perfectly appreciated. Yet it is certain, and it is obvious. The United States Board of Agriculture puts the matter in a nutshell when it says: 'We lose more by not improving roads than it costs to improve them; so that we may say we pay for improved roads whether we have them or not, and we pay less if we have them than if we have not.' ... Mr Churchill's policy in raiding the Road Fund was a heavy and quite wanton blow at British trade.

The case was not tested, the Liberals were badly defeated in the election. But the point here is not whether the expansionists of 1929 were right or wrong; rather it is that the automobile industry and the roads industry that went with it were now publicly treated as powerful economic activators. At the time people would be likely to look to the United States for evidence as to how far that was true, for there automobile production was regarded as one of the best indicators of business prosperity. However, it was not in America, but in Germany, where the automobile as galvanizer of the economy was to be seen at its most dramatic.

The effect of the Depression on Germany was dire. In the winter of 1932—3 two out of every four Germans employed in 1929 were out of work. Hitler, coming to power in January 1933, had no choice but to inflate the economy somehow: the level of unemployment had been a key plank of the Nazi attack on the Weimar government, and without economic recovery it was doubtful whether the party could survive. At all costs work must be provided. Various measures were taken to stimulate demand and jobs — a 'marriage loan' for one, and, in 1935, conscription, which of course served two purposes. But to launch recovery, the government relied above all on public investment in civil engineering, at the forefront of which was a sweeping roads programme. In the first years, rearmament as an energizer of recovery was secondary. The huge sums spent on roads went first on the renewal of those in existence and then on new motorways. The motor industry itself, in a wretched state in 1933, was stimulated by tax concessions to buyers. By 1935 it had become Germany's largest manufacturing employer, and by 1938 was the largest contributor to the country's manufacturing exports. What was just as important, possibly more important, was the sequential effect of the investment in road transport, the revival of other industries, motor component manufacturers and machine tools, and the heavy industries of iron and steel, cement and mining. The economy took off, and business confidence returned.

To replicate the German 'economic miracle' in Britain, where the pressure anyway was much less, would have been out of the question, for its success depended on stringent rules to protect foreign exchange and controls on wages and the right to strike. Nevertheless, expenditure on roads was regarded by the British government as important in reducing unemployment. Indeed it was for that reason that many of the new roads were built in areas such as the north of England, where unemployment was most severe (and, from a strictly transport point of view, almost by definition, the less necessary). Controls, though, were not wholly absent, for there was a $33^1/_3$ per cent duty on car imports.

On that feature of the German programme, *Autobahnen*, the motorways, which attracted worldwide attention, Britain was ambivalent. The Italians built them, and the Americans, who had got in first with William K. Vanderbilt's Long Island Parkway, constructed between 1906 and 1911. The RAC, for one, in those days opposed special roads for motors, fearing that as a consequence they might be banned on ordinary roads. In his *Anticipations ...* of 1902 H. G. Wells speculated that special roads for automobiles might well be built in Britain during 'the present decade', though he added no doubt they would come about first in the United States and Germany. In Britain, a plan was mooted in Parliament — within Wells's decade — for a fast motor highway between London and Brighton, but was dropped early in 1906. In 1923 a company was formed with Lord Montagu as chairman to build a motorway linking London, Birmingham, Manchester and Liverpool. In the following year it went to Parliament for authorization in the form of a private member's bill enjoying all-party support, with a clause providing for the compulsory acquisition of land. However, the government and the Ministry of Transport were opposed: it bypassed the minister and, so it was argued, marked a return to the old turnpike system, remembered with displeasure not least because it had been so costly to wind up. Other opponents included the Manchester and District Joint Planning Committee, which submitted that the 'construction of a Motorway is in effect equivalent to the construction of a railway'. The railway companies were against it for obvious reasons. So the bill was quashed. A few years later there were hopes of a Channel Tunnel and a 'marine motor road' running along the south coast of England.

But there were still no motorways in Britain in 1939. Far from it, in fact, for the Great North Road, 276 miles long from London to Newcastle, was without a single mile of dual carriageway. Nevertheless, the idea, beset by scepticism, stayed alive. The trouble was the expense and the prospect of tolls. The Royal Commission on Transport (which was so rude about the railways) rejected a proposal from Rees Jeffreys that the depleted Road Fund should pay, but it also strongly opposed the construction of toll roads, again most probably influenced by memories of the turnpikes. Even the *Motor* (19 February 1929), referring to the south coast project, was uncertain. It too disliked toll roads. The official view was that existing highways could be widened and verges incorporated in the roadway. To quote C. D. Buchanan in his book *Mixed Blessing*:

> We always seem to have been a lap behind the motor car: by the time we had thought of 30-foot carriageways, it was dual that were really needed, by the time we had though of duals it was motor roads that were wanted, by the time we had thought of roundabouts it was flyovers that were needed.

A lack of initiative, an indecision, was only too apparent. By the end of 1929, though, there were signs of a more effective approach. The Road Traffic Act of 1930, besides reforming public passenger transport, abolished the speed limit for cars and motor cycles and, among other measures, made third-party insurance compulsory. It signified too that the state was coming to terms at last with motoring.

The number and diversity of organizations concerned with motoring and its effects by this time are astonishing. A meeting with civil servants might involve representatives of the RAC (and its affiliate the Royal Scottish Automobile Club), the AA, the Commercial Vehicle Users' Association, the Society of Motor Manufacturers and Traders, the British Road Federation, the Long Distance Road Haulage Association. And others too. In 1929 Viscount Cecil of Chelwood got so fed up at the slow progress towards what became the Road Traffic Act that he introduced his own very radical private member's bill to give matters a push. (His plan worked.) During a debate in the House of Lords, Cecil deplored the corporatism, the formal associations and their influence. He contended that the delays in tackling the problems brought about by the automobile, for which they were partly responsible, were unacceptable to public opinion and especially to the poorer classes, who had no means for such formal representation.

> Nowadays, if you want to get anything done, you can only do it by combining and making some kind of society, or league, or association, in order to press it in some way or other upon the people. The motor trade has an immense number of these associations. I was amazed at the number of them who came before the Committee [which considered his bill]. Motor manufacturers, automobile clubs, automobile associations one after another came in a kind of procession, all saying much the same thing; all saying: 'Whatever you do don't touch the motor trade.'

While they might be unanimous about independence, the various organizations could disagree sharply among themselves. Private car interests and those representing heavier goods vehicles were often at odds. The AA was strident in its demands that motor taxation should be based on a petrol tax rather than the existing vehicle duty, while the commercial bodies preferred the system as it stood. Then there was the natural rivalry — and competition for members — between the AA and the RAC. The AA continued to be more belligerent. The difference of approach was highlighted when the chairman of the RAC broke ranks over the sanctity of the Road Fund,

conceding that the original pledge could not be regarded as binding for ever. The dissension — if not in this case — often made it the more difficult for the government to introduce reforms.

An early road sign, one of many paid for by the motoring associations.

The prominence of the RAC and the AA, the latter of them by now much the larger and the more energetic, reflected their lobbying power and also the services they provided for their members. Scouts were still employed to sniff out police traps — dangerous driving of course remained an enforceable offence — but, backed by workshop vans, they supplied valuable support in the case of breakdown. The two organizations put up road signs, helpful to motorists in general as well as to their own members; they drew up travel itineraries and helped with the red tape incidental to journeys abroad. Their

Filling up with petrol at the first roadside filling station, set up by the Automobile Association at Aldermaston in Berkshire in 1919. As soon as others followed suit, the AA withdrew.

engineers continued to test cars, a very useful service for those buying second-hand, and advised on accessories.

The breadth of service was impressive. Nothing could better illustrate that and the imagination behind it than the establishment by the AA of the first roadside filling station in 1919. Up until then, while some petrol pumps existed at garages off the main road, motorists generally relied on petrol cans they carried about in their cars. The AA followed up this first filling station — at Aldermaston in Berkshire — with seven others sited about the country. They were careful, though; they had no intention of going into business, and while the pumps were manned by their employees, supplies were obtained from local agents and sold at the standard retail price. Once the oil companies and others provided their own roadside filling stations, the AA withdrew.

There were also non-motoring consumer organizations with axes to grind. Lord Cecil may have been astonished at the number of bodies which appeared before the committee considering his private bill, but he had already drawn the lesson. He had himself founded the Pedestrian Association for Road Safety. Environmentalists, of varying types, realized what they had to do. Unify, speak with one voice, speak coherently and realistically if they wanted effectively to resist the malign influence of motoring on the countryside. The Pedestrian Association was small fry compared to the National Trust and the Council for the Preservation of Rural England and its constituent parts in Scotland and Wales. The National Trust, which had especially good links with the government, dated back to 1895 and although its main function was that of landholder, it was also a national champion of the preservationist cause. The CPRE was something of an umbrella group, founded in 1926 to coordinate preservationist activity. It comprised twenty-two constituent organizations which included the National Trust, the Royal Institution of British Architects ... and the Royal Automobile Club. A key figure was Patrick Abercrombie, the author of *The Preservation of Rural England*.

Preservationist policy evolved. In Victorian times, with notable exceptions such as the campaign to protect common land, the effort had been directed first towards persuasion and the purchase of endangered buildings and, if that failed, to what could be accomplished in the courts. Now more attention was given to political lobbying. Moreover, as the automobile extended its ravages far and wide, preservationists were often obliged to think in broader terms, to consider an environment as well as a place. The broader too as the passion during the inter-war years for hiking, for tough walking over moors or hills, enlarged the definition of scenic beauty. In the early 1930s the preservationist forces were strengthened by the formation of the Youth Hostels Association and the Ramblers' Association. There was the added advantage that rambling was popular with younger Labour Members of Parliament.

The preservationist books discussed in Chapter 6 tended towards invective but a chapter by Geoffrey Boumphrey in Clough Williams-Ellis's *Britain & the Beast* minced no words in warning against too emotional an approach. To quote: 'In our reaction from the evil of the town, we turned to the country and became romantic and sentimental about it. To-day we are so maudlin that we are in danger of forgetting it has any utilitarian purpose at all.' Appeals for something to be done, so Boumphrey argues, had been addressed too exclusively to an educated and cultured minority. It was essential to convert and 'fire the energies of the new class into whose hands the stewardship of the countryside is passing. It's no use going on talking about the past.'

It was well said, since the organizations with the most immediate powers over planning were the local councils, whose members might be educated but were certainly not universally cultured. And the same was true of the ratepayers who had to pay up when it was a question of compensation, and of the general public who elected the councillors. There was a track record of sorts where local authorities had attempted to preserve areas of especial beauty. On the south coast, the Eastbourne Town Council bought Beachy Head to save it from the shanties and bungalows, a sensible move from both an aesthetic and a commercial point of view. But not every municipality could afford to buy endangered countryside. Even Brighton, rich as it was, ran into trouble with 10,000 acres of the South Downs which it bought in 1934. The council's hope of obtaining a contribution to the cost from central government and from other, neighbouring, local authorities came to nothing. So it tried to recoup some of the money by leasing out a part of the land as a motor-racing track — not at all an alternative to appeal to preservationists. In Cornwall buildings were intruding on some of the small and beautiful coves. The county planning committees were indecisive, which was not surprising given that they might have to pay heavy compensation should they prohibit such building.

As was to be expected, the problem was nowhere more acute than in Surrey. Great tracts of land had already been built over, around Croydon and along the south bank of the Thames. In 1929 the threat was to the famously beautiful Box Hill, twenty-five miles from London. Local residents protested vigorously and there was widespread publicity. To forestall speculators, a member of the county council bought the Norbury Park estate, on the market and overlooked by Box Hill. When an adjoining estate also came up for sale, he bought that too. In each case this buyer was reimbursed by the county council. Essential time had been gained, but the county council still had to recoup what they had paid up. It could meet some of the cost by selling off part of the land for building development, but to do that it needed special powers which only Parliament could grant.

Surrey was fortunate enough to have the right man available. He was James Chuter Ede, an MP and a long-serving county councillor, who became known to the public generally after the Second World War as Home Secretary in the Attlee administration. He was long-serving there too, holding that vulnerable post for longer than anyone in more than 100 years. In his ministerial days, Chuter Ede looked a bit out of place, original Old Labour, more attuned to one of Ramsay MacDonald's early administrations, 1929 or even 1924. Dignified, undoubtedly worthy, but not, one would have thought, possessed of great energy or originality. Such a judgement would have been quite wrong. To Chuter Ede, the car had made development of the countryside inevitable. People who before would never have thought of moving to the country could now do so, and were determined to do so. He sympathized; homes must be built for them and access to open spaces encouraged, but at the same time it was important that the countryside be preserved. Development and preservation must be balanced, part of an overall scheme. The land sales and the economic boost delivered by the migrants would pay for it.

Chuter Ede became the driving force behind a series of local bills to Parliament promoted by district councils which sought authority for planned development of this sort. However, it was hardly practicable for small districts everywhere to present individual bills to Parliament each time some choice piece of country was threatened. So the next step was an overall plan, the Surrey County Council Bill. Other counties followed and a precedent had been set. The Town and Country Planning Act of 1932 enabled all local authorities to apply for the powers they required.

The Road Traffic Act of 1930 had set things moving. Further legislation in the early 1930s, whether in the form of county planning acts or more comprehensive national planning laws, was directed towards reducing damage to the environment. But, with the frightening number of road accidents, what about damage to people?

Was it possible to identify people who were especially accident-prone? This was one approach studied by the Ministry of Transport. It did not get far, partly because the Medical Research Council considered that they could not endorse any known test as being accurate, and also because of opposition from trades unions, which saw a test as likely to discriminate against workers. The *Daily Herald*, a Labour paper, called the proposal 'a scientific third degree' which might make motor drivers unemployable. Ernest Bevin, the general secretary of the Transport and General Workers Union, commented, 'if there were psychological tests for employers I am sure that more than half of them would be out of business'. A request from an MP that the Minister of Transport consider setting up a committee to investigate the role of alcohol in road accidents again led to consultations with medical experts. Matters started on the wrong foot: the Medical Research Council was affronted that the minister had approached the British Medical Association first. (No wonder that he had — the Research Council was chronically ver-bose and repetitive.) Anyway, the Council was unenthusiastic, believing that an inquiry was 'likely to prove troublesome out of pro-portion to the results which may be expected'. The BMA thought that a very small proportion of fatalities on the road were due to alcohol and were dubious about the existing methods of testing, some of which were already in use, so it was reported, in Germany, Sweden, the United States and Turkey, where police had powers to take blood tests of those involved. There was, though, a possible bonus in all this, for the minister and his parliamentary secretary received an offer of membership from the honorary secretary of the Society for the Study of Inebriety. (They turned it down.)

Then there was the question of traffic lights, or 'traffic control robots' as they were called in early days, which in Britain were first installed in Wolverhampton and Leeds in 1927, arriving in Man-chester and other cities in 1928 and 1929, and in London on a per-manent basis in 1931. The German visitor Karl Silex was unimpressed by some of the experimental lights in London. They do not seem to have been well thought out:

> light signals controlling the traffic from the side-streets have been put up in Oxford Street. But the driver of a car cannot see the sig-nals because they do not hang over the road, but stand on the pavement, with the consequence that a policeman has to be sta-tioned beside them to instruct drivers.

At Manchester both pedestrian-operated and automatic versions were tried out, but police reported that people seemed diffident about using the former. The Ministry of Transport and the London police kept a close eye on progress, and so great was the interest gen-erally that the manufacturers, the Forest Hill City Electric Com-pany, ran out of explanatory leaflets. They must have done well, however, for they continued as leaders in the market, to be consulted in 1938 on the construction in London of Western Avenue (which

they consistently referred to as 'Weston Avenue'). Here they were up against some disagreeable competition from footbridges. The company had to struggle to persuade their employers that these did not work well, and were disliked by the public.

But traffic lights were unpopular with many people. A correspondent to *The Times* in July 1934, signing him- or herself 'Safety First', claimed that pedestrians raced over crossings on the green light if they were close by when the lights changed. Otherwise, however, uncertain as to how long the green light would last, they preferred to wait until it came round again. The answer, said 'Safety First', was 'that in the place of the yellow light there be substituted a slowly revolving arm, or clock hand ... The arm, on arriving at the red light, will automatically switch it on and switch off the green light, and vice versa.'

Reading the Ministry of Transport's files gives one sympathy for the civil servants and admiration for their patience. At all stages of a project or an inquiry they needed to consult with some of the now numerous organizations that demanded a say. In 1933 Clarendon Street in Paddington was closed to traffic, with a notice posted outside announcing it now to be a play-street for children. The secretary

Traffic lights confused pedestrians, claimed 'Safety First', writing to *The Times* in July 1934; they never knew how much time they had for crossing the road. Better, he suggested, a revolving arm, enclosing this sketch to show what he meant.

of the RAC wrote to the Roads Department of the Ministry of Transport inquiring why, by what authority. (None, Paddington had acted off its own bat.) That was on 1 November 1933. On 8 November the ministry acknowledged the letter, saying that the matter was being discussed with the Metropolitan Police and that it was proposed in due course to refer it to the London and Home Counties Traffic Association. On 30 November the RAC sent a reminder. 'Enquiries are not complete', replied the ministry. On 8 December the ministry wrote to remind the police, mentioning that they needed an answer as they were anxious to discuss the question with the London Traffic Advisory Committee as well as with the London and Home Counties body. No answer, so on 12 January 1934 they wrote once more to the police. The London Society and the London Safety First Council now joined in — which did not speed matters up. Indeed, on 16 July the affair of little Clarendon Street was still unresolved and the minister himself had to intervene. And if motorists and others were involved with children's play-streets, so of course were residents. In one case, according to a report in the ministry's files, there was almost pandemonium. Nightworkers living in the street who were obliged to go to bed early in order to get up at four or five in the morning lost half their night's sleep because of the noise made by children.

One reason that the government took so long to come to grips with the consequences of motoring was the low priority given to the Ministry of Transport. For a period it was bereft of any minister at all; then it had too many. Between the formation of the ministry after the First World War and the middle of 1934 there were no fewer than nine ministers of transport. Such frequent changes were not calculated to get things done. If by the early 1930s the controversy over how motorists should be taxed and the effect on road building had faded, the number of road deaths and accidents had built up into a national scandal.

All sorts of attempts were made to spread the blame. Pedestrians (who accounted for nearly half the road deaths in these years) got a lot of it. A writer to the *Listener* in 1932 denounced people in towns for 'hurling' themselves about among moving traffic, and as for the country, there were 'many people of the bumpkin class who think it clever to stroll about in the middle of the road and only get out of the way at the last possible moment'. Another correspondent declared that everybody knew that motor traffic was now necessary to our very existence, and that roads were not built for pedestrians — it was as if they were to walk along a railway line. A future minister of transport, the veteran motor pioneer and aeronaut Colonel Moore-Brabazon, demanded in the House of Commons why such a fuss was made about road deaths: 'Over 6,000 people commit suicide every year, and nobody makes a fuss about that.' Others gave a different twist to the statistics. Another correspondent to the *Listener* in 1932 calculated that in the previous three years more people had been killed on the roads than on the battlefield — he was talking of the British regular army — during the entire twenty-two years of the revolutionary and Napoleonic wars with France.

Moore-Brabazon's cavalier dismissal of the casualties was shared by others. A doctor writing in the *Practitioner*, referring to the comparisons made with nineteenth-century wars, considered that people had become reconciled psychologically to numbers that would have made an earlier generation shudder. To the doctor, road rage and reckless driving were to be ascribed to a state of persistent hypomania. He knew one case where 'an impulse to charge oncoming vehicles has ... stopped one gentleman from driving'. Another distressing symptom which he mentioned was a phobia induced 'by the impossibility of seeing ahead when following behind another car, which led a driver to pull out of line even when he had no intention of passing'.

There is an unexpected mixture of horror and wry detachment about the heavy road accident casualties. Jokes in *The Best Motoring Stories*, published in 1931, read strangely. Many of them are old chestnuts dressed up in motoring garb, as for instance Irish jokes and mother-in-law jokes. In this latter case, the magistrate demands sternly of the accused why he was driving so recklessly up the high street; what excuse can he give? Only, the man replies, that he was on the way to the station to fetch his mother-in-law. Case dismissed. That is good-humoured enough, as is the one about the Brighton Road which prefaces this chapter. However, there are others in a taste which would be almost unthinkable now.

'First aid classes for pedestrians should be organised,' declares a Harley Street doctor. 'But surely all really workmanlike motorists take care that their victims are past first aid.'

'A serious rival to the vogue of greyhound racing is dirt track racing for motor cyclists, and it was clearly a brain-wave on the part of somebody who suggested the pursuit of an electric pedestrian.'

The Road Traffic Act had removed the speed limit altogether for cars (while raising it for heavier vehicles) on the grounds that most motorists could be trusted to drive reasonably. But accident figures climbed relentlessly. The motoring lobby was successful in holding up legislation. The RAC and the AA opposed speed limits, a driving test, pedestrian crossings, and what they regarded as excessively heavy punishments for driving offences. They decried frequent release of accident statistics and they fastened the blame on pedestrians, along with bicyclists. Their remedy was always to spend more on roads. The National Safety First Association, despite its reassuring title, was largely financed by motoring interests.

In June 1934 the Prime Minister, Ramsay MacDonald, appointed the financial secretary to the Treasury, Leslie Hore-Belisha, as Minister of Transport. A year or two later any moderately alert town child of over say the age of seven, unaware as he or she would be of Halifax or Simon or Hoare, would know about Hore-Belisha. You could not miss him: almost every time you crossed the street, you did so at crossings illuminated by flashing lights, the Belisha Beacons. As the Conservative MP Chips Channon noted in his diary in January 1935, 'Belisha Beacons, unheard of a few weeks ago, are now world famous.' A board game called Belisha went on sale; it was a form of rummy portraying 'a motor journey from London to Oban', carefully designed, according to its makers, 'to stimulate road consciousness especially among young people'. At Blackpool the idea was less worthy: an arcade game, Belisha Beacons, encouraged visitors to throw balls at traffic signs.

Hore-Belisha himself would have been happy either way. Publicity — few people ever relished it more, few politicians have been better at it. Channon, who grew increasingly fond of him, is a perceptive witness to his career and to his personality. Flashy he certainly was — his inspiration was Disraeli, a bust of whom held pride of place in his library. His was a 'Hollywood mentality', said Channon. Ambitious of course: at a party, overexcited, 'Leslie ... became "the Jew boy", bungling and self-important, and talked of what he would do when he was Prime Minister'. Vain — Channon and he were in a car when a lorryman, recognizing him, called out 'Hallo Leslie!' He was as pleased as Punch, noted Channon.

But then how many ministers of transport are recognized by lorry drivers? What Hore-Belisha intended to do — and what he accomplished — was to focus the public's attention on road safety, to make everyone conscious of the importance of stemming the ever-growing figures of death and injury on the roads. At the same time he also wanted people to understand the achievements of modern transportation. 'Tell me of another age,' he demanded rhetorically in a speech on the opening of a new road to the London docks, 'which in one twelve-month could see open in the public use a Mersey Tunnel — the greatest under-waterway in the world; three fine bridges over the Thames ... a road uniting Liverpool with Manchester and a highway such as this.' His intention was always to involve the public. Nevertheless, Hore-Belisha needed more than oratory — and he was an excellent speaker — and a mastery of public relations; he needed determination. (He proved that he had that all right when, as Secretary of State for War, he was to put his career at risk in inducing a reluctant Neville Chamberlain to introduce conscription in the spring of 1939.)

At the Ministry of Transport, his reforms were challenged by a variety of special interests. From the motorists came grumbles that pedestrians were too indecisive when using the crossings, which anyway were 'provided ... without the motorist's consent, but out of the motorist's pocket'. There was criticism from some of the press, with the *Spectator* objecting that the beacons made London look as if it were preparing for 'a fifth rate carnival'. The doctor quoted above feared that motorists might be dangerously provoked by a requirement that they cede right of way. The cyclists' organizations objected to the introduction of separate bicycle tracks along main roads, despite evidence that they made for increased safety. It was a question of principle, they insisted, that all vehicles should have equal rights to use the main highway. They objected too when Hore-Belisha criticized their members' custom of riding several abreast. If an incident related to Hore-Belisha by the Prince of Wales in December 1934 is anything to go by, cyclists may have occupied the centre of the road not just because riding side by side was more friendly but also as a form of protest. The Prince had jumped out of his car and expostulated with a cyclist who told him that he rode in the middle of the road in order to annoy the idle rich.

Moreover, the whole enterprise seems only just to have escaped disaster at the very start. Soon after his appointment, the minister, a physically clumsy man, was demonstrating personally in Camden Town, London, how a pedestrian on a crossing could claim right of way when he was almost run down by a small sports car. Still, it was reported in the press, it was publicity.

Hore-Belisha pressed on, driven by what *The Times* called his 'unresting energy'. In the autumn of 1934 he was badgering the Chancellor of the Exchequer, Neville Chamberlain, to alter the rules so that local authorities might have an idea in advance of how much money for roads they could expect from the Road Fund ('raided', but still in operation). No prudent authority, he argued, could plan ahead effectively without knowing roughly how much of their spending was likely to fall on their ratepayers. Sometimes he obtained encouragement from his colleagues, as when MacDonald, writing about ribbon development, described the transport ministry's long neglect of the tax implications as 'criminal'. Sometimes he went too far. Angered by the London County Council's negative attitude towards what he regarded as urgently needed road schemes in London, Hore-Belisha proposed in early 1936 to Chamberlain, now Prime Minister, that the government should obtain from Parliament direct powers to act. Chamberlain was 'not at all happy', such a plan went much too far, and anyway, with increased spending on defence, this was hardly the time for more money to go to 'prosperous London'. In fact, Hore-Belisha had already commissioned Edwin Lutyens to prepare a plan for London in conjunction with his ministry's Roads Department. It envisaged a new capital, encompassed by ring roads, crossed by arterial roads, with tunnels under the parks. A model was exhibited at the Royal Academy and a report was published in 1938, but the project became a casualty of the war. It has been described, however, as 'the most comprehensive and imaginative survey ... since Sir Christopher Wren's abortive design after the Great Fire'.

But if road planning stalled in London, in other parts of the country it prospered. It is worth quoting a (slightly arch) tribute from Scotland contained in a letter to Hore-Belisha from Sir David Cameron of Lochiel:

Never, during my long Association with the County Council, have we had a Minister who has done more for our Roads in the Highlands of Scotland, & we Highlanders will never forget that it was you ... It may be that your name is facetiously connected with Beacons but your Beacons in the Highlands will be our roads.

In May 1937, after not quite three years as Minister of Transport, Hore-Belisha — who was already in the Cabinet — was promoted to be Secretary of State for War, possibly at that time, after the Prime Minister's, the most crucial of all posts. He had succeeded in halting what had seemed to be an inexorable rise year by year of road deaths and injuries. In his first full year in office, 1935, deaths fell by 841 to 6,502 over the previous year and injuries by 10,877 to 221,726. Since the number of vehicles on the road had increased, the fall was significant. He tightened the rules for driving by imposing driving tests and reimposing speed limits in towns. He had introduced the Restriction of Ribbon Development Act of 1935. He had brought about a clearer public understanding of the implications of motoring, both constructive and destructive.

If by the time the Second World War broke out, there were no motorways, there was undeniable progress. British roads were well paved and many towns had been bypassed. The Mersey Tunnel was not unique in imaginative planning and construction. The Trunk Roads Act gave the Minister of Transport control of more than 180,000 miles of highway previously administered by county councils. The automobile had been accommodated. But the network of roads, new and reconstituted, did much more than that, for perhaps the most important consequence of the motoring age — so far only touched on — was the radical alteration it brought about in where people lived and worked.

9
Metroland Magnified

'*The rapid development of mechanical road transport has been one of the outstanding events of the post-war period, and in a single generation it has reacted in a marked degree on the whole economic and social life of the country. It has opened up the country to an extent never before possible and it has stimulated a more intense economic activity in all parts of the Kingdom, even the most remote.*'
British Association for the Advancement of Science, 1935

J. B. Priestley, the author during his lifetime of twenty-nine plays and innumerable books and articles, was well known by the time the Second World War broke out. What made him more than that, transformed him into a household name, was a series of talks he gave each Sunday night on the BBC between 5 June 1940, just after Dunkirk, and 20 October, by which time the Battle of Britain had passed its climax. It was estimated that he was listened to by 29 per cent of the adult population. The message was straightforward, about how Britain was standing firm against a barbarous enemy; it was not preachy or sentimental or declamatory, but reassuring and robust and larded with homely anecdotes. Priestley talked of a duck and her duckling which he had seen one week on a Hampstead pond; he made light digs at pompous officialdom; he described Margate beach, once so crowded with tourists but now barricaded against invasion, with its rows of boarding houses shut down. He recalled to his listeners' minds the bits and pieces of British life, the things that we were fighting for in terrible times. But there was another message as well; we were fighting to survive certainly, but we were fighting too for a better world in the future, one that redeemed the errors of the previous twenty years. It was on that note — as the air battle raged — that Priestley spoke of a young RAF pilot and his wife, and how the husband might be killed at any moment. Last time, he said, we did nothing for such people, 'except to let them take their chance in a world in which every gangster and trickster and stupid, insensitive fool or rogue was let loose to do his damndest'.

It is this feeling, a bitterness for the wasted years between the wars, a memory of the unemployment and poverty, of the degradation that awaited so many returning servicemen, which permeates much of Priestley's classic book *English Journey,* his 'rambling account of what one man saw and heard and felt and thought during a journey through England during the autumn of the year 1933'. In the last chapter he sums up: what he has found are three distinct Englands. The first is 'Old England', a land of cathedrals and minsters and manor houses and inns, of quaint highways and byways. The second is 'nineteenth century England', the terrain of coal, of iron and steel, of cotton, wool and railways, a region which for more than 100 years had been the industrial powerhouse of the world. The third England is new altogether, post-war and 'belonging far more to the age itself than to this particular island', a country of

> arterial and by-pass roads, of filling stations and factories that look like exhibition buildings, of giant cinemas and dance-halls and cafés, bungalows with tiny garages, cocktail bars, Woolworths, motor-coaches, wireless, hiking, factory girls looking like actresses, greyhound racing and dirt tracks, swimming pools, and everything given away for cigarette coupons.

This was the country he described as 'rapidly Blackpooling itself'. And it was too the country that created the wealth that made the period from 1926 to 1938, despite the slump, despite the huge numbers of unemployed, despite the disappearance of export markets, economically the most successful for many years. And, incidentally, it was this country which produced the money so lavishly spent on automobiles.

211

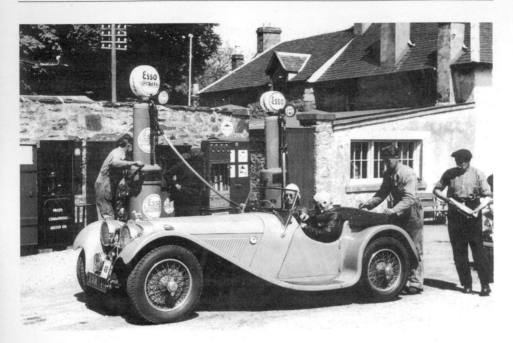

By the 1930s villages possessed their own manually operated petrol pumps.

The first lap of the journey ran from London to Southampton with Priestley, who usually travelled by chauffeur-driven Daimler, sitting, for the first time in his life, in a motor coach. He was impressed: motor coaches, he noted, seemed to be going everywhere in the island. What was more, they were amazingly fast and comfortable, with deep, plush seats that reminded him of the 'vast' new cinemas. Travelling out of London down the Great West Road, he caught his first glimpse of the new 'third England'. It did not look English: 'we might have suddenly rolled into California', he thought, as along each side of the road glittered a line of new factories. They were not at all like the factories he remembered as a youth in the West Riding of Yorkshire; they were not grim, blackened rectangles with a chimney at one corner, rather they were 'decorative little buildings, all glass and concrete and chromium plate', which seemed to his mind 'merely to be playing at being factories'.

Priestley's journey led him, sometimes by coach, sometimes by car, occasionally by train, through the prosperous south-west, from Southampton with its great ocean liners to Bristol, an admirable place, he thought, at once a genuine city and an ancient metropolis. Then on to Bath, to Swindon and to the Cotswolds, still unspoilt,

still arcadian, a 1920s dream-landscape, except perhaps for Broadway, which was 'loud with bright young people who had just arrived
from town and the Tatler in gamboge and vermilion sports cars'.
However, as he travels into the Midlands, through Coventry, Birmingham and Leicester, the tone changes. This is still booming country, the roads notable for gaudy pubs, some admirably designed,
others 'inspired by the idea of Merrie England, popular in the neighbourhood of Los Angeles'. A few of the more ambitious ones were
evolving into roadhouses. But as he goes north into the Black Country, his 'second England', Priestley's mood darkens. Even the motor
bus which took him from Leicester to Nottingham, with its rattles
and shakes, and which at 40mph 'seemed to be swaying on the edge
of catastrophe', was a reversion to an ancient type. And as he tours
the broken industrial cities it never — or so it appears — stops rain-
ing. Except in Manchester, buried in fog, where 'we crawled to the
Midland Hotel through a turgid sooty gloom that was neither day
nor night'.

The old Lancashire adage, 'Where there's muck, there's money',
was out of date. For now in 1933 there was still plenty of muck but
not much money. He visits Liverpool, where by the end of the 1930s
trade would have dropped to 75 per cent of its level in 1914. He
passes by Stockton, where the shipyards had long been closed and
their skilled workforce unemployed. In Jarrow one out of every two
shops appeared to be permanently shut; among those still open,
Priestley remarked drily, were those selling funeral wreaths. He looks
on the ruin of the cotton industry. At Blackburn he reflected that
the 'whole district had been tied to prosperity, to its very existence,
with threads of cotton; and you could hear them snapping all the
time'. The very day he arrived, a large cotton mill, built perhaps
twenty years before, was put up for auction without reserve. There
was not a single bid.

It was natural that Priestley was affected most by the decay of his
hometown, Bradford. To him its plight epitomized the change in the
relationship between the north and south of England. Before 1914,
people in Bradford were largely indifferent to the south. It would
never have occurred to his father, he reflected, to envy London, and
he himself had been unmoved by the prospect of a university place
in the south. In those days Bradford seemed to offer all he wanted
from a town. The centre of the worsted trade, it was cosmopolitan,

'a city of travellers', with its citizens buying wool wherever it was to be found and selling yarn and pieces 'from Belgium to China'. And foreigners came to Bradford too, colonies of them lived there, particularly, Priestley remembered, a colony of German Jews. Indeed, in those days a Londoner was a stranger sight than a German. But a lot had changed by 1933. The self-confidence was enfeebled, and much of the cosmopolitanism gone. (Although it should be added that even in the 1950s there remained a colony of French businessmen, to be seen playing billiards together at the Bradford Club.)

This disjunction between the north and south of England, even after the First World War, is recalled by others. For one by Richard Hoggart, brought up in Leeds, next door to Bradford, for whom the south of England was

> the softer South, the property-owning South, the executive South, the clean South, the suburban South, the mock-Tudor and half-timbered South which, on the rare occasion one passed through a swathe of it on the way into London, had all the tugging attraction of an Ealing film, and made a Northerner feel more than ever outside, cut off from an altogether softer, more wrap-around, less hard-edged England.

Softer perhaps, but sometimes exciting. Don Haworth in Burnley remembered the arrival one day of some insurance men on their bicycles. With them, but in a car, was a blond young man with a slight moustache and plus fours, who made it known that he had motored to the south of England, and described his expedition as though he had been up the Amazon. 'We were left with a notion of wide roads and glass factories, lush fields and woods, and of brisk people of sharp speech and punctilious driving habits, living in green and spacious towns.'

How far did the automobile affect the decline of the old industrial England? Indirectly, as we shall see, a good deal. From a direct point of view, it brought its universal, immediate benefits, as witness the quotation from *Britain in Depression* at the very beginning of this chapter. Trade and industry which survived gained from faster and more flexible transport. As in Laurie Lee's Gloucestershire, the motor bus transformed the life of rural communities. Priestley relates that on the morning after the regimental dinner which coincided with his visit to Bradford, he and some old comrades from the

First World War set out to walk the lovely moors that lie to the north of the city by Ilkley and Grassington. Deep in the moors, they come on the tiny hamlet of Hubberholme, the end of the world, they think, miles from anywhere, certainly from any railway station. 'It is the internal-combustion engine that has brought such a place as this on the map', notes Priestley. And again, among the collieries of East Durham, Priestley can say that at least the traditional isolation of the mining communities is less than it used to be, thanks to road transport.

The great traditional industries of the north, textiles, coal mining and shipbuilding, went into decline partly through the loss of export markets, some of them crippled by the war, others captured by competitors overseas. Many family firms found it difficult to raise new capital or to strike out afresh. Priestley comments on another weakness of such businesses. Bradford, he says, has suffered not just because the wool trade has dropped away but because the richer merchants and manufacturers no longer live in the city. They work there, but live well outside. Originally it was the railway that made this separation feasible, but 'the motor has, of course, encouraged this migration which is common, I suspect, throughout the north, where the wealthier industrialists are busy turning themselves into country gentlemen and are leaving the cities to the professional, clerking and working classes'. It was the same in Hull. As a playwright Priestley was especially conscious of the cultural effect, of the loss of 'the very people who, at one time, would have been the chief supporters of local music and drama and so forth [and] now spend their evenings with bridge and the wireless twenty-five miles away'. Katherine Chorley makes the same point in her book *Manchester Made Them*: the wealthy of Manchester have been able to move their homes out into the Cheshire countryside. Priestley approved the criticism of a foreigner who declared it would be much better if, like continentals, the British were to live in town but have bungalows and cottages outside in which to spend two or three months in the summer.

Such decampment, harmful to morale and to labour relations as it must have been, is of small significance when seen in the context of that shift in population from north to south which was so important a feature of the inter-war period. Much of it was a direct result of the collapse of northern industry, which forced the unemployed to seek work in Priestley's third, new England. In 1933 (the date of his journey) the unemployment rate nationally was 19.5 per cent, slightly less than it had been in the depths of the Depression two years before. There were marked variations: in north-east England, for example, the figure was over 25 per cent, while in the south-east it was under 10 per cent. And take the population as a whole. During the period 1921—39 the overall population of Great Britain increased by about 7.5 per cent to 46 million. The increase in the south-east was 18.6 per cent and in the West Midlands 13.8 per cent, but in the industrial north of England the population was virtually static. (In Scotland there was an increase of 12.7 per cent.) The motor industry provides a good illustration of the effect of the migration of workers during the 1930s. In 1931 the population of Coventry was 167,083, of which 3,459 were recent migrants. By 1939 Coventry's population had risen to 224,267 (the increase partly the result of the rearmament programme), which included 42,148 new migrants, something like a quarter of whom came from Wales. At the newly established Ford plant at Dagenham outside London, 28.7 per cent of the labour force were migrants, mostly skilled workers transferring from Manchester and its surrounds. At Luton, with its Vauxhall plant, the population increased by more than three-quarters over the period 1921—39, of which 83 per cent were migrants.

Laurie Lee's description of his own migration from Gloucestershire to London breathes life into these figures. Chapter 6 left him playing his violin to elderly and appreciative ladies on the front at Worthing. He then turned northwards on the last lap of his journey:

> I was not the only one on the road; I soon noticed there were many others, all trudging northwards in a sombre procession. Some, of course, were professional tramps, but the majority belonged to that host of unemployed who wandered aimlessly about England at that time ... One could pick out the professionals; they brewed tea by the roadside, took it easy, and studied their feet. But the others, the majority, went on their way like somnambulists, walking alone and seldom speaking to each other ... They were like a broken army walking away from a war, cheeks sunken, eyes dead with fatigue. Some carried bags of tools, or broken cardboard suitcases; some wore the ghosts of city suits; some, when they stopped to rest, carefully removed their shoes and polished them vaguely with handfuls of grass. Among them were carpen-

ters, engineers from the Midlands; many had been on the road for months, walking up and down the country in a maze of jobless refusals, the treadmill of the middle-thirties ...

As he drew nearer to London, Laurie Lee was struck by conflicting impressions. One was depressive. Bagshot Heath, two days out, where he slept a night, 'all birches, sand and horseflies', felt sinister and 'wasted like the vast plains of Russia'. Then a bit further on and he was walking in parkland, where every car which passed was either a Rolls-Royce or a Daimler packed with girls and hampers and 'erect top-hatted men'. He had never seen more than two such cars in his life; were they, he asked himself, intimations of treasure to come, was all London as rich as this? Then his wondering was interrupted by an almost surreal moment. From one of the Daimlers stretched a beckoning arm. Lee hurried over as the car stopped. 'Want a pheasant, my man? We just knocked over a beauty a hundred yards back.'

London of course was not all that rich, not all Daimlers and Rolls-Royces. But anyway few of the thousands and thousands of migrating workers were going to the county of London at all. They headed to outer London, to the ill-defined Greater London — ill-defined because it was in a state of constant flux — and to all over south-east England, to Dover, to Slough, to Welwyn, to St Albans, to Letchworth, to Canterbury, to wherever new factories or depots were to be found. Here were the new industries of the twentieth century — motor vehicles and their components, aircraft, electric lamps and valves, rayon, plastics, chemicals, radio and a multitude of consumer goods.

No longer did industry rely on the coalfields of the north, no longer did factories need to group around railway stations, nor, for the high cost of transport by horse dray no longer mattered, was it vital to settle close to suppliers and customers. And, if they wanted a port, there was a flourishing one in London. Sir Arnold Wilson, MP, visited a factory in his south of England constituency which was producing a new type of steel and, remarking how many of the workers were migrants, thought how ominous this was from the point of view of the north of England. Manufacturers wanted to be in close touch with their markets and with the banks and other financial institutions of London. Foreign manufacturers, faced with formidable tariff barriers, opened factories in Britain and found it natural to establish them in the south, which anyway was the region they usually knew best. The government could have intervened — as it was to do after the Second World War — by directing industry to regions with exceptionally heavy unemployment and so, in theory anyway, provide a better balance to the economy. In fact, it did introduce subsidies for work in distressed areas and from 1936 put pressure on foreign manufacturers to locate in the north. There was a boost to northern industry in the late 1930s with the rearmament programme, which came about partly because of the government's concern to disperse the likely targets for enemy bombers. However, generally speaking, there was little enthusiasm during the inter-war years for the higher taxes which would have followed a more thorough regulation of industry.

The modern communications which enabled industry to develop in new territory meant above all roads and the use of automobiles, and the government set up two royal commissions to study the social consequences. The first, its report known as the Barlow Report and presented to Parliament in January 1940, dealt with the demography of the industrial population. The commission agreed that economic rather than social considerations must normally determine where factories were established, but it was dismayed at the social price that was being paid, at the pull of London. The 'macrocosm of London', it declared, was spreading at an alarming rate. The other commission, its findings recorded in the Scott Report, presented in August 1942, was concerned with the protection of agriculture and rural communities. Neither royal commission was in any doubt as to the importance of the automobile. Scott declared:

> A factory can now be established in a field at the edge of the town, or right out in the country some miles beyond. Its choice of site is indeed only limited to being near a reasonably good road and a 'bus route along which its workers can travel out from the town and its suburbs where they live.

We were living, the report went on, at the time of a new Industrial Revolution, with social and economic consequences as far-reaching as those of the earlier Industrial Revolution. The two most important causes of this revolution were the automobile and electricity.

But if in the overall plan of things the two industries, automobiles and electricity, made natural partners, in the narrower sphere of short-distance transport they were in fierce competition. In the towns and cities it was a battle between the motor bus on one side and trams and trolleys on the other.

J. B. Priestley, during his journey, mentions trams several times. On one occasion, coming into the West Riding at night, he sees trams, far away, climbing the hills like 'luminous beetles'. Usually though the context is much less romantic. In Liverpool, he writes of trams 'going whining down long sad roads; a few stinking little shops; pubs with their red blinds down'. And at Birmingham:

> Then followed one of the most depressing little journeys I ever remember making. No doubt I was tired. And then again the electric tram offers the least exhilarating mode of progress possible. It is all very well for the Irish poet 'AE' to call them 'those high-built glittering galleons of the streets'; but no man inside a tram, no matter how he strains his fancy, really feels he is inside a glittering galleon. The people show a sound instinct when they desert the tramway for any other and newer kind of conveyance. There is something depressing about the way in which a tram lumbers and groans and grinds along, like a sick elephant.

But however they seemed to Priestley in 1933, trams, at the start horse-drawn, then steam, then electric, introduced new flexibility, and gave an impetus of their own to the movement from town centres to the suburbs. Indeed, they were precursors of the automobile, for they encouraged settlement at a distance from railway stations. They had too the doubtful honour of introducing that ribbon development along highways which was to become so much a mark of the automobile. Back in 1909 the chief officer of the London County Council tramways had forecast that 'twenty years hence motor buses will be exhibited as curios in museums'. But trams suffered under serious disadvantages when compared to motors, quite apart from any tendency to groaning and grinding. They took up more road space than motor buses; passengers disliked boarding and dismounting out in the road, away from the safety and convenience of the kerb; their difficulties in manoeuvring caused congestion, which meant they were often forbidden in towns. By the 1930s in London, trams were tending to draw their power supply from underground conduits rather than through overhead cables, an improvement, but not a wholly satisfactory one, since readjustment to the old system was often necessary when they reached the suburbs. The Royal Commission on Transport, in its final report presented to Parliament at the end of 1930, appreciated some of the advantages of trams. Unlike automobiles, they did not consume imported fuel, they were without fumes, they made little noise and — whatever Priestley said — usually provided a smooth ride. However, the commission considered them to be an obsolescent means of transport, best replaced by trolleybuses, 'trackless trams', which drew their power from overhead lines but required no rails on which to travel.

Trolleys were safer and more manoeuvrable and could take advantage of power plants and infrastructure already in place. But the royal commission had no doubt that for through-traffic anyway the future belonged to the motor bus. It had the supreme advantage of being a 'self-contained mobile unit', able to operate on any route and easy to withdraw should a route prove uneconomic. It required far less capital investment. In the old days the bus could not match the reliability of its rivals and was more expensive to run, but now technical advances had improved running costs and comfort.

Trams did not, so to speak, go quietly. Whatever the attractions of the motor bus, town transport managers in the 1920s and 1930s were often the same people who had originally introduced the trams. They were deeply loyal to them. Dr Smithies, in his thesis on contrasts between North and South between the wars, describes the situation in Halifax, where the municipally owned tramway system (by this time most tramways were municipally owned) was losing money fast. Fares were reduced, and then raised again when the hoped-for increase in passengers failed to materialize. In 1927 a new chairman of the tramways committee was elected; he was determined to replace the trams by buses but had to move cautiously. In 1929, with the loss of revenue becoming intolerable, he was only just able to squeeze his proposals through the council. It was very much a political matter. Just as the conservatives of Eastbourne had turned up their noses at trams on the grounds that they were plebeian vehicles, so, for the same reason, did Labour councillors and MPs fight to keep them. In 1929, in London, the Labour members of the London County Council opposed a bill to Parliament proposing the coordination of road and underground services, believing that it would lead to the dissolution of the tram network. With the election of a Labour government at Westminster, the bill was thrown out, to be revived successfully when the national government came to power two years later.

Trams were a special case. For the 1929 Labour government, with Herbert Morrison as Minister of Transport, was enthusiastic about the coordination of all forms of passenger transport (other than main-line rail) in the county of London area. In turning down the Conservative-promoted bill, it promised its own legislation. In any event, new legislation in 1933 created the London Passenger Transport Board, soon to be known more simply as London Transport. There was overall control, with shareholders of existing private companies compulsorily bought out. Even before, there had been coordination of transport activities, as, for instance, with buses acting as 'feeders' for underground lines and even for trams. New tube stations and bus stations incorporated car parks. Strong arguments existed for rationalization, but again, as in the case of transport nationally, an important reason behind it was the need (as it was considered) to protect the older services from the automobile. *The Economist* in 1937 eschewed pieties. A compelling argument for unification, it declared, was that 'in free competition the petrol bus can drive any other form of transport (save, perhaps, the suburban services of main line railways) into bankruptcy'. But however its transport was organized, London faced a special problem, for, as *The Economist* noted, of all the world's capitals it was the most dependent on buses. The greater challenge, however, that of coping with a huge growth in population, it shared with many large cities, with London unusual mainly in the amount of land consumed per building. In London, or rather Greater London, the population, between 1890 and 1940, increased from 5.6 million to 8.7 million. In the same period, the population in the three departments of the Paris region rose from 4.1 million to 6.6 million; in Berlin the figures were 1.6 million and 4.3 million. Between 1900 and 1940 the numbers in the metropolitan district of New York went up from 4.6 million to 11.7 million and in Tokyo (1889—1942) the population increased from 1.4 million to 7.35 million.

An early-twentieth-century suburb of London particularly lavish in its use of space was what became known as Metroland or Metro-land. This was a region developed by the Metropolitan Railway to the north-west, out towards Amersham and Aylesbury. The railway provided the transport and sold land for building along the route. (It was the only railway company allowed by law to market land in this way.) Rural charms were emphasized in its bucolic publicity:

> The song of the nightingale for which the neighbourhood is renowned; its mingled pastures, woods and streams; its gentle hills clothed with verdure; the network of translucent rivers traversing the peaceful valley render it a Mecca to the City man pining for country and pure air.

Rural charm was an important selling point, but care was necessary, for not all buyers were as yet fully acclimatized. In the 1920s apparently developers preferred to use black cars to meet prospective customers at the station — they did not show up the country mud. By 1905 the Metropolitan Railway had introduced electric trains and was creating an extensive suburban area. It published an annual guide which extolled the converted countryside and at the same time publicized London theatres, famous buildings and other sights. When in 1933 the company was unwillingly subsumed in the London Passenger Transport Board, Metroland as a name disappeared from official terminology. But it had entered everyday language, first as a reference to the north-western suburbs of London, and then more generally to the new suburbs sprouting up around the city. (And now more generally yet: a television programme shown in December 2002 about a house in Soho Square, rated as central London since the seventeenth century, carried the title *Metroland*.)

In the case of Metroland, communications came first, suburban development followed the rail line. The railways fathered, not just peripheral developments, but whole new towns, perhaps creating them from scratch, perhaps from existing villages. The outstanding example is not in Britain but in the United States, in southern California, where Henry E. Huntington's inter-urban electric trains transformed Los Angeles and its district. Or it might be tram lines or the tube which led the way. Indeed, even during the railway age, roads might on occasion act as precipitators of building development. Glasgow in the 1840s was an example: private investors constructed the Great Western Road leading from the city centre into the country, totally straight and a mile long. On the undeveloped land was then built the new suburb of Blythswood.

The process, however, did not always work that way round — the building might go up before the communications were in place. After all, in the 1890s large numbers of workmen living in the south London suburbs walked to their work in the centre of town. It might be that public transport was too expensive, or it might equally be that there was none, that a new suburb lacked transport links with the city proper. The Metropolitan Railway was untypical, dealing, as it did, with a particularly affluent market. Sometimes, as with the Great Western Railway at Paddington, the terminus was ill-placed, too distant from where most commuters worked. In any event, by and large the big railway companies were interested mainly in their long-distance business; they supported middle-class suburbs such as Surbiton and Ealing but were less happy about the poorer ones. The government intervened. For instance, the Great Eastern Railway needed to build a terminus in the City and to occupy a great deal of land in doing so. Government permission was required, and to get it the company accepted an obligation to run trains, charging cheap rates, to the working-class districts of Walthamstow and Edmonton. Cheap workmen's train tickets and tram fares were important in persuading poorer families to move away from the centre.

Central to the coalition government's platform in the snap election of 1918 was the pledge to build 'homes fit for heroes'. The promise was honoured, for an immense number of houses and flats were built in the twenty years between the wars. Some 4 million residential buildings, houses and flats, were built in England — enough to accommodate nearly a third of the population. Between 1921 and 1938 the population of Britain increased by 7.8 per cent while there was an increase of 37.5 per cent in the stock of housing. And building was mainly in the suburbs, with the inner cities continuing to lose population. The German Karl Silex lived in London, and wrote a book about Britain for his countrymen which was published in English in 1931 under the title *John Bull at Home*. Silex was unenthusiastic about British homes. They were poky compared to their German equivalents, and cold and generally uncomfortable. The sleeping quarters allocated to servants, he said, defied description. He was, though, full of admiration for the ambitious building programme, describing it in fact as the only great achievement of the English people since the war.

On the other hand, Silex considered the suburbs of London more generally as eyesores, as 'a hermetically sealed girdle of mean and dirty streets'. Others agreed, for if the new houses and sometimes

flats were often superior to what was already there, they were adding
— and on a gigantic scale — to an already extended concourse. In
the 1930s Cicely Hamilton described the northern suburbs flung out
layer after layer, ring after ring:

> Journeying from the centre to the outer rim of London, one per-
> ceives the various strata of suburban growth. Brick of a dirty-grey
> colour, which begins in the inner regions, near King's Cross,
> denotes mid-Victorian expansion; then farther on, comes the ugly
> red of the late Victorian builder; while here and there, as you draw
> towards the rim, there will be a little house of older date which,
> sandwiched into a terrace of yesterday, survives from that van-
> ished countryside of Middlesex in which its foundations were laid.
> The last and newest layer of London is the layer of suburban flats.

As another writer pointed out, after about eight or ten miles of
suburbs everything became reduced in scale — the windows and
doors of the houses, the tube stations and shopping precincts, all got
smaller. Sometimes the rings occurred in a different order, where the
inner mid-Victorian suburbs had been pulled down and replaced by
row upon row of small mean houses. Professor Joad, in his *The Horrors of the Countryside*, describes what he saw on a train journey
through Surrey and Sussex, from London to Worthing. He talks of
the immediate drab and squalid suburbs which culminate in a
'climax at Croydon', in its centre the familiar tangle of mean streets,
'undistinguished shops and radiating tram lines'. Then on edge was
a fringe of large detached Victorian houses, each approached by its
own carriage drive, each built in yellow brick, imposing and very
ugly.

The great incoherent urban sprawl unchained by the automobile
enormously complicated travel within the metropolis. 'Nowadays',
asserted a writer in the *Listener* in 1930, 'a resident at Hendon considers a journey to Bromley as serious a business as a journey to
Birmingham'. Much better, argued the popular writer Douglas
Goldring, to set up business in the north of England; compare trying
to escape from Finchley and Croydon with leaving Newcastle,
where you find ravishing country immediately on your doorstep. No
wonder that Laurie Lee, champion walker though he was, lost heart
on that score when finally he reached the outskirts of London.
There lay the city, 'a long smoky skyline hazed by the morning sun

and filling the whole of the eastern horizon', and dry, rusty-red, 'like a huge flat crust, like ash from some spent volcano, simmering gently in the summer morning and emitting a faint, metallic roar'. But the suburbs were long and empty. He took the tube.

So again, with motor transport established, which came first, the road or the building? In the case of Manchester, the new suburb of Wythenshawe was entirely dependent on road transport. The city's corporation had bought the main block of land from a local landowner in order to rehouse slum dwellers. Wythenshawe was a 'garden city', meticulously planned, complete with a permanent 'green belt' and generous playing fields and open spaces. By 1931, when the main construction work got under way, it was already larger than the original garden cities of Letchworth and Welwyn, with such well-known planners and architects as Raymond Unwin and Patrick Abercrombie concerned in its design. It included two parkways, the first in Britain, for free-flowing traffic, segregated from housing and minor roads. Birmingham, the third-largest city in Britain (to replace Glasgow as the second largest in 1951), was a centre of the motor and engineering industries. Here a steady migration to the suburbs had been under way since the very start of the century. By the 1920s the stream had turned into a torrent, with large municipal estates surrounding the city, to the north, east and south, and with the ever-swelling suburbs dependent on ring roads. By 1938 one in seven of the population lived in the innermost ring of the city, two in seven in the middle, and four in seven in the outer ring. By the end of the 1930s, what Goldring had written of Newcastle was out of date. 'Once the flight started', wrote Thomas Sharp, 'there has been no stopping it.' He added that Hartlepool, Stockton and Darlington were all acquiring the 'biological structure of the octopus'.

As far as London was concerned, roads or other means of communication might or might not follow development. Patrick Abercrombie described the London Passenger Transport Board as 'now pioneer, now camp follower'. Sometimes developers started building on an isolated site, anticipating that once the potential was evident, transport links would follow; should they be delayed or insufficient, the developers might organize their own services. Karl Silex singled out for praise the London County Council's new estate at Becontree, in east London, some twelve miles from Charing Cross. It was enormous, planned to provide for more than 100,000 people, a housing

Edgware from the air in 1926.

estate, mainly in the form of two-storey houses. Transport of all kinds fitted in almost automatically. As it turned out, those who managed to find work within five miles of their new homes either walked or used motor cycles or buses, while those going further afield travelled by train or, sometimes, tram.

As the suburbs stretched further and further from the centre, so did travelling to work take up more time. (A concern among employers was that longer journeys would intensify pressure for the eight-hour day.) On the face of it, the answer could be to locate homes and places of employment close to each other. The Becontree estate would seem to have been admirably placed, for in the early 1930s Ford moved from Trafford Park to Dagenham, immediately next door, bringing with them Briggs Bodies and Kelsey Hayes Wheels. For residents of the great housing estate it was an exciting prospect — local jobs and motor-industry pay levels, which were well above the norm. But it did not happen that way, for Ford wanted skilled workers whom Becontree could not supply. And since the Becontree estate was, for a period anyway, reserved for transplanted Londoners, it was itself of limited use in housing the skilled workers the company brought in from outside. In 1934 a Fabian booklet, demanding

stricter planning, denounced the existing state of things as a 'headlong charge to urban perdition', stating:

Edgware from the air in 1948. The site shown in the earlier photograph is to be found at the road intersection, centre right. The automobile, bus and car, led to an enormous and incoherent spread of suburbs. Edgware (where the underground was also a powerful force) was just one of them.

> The typical Londoner who works in the centre has at the best the choice of life in a tenement, necessarily cramped and rather poorly lighted, without garden, and out of reach of playing fields; or daily journeys by tube, train or 'bus from and to a house 12 to 20 miles out.

Remoteness of workplace and home was evident elsewhere too. Glasgow might congratulate itself, or at least its nineteenth-century self, on the foresight shown in building the Great Western Road, but it had little to be pleased about when it found its trading estate of Hillington to be located five miles on one side of the city and its local authority housing development on the other. But London, being so enormous, with Greater London something like thirty miles across, was in a category of it own. Its share of new factories emphasizes how exceptional it was: between 1932 and 1937, of the net increase of 644 factories in Britain no fewer than 532 were in the Greater London area. In the inter-war period Greater London accounted for one-third of the total expansion of built-up land in England and Wales, with most of its industry located to the west and north-west, while most industrial workers lived to the east and south-east. As a result huge crowds daily moved from one place to another, usually concentrated within short periods in the morning and evening. So decentralization of industry and of homes for industrial workers actually led to more congestion not less, and the pressure was the more severe since office workers as well now had further to travel. Banks, insurance companies, stockbrokers and other services were concentrated in the centre, in the City of London. The London Passenger Transport Board estimated that whereas in 1921 between 850,000 and 900,000 persons converged on the centre each working day, by the late 1930s the figure had more or less doubled.

The automobile was instrumental in making it possible to establish factories pretty well anywhere, and indeed now they were to be found in previously unimagined places. However, the factory owner already established somewhere near a city centre was not in the same position as the Fabian Society's 'typical Londoner'. He was not going to miss the gardens and playing fields — for he did not actually live in his factory anyway — and the shortage of other amenities was not necessarily going to drive him to the expense and trouble of relocating, even given that suburban rates would be lower. An immediate lack of space might not shift him, for he might be able to make up for it by occupying premises or land vacated by families who moved out to the suburbs. Thus away from London, in areas where new factories were not so thick on the ground, industrial decentralization was less common. However, in London and the south-east, factories did habitually establish themselves at the edge of town. As the plan published by Douglas Smith in his *The Industries of Greater London* of 1933 shows, they tended to settle in clusters and then to straggle out along the main highways, to the north towards Ware, for instance, to the north-west towards St Albans and along the roads set out lower down on the plan, which include Priestley's 'California in England', the Great West Road, that runs in the direction of Southall, Hayes and Yiewsley. As Smith notes, 'arterial roads are a cause of the location of factories, and not an effect of the factories'. There are two points, though, to make about the plan. First, that the new factories, though they push out along the new roads, are often still within easy distance of pre-First World War factories, con-

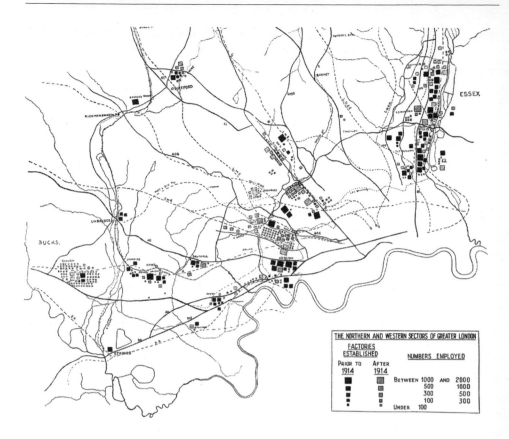

THE NORTHERN AND WESTERN SECTORS OF GREATER LONDON

FACTORIES ESTABLISHED		NUMBERS EMPLOYED	
PRIOR TO 1914	AFTER 1914		
■	▨	BETWEEN 1000 AND	2000
■	▨	500	1000
▪	▫	300	500
▪	▫	100	300
·	·	UNDER 100	

structed at a time when the automobile's influence was non-existent or negligible. Secondly, that Smith's book, indicative as it is, counts as a preliminary study, since it is concerned with the situation at the beginning of the 1930s, before the main influx of new factories (and other commercial premises) had taken place.

Factories, freed from dependence on railway stations, multiplied along the roads out of London. This plan was published in 1934 by Douglas Smith in his *The Industries of Greater London.*

Nowadays drivers travelling due west out of London normally follow the M4 motorway, but anyone who instead takes Priestley's old route, the A4, will find it changed certainly in detail, but with a character still recognizably of the sort he described. All the way to Heathrow it is lined with factories, warehouses, garages, and hotels, and with pubs, sometimes like those in the Midlands in old road-house style. To the north of the M4 motorway is the M40 to Oxford, its London end, Western Avenue, being a reconstructed version of what was there in the 1930s. Unreconstructed and happily still in place, now distinguished as a listed building, is one of the finest of inter-war factories, the art deco Hoover Building, designed by a leading architect of contemporary industrial buildings and described in its day as 'magnificently placed for road and rail transport and for the housing of our workers'. The road has had a long and difficult history. Back in 1903 Rees Jeffreys, on behalf of the Roads Improvement Association, proposed its construction, and eighteen years later, with permission granted by the Ministry of Transport, work started ... and then stopped as the government cut back on road schemes. In 1937 it began again, and, with the war, stopped again. In the 1990s Edward Platt took up the story in his *Leadville: A biography of the A40*, an account of the decay of the original road and of the industrialization that took place. Platt travelled up and down a stretch of Western Avenue, talking to the residents and squatters faced with eviction to allow for widening of the highway and its segregation from local traffic. By the time the evictions were just about completed and the bailiffs ready for work in more promising territory, in came the news that construction on Western Avenue was to be halted once more. (It has now again been resumed.)

Here and there, as Edward Platt moved up and down the road, were vestiges of the housing estates built for employees of the new factories. It was not for them to waste time travelling; they would not be adding to the congestion of central London. What is more, Western Avenue and particularly, when it was finished, the North Circular Road provided extra relief from traffic congestion by enabling motorists and buses to travel to work around the periphery, rather than through the middle of town. On the other hand, a result was residential ribbon development, with local traffic cluttering up what was intended as a safe but fast highway. Matters got worse as shops followed, and a cinema and a church. Intersecting roads proliferated, accidents mounted. Residents were usually happy, though, what with easy access in front and a view over open country behind. According to the Scott Report, another thing they liked about ribbon development was that it allowed them to avoid road charges and other service expenses.

The new Western Avenue suburb actually became rather smart. The residents interviewed by Platt were poor, occasionally almost destitute, but their predecessors back in the 1930s were the sort of person you might have found in Dulwich or another of the wealthier

London suburbs, people who certainly had no intention of asking Hoover for a job. One old inhabitant interviewed by Platt remembered these superior beings, now long-departed, who lived in what was known as 'Toffville', a group of big houses along Western Avenue.

For in their day these motor suburbs possessed a sort of romance. Admittedly not everyone greeted them with joy: not, in 1922 for instance, the allotment holders of good horticultural land threatened by the Western Avenue development, nor later, after the Second World War, when workers arrived to peg out new territory. But in the early 1930s the local paper, the *Acton Gazette*, could claim happily that 'we are now entering upon a new concrete age', could greet Western Avenue as 'one of the finest thoroughfares in the London area', while at much the same time describe its spirit as that of Ealing, which it hailed as London's 'Queen of the Suburbs'. A brochure of the early 1930s went into full Metroland mode, rhapsodizing about an Enchanted Land where you could ramble in the countryside.

For all the hyperbole, it is the spirit of the period, the machine age, the 'new concrete age', which in its fusion of romance and utility was so perfectly embodied in the motor car. And, to an extent, in the suburban ethos as well. This book has examined the influence of the automobile in terms of the rich, the poor, the sporting, the amorous, the aesthetes, the country lovers and so on. The 'suburbans' rate their own treatment, not just because of their numbers, but because they are so much in tune with their age. In the words of one historian, the suburbanite is to be seen 'as the leading example of the mass-produced man'. The suburbans emerge famously in literature in the fictional person of Mr Pooter from the Grossmiths' *The Diary of a Nobody*, first published in 1892. They are treated more as a class than as a group in C. F. G. Masterman's classic, *The Condition of England*. In George Greenwood's *England Today* of 1921 they appear again as a distinct type, this time disconcertingly as a class on the verge of revolution, victims of the acute inflation between 1918 and 1920, when prices jumped by nearly a third before falling back again. They are people with largely static earnings, the counterparts of those who were totally ruined by the (infinitely worse) inflation in Austria and Germany. Greenwood has in mind middle class and, like Mr Pooter, lower middle class. Indeed, while warning that they can no longer be relied on to vote Tory, the suburbans are, he says, 'united in fear and dislike of the workers'. That in the 1920s, though not in the 1930s, the migration to the London suburbs was to introduce large numbers of blue-collar workers hardly seems to have affected the outside world's perception of suburbia. (There is also the irony — given the intention of local boroughs to clear central city slums — that the finer the motor highway built, the more expensive would be its ribbon housing.)

By 1926, when the second edition of Greenwood's book appeared, the inflation was over. Now the author refers to motor cycles in the backyard and charabanc trips to the countryside. Certainly his bank clerks earning between £250 to £300 a year (say £9,500 to £11,500 today) could have afforded nothing more exotic. However, Greenwood takes £700 to £800 (£26,500 to £30,500) as a more typical level of income. While gardens and gardening seem to have been popular subjects of conversation on the commuting trains, they would by now have had to share their place with motoring. James Kenward has described his upbringing in his *The Suburban Child*, published in 1955. In suburbia, as Kenward remembered it, there was a prolonged phase after the horse was gone (other than for commercial use) when the bicycle was the normal form of transport. When he himself grew into being what he called a 'definite member of the family' — apparently shortly before the First World War — he was to be taken on excursions. The question was whether his parents should acquire a sidecar to carry him in or a trailer. The trailer was chosen, 'a wickerwork contraption, a direct descendant or collateral relation of the bath-chair' in which he and his mother plus picnic equipment would be hauled by his father on a bicycle. It was hardly ideal and Kenward senior kept his eye open for motors. It was a fastidious eye apparently. One day James and his father came on a parked car. Intrigued and admiring, they went over for a closer look: 'Oh, but it's only a Ford,' said his disappointed father. No doubt Mr Ryder of Burnley (see Chapter 5) would have been equally disappointed. But Mr Ryder would have been less playful in his approach to cars than were members of the Kenwards' suburban London community. They tinkered with them, James said, they enjoyed their glossy appeal, but treated them a bit as they had their bicycles. The car was, so James Kenward insists, a plaything, not a machine prized for its utility. (They shared that view with Mr Ryder.) Nor does it seem that ownership of a car, even at this early stage, brought with it social distinction, as, in its day, a carriage would have done. The car, concludes Kenward, was 'the dream of the Suburban child come true'. This surprisingly romantic attitude is given the more credence by one of the most perceptive writers on suburbia, J. M. Richards, who declared that 'the very spirit of suburbia was a kind of rural-romantic make-believe'.

In fact, defining 'suburbia' is sometimes rather like defining 'Metroland': there is a lot of elasticity about the meaning. Suburbia, Kenward propounds, was not only a geographical state, it was an historical state, and a state of existence and a state of mind. He backs up his metaphysics with an interesting illustration: 'the heart of Suburbia is at its frontier, while its frontier goes rippling forward. Thus, although it is continuously advancing, it remains in the same place relatively — relatively to the shops and to the fields.' His grandfather had lived on the frontier, on one side a few streets and on the other green fields where his children went haymaking and blackberrying and looking for mushrooms. His office in the City was within walking distance, less than five miles away. But the 'ripple' carried the family onwards. For his father, his workplace was ten miles off and he went by train. By James's time the distance was twenty miles.

Paul Vaughan gives another excellent account of life in the London suburbs between the wars in his *Something in Linoleum*. (Another book of his that sounds worth reading is *Exciting Times in the Accounts Department*.) Vaughan defines his objective as being 'to show what it was like to live in a certain district of England in the 1930s, and to have been part of the mass migration to the outer edge of London'. Here the characterization of suburbia is more familiar. Vaughan's parents were second-generation Londoners, living in a flat over two floors in the inner suburb of Brixton, less than two miles south of the Thames. It was a district developed for prosperous City merchants, which while it still retained a few signs of old prosperity, was going downhill very fast. Paul Vaughan describes it in his childhood as clattering and grimy, not at all satisfactory for his parents, who were determined to get on in the world. Their attitude, says their son, was shared by many of the suburbanites: 'the idea of getting on', as he puts it, 'was to hang around those suburban estates like the smell of cooking on Sunday mornings'. Private cars were still scarce in Brixton even by the late 1920s, but the Vaughans possessed

The Kingston By-pass, leading south-west from London, on a quiet day. What were intended as motor roads (though not as motorways in the modern sense) were much less effective than intended because of 'ribbon development'.

one — first what Paul remembered as a small, red open sports car, then a Morris saloon and then, after Mr Vaughan was appointed secretary of the Linoleum and Floorcloth Manufacturers Association, a 15hp Wolseley.

In 1934, as they rose financially and socially, the family moved, to become participants in what their son called 'the rush to an illusory Arcadia'. Their choice fell on New Malden, just on the edge of the London postal district SW20, once fertile farmland, now at the sharp edge of suburban expansion. The farmland by then would have been a very distant memory even had there been anyone left to remember it at all. The area, the urban district of Malden and Coombe, had doubled in population every ten years between 1901 and 1931. In the 1930s — the Vaughans arrived in 1934 — it was to go up by another 75 per cent. Still, the countryside was no more than a short walk away from their house. More in evidence, however, visually and aurally, was the Kingston By-pass. It was no parkway, no safe route out of London, and it had its fair share of ribbon development. Paul Vaughan remembered the spectacular accidents that occurred just by their house and the large cars sweeping down the road as they made for the Ace of Spades roadhouse or the Bear Hotel at Esher.

It is illuminating to look at house and car prices side by side. The Vaughans paid £1,000 (say £38,000 today) for their house, 14 Malden Way. It was on a corner, semi-detached, Swiss chalet style, with its façade in pebble dash to protect the brickwork underneath. There was a garage at the end of the garden. Metroland houses at the time were in much the same price bracket. The 'House Seekers' section of the Metropolitan Railway Company's guide took up nearly half the space in the last issue, published in 1932. A fairly typical house on the Eastcote Hill Estate, four miles from Uxbridge, was advertised at £975, with a £25 deposit. Priced at £1,225 (£46,500) was a rather grander affair at Amersham, 'exclusive Tudor Type', set well back in woodland, with three large bedrooms, one bathroom and built-in garage. While Stanmore Ideal Estates were asking no less than £3,500 for some of their houses, there were plenty, if you did not require a golf course or tennis courts next door, which were listed at under £1,000. The price of the average London house at the time, incidentally, was only £500. Contrast these figures with car prices. The cost in 1932 of a middle of the range Humber Snipe, for instance, was £435. The most expensive Hillman, the Vortic, was priced at £375, while the most opulent Rolls-Royce was going at just under £2,500. It is the easier to see what Mrs Peel meant (see Chapter 5) when, writing at almost exactly the same time, she stressed the high priority given to the car. She added, 'In order to afford it the house becomes a bed-and-breakfast dwelling which may be run with little trouble and expense.'

Metroland was at the upper end of the suburban market and no doubt the Humber Snipe and a smart Hillman were familiar sights in the golf-club car parks. Most 'suburbans' made do with the cheapest models, the small Fords, Morrises and Baby Austins. For by the 1930s the slump was changing the market. The expensive brands were doing badly or tending to stagnate and there was a noticeable fall in demand for cars of over 16hp. On the other hand, there was spirited buying of Sevens, Eights, Nines and Tens, as well as the cheaper sports cars. With an echo of Mrs Peel, a more recent writer on motoring in the 1930s mentions that commentators of the period, at least the more cynical of them, held that in the suburbs a Baby Austin in the garage was more important than a baby carriage in the hall. For it was the Baby Austin, the Austin Seven, which became almost a suburban emblem.

Like William Morris, Herbert Austin was a trained engineer and had been involved with cars since the beginning; in fact, in 1895, while working for Wolseley, he had built the first British petrol-driven car. Austin was less of a pure assembler than Morris, making many of his own components at his Longbridge factory at Birmingham. He had only just escaped disaster when the motor bubble burst in the early 1920s. However, it was at that time, in 1922, that he designed and first built the Austin Seven, the Baby Austin, which was to prove his most successful car. Greenwood referred to the motor cycles in the suburban backyards — it was they, and cyclecars, that Austin was intending to displace, by persuading their owners to graduate into being what he considered proper motorists. His challenge could not have been more direct. At the annual dinner of the Birmingham Motor Cycle Club in 1922, as the guest speaker he declared, to the outrage of some of his listeners, that he was going 'to knock the motor cycle and sidecar into a cocked hat and far surpass it in comfort and passenger-carrying capacity ... I cannot imagine anyone riding a sidecar if he could afford a car.' He designed the Austin Seven so that it would occupy no more space in a garage (or backyard) than a motor cycle and sidecar. Soon after its launch, the price was lowered to £165, the motor cycle/sidecar range. The Austin Seven was distinctive: it hummed like a gnat, said one expert; indeed, it seemed also to imitate gnats in its method of progress, darting forward and bouncing from bump to bump. Top speed initially was 52mph and fuel consumption, so it was claimed, 50 miles per gallon. Part of its success was due to Austin's adroit handling of credit arrangements with dealers, and part also to the prestige gained by an adapted model in motor racing. Above all, it was reliable, remaining in production until 1939. It was the reliability that Austin emphasized, not the selling price, for indeed the Morris Eight and the most modest Ford, when they came on stream, were cheaper.

In Jacques Tati's film *Traffic* (1970) the tourists are marooned in the Paris suburbs, severed by impenetrable traffic from the authentic city, of which they glimpse no more than momentary reflections, of the Eiffel Tower and Notre-Dame, for example, mirrored in windows or glass doors. The film is a brilliant allegory of twentieth-

century life (and twenty-first-century life too for that matter), of the individual lost in megalopolis, an inhabitant of one of the agglomerations, urban with rural decoration, that grip such vast areas of the developed world. The philosopher and critic Lewis Mumford described the predicament the other way round, how the driver is thwarted in a quest for authentic country:

The Austin Seven was on the market from 1923. Some 350,000 were built. Herbert Austin announced that they would 'knock the motor cycle and sidecar into a cocked hat'. They went a long way towards doing so.

> In using the car to flee from the metropolis the motorist finds he has merely transferred congestion to the highway and thereby doubled it. When he reaches his destination, in a distant suburb, he finds the countryside he sought has disappeared; beyond him, thanks to the motorway, lies only another suburb, just as dull as his own.

To many sensitive people of the inter-war years the sprawling conurbations, urban blight run wild, it seemed, evoked horror. Of one town close to London, laden with a large industrial estate, John Betjeman wrote:

Come friendly bombs and fall on Slough!
It isn't fit for humans now,

There isn't grass to graze a cow.
Swarm over, Death!

Betjeman, the poet of Metroland, mourned the devoured county of Middlesex, where, 'In my mind's eye I see dark cedars behind garden walls of brown and red, orange and gold Middlesex brick, the most beautiful brick in England.' Opinion formers tended to ignore what was happening, the BBC showed little interest, the parochial and mannered British film industry virtually none at all. Intellectuals were disdainful, depressed by what Karl Silex deplored as London's 'dolls' houses "ad infinitum"', by the cultural sterility, by the aspidistras and twitching net curtains, bogus romanticism, the Tudor inglenooks, an excessive genteelness of manner, and by what George Greenwood described as a 'life of undisturbed routine'. And you did not need to be an intellectual to despise streets which, according to Paul Vaughan, were never called streets, but Close or Rise or Drive or Crescent, or whimsical house-names like Dunroamin. Contemptuous or, like the writer H. J. Massingham, angered, when driving along an arterial road, he caught sight of a house-name Rookery Nook. How ludicrous and inappropriate, how tragic even, he thought. Here we were, 'all of us, speeding without purpose or question into the future with our minds stock-still in the past ... and conquering nature for the most trivial of ends and progressing, always progressing in an awful automatism'.

Massingham was a romantic, a celebrator of a pastoral and agricultural past, unlike George Orwell who addressed the same subject from a different point of view. Orwell, and Aldous Huxley too, assumed that the tendency of mechanical progress in general was to make life safer and more soft. He takes the transition from horse to motor vehicle as an example. Leave out of account the heavy accident toll, for that would be corrected by serious road planning; leave out too motor racing, which was undeniably dangerous. But for the rest, 'The motor-car has evolved to a point at which anyone who is not blind or paralytic can drive it after a few lessons. Even now [1937] it needs far less nerve and skill to drive a car ordinarily well than to ride a horse ordinarily well.' To Orwell, to attempt to hang on to skills which were made redundant by the machine was dilettantism, behaviour that amounted to nothing more than 'pretty-pretty arty and craftiness'.

Orwell by no means relished the suburbs for their beauty. In *Keep the Aspidistra Flying* (1936) — the title itself a joke at the suburbs' expense — he refers to 'straggling villages on whose outskirts pseudo-Tudor villas stood sniffishly apart, amid their garages, their laurel shrubberies, and their raw-looking lawns'. In *Coming up for Air* (1939) he places his hero, George Bowling, in Ellesmere Road (there are a number of that name in real-life London) in a west London suburb. There are fifty others like it, says Bowling, always with the same long, long rows of little semi-detached houses, with stucco front, creosoted gate, privet hedge and green front door. He rolls out the jokey names — the Laurels, the Myrtles, the Hawthorns, Mon Abri, Mon Repos, Belle Vue. Mortgages are provided by the Hesperides Estate, a subsidary of the Cheerful Credit Building Society.

The book contrasts past and present. But the present is overshadowed by approaching war. 'There was a bombing plane flying low overhead ... for a minute or two it seemed to be keeping pace with the train'; 'a fleet of black bombing planes came over the hill and zoomed across the town'; 'the next war ..coming over the horizon. 1941, they say.' This is *fin d'époque*, the end of an era that coincides with Bowling's own lifetime. He resolves to revisit Lower Binfield, in Oxfordshire, the village where he grew up before the First World War, within bicycling distance of Burford. As he drives along, memories tumble into his mind: of how his father, a corn and seeds merchant, would think it wonderful that a son of his should own a motor car and live in a house with a bathroom; of how his father's business, and those of many other solid tradesmen too, slid away towards bankruptcy; of how even 'Lovegrove the saddler, with cars and motor vans staring him in the face, didn't realize that he was as out of date as the rhinoceros'. And of how the schoolmaster, Porteous, a kind man, was, like the others who could not understand the new world, in reality dead.

And Lower Binfield when he gets there? He drives over the hill on the remembered road, now tarmac, then macadam. It has gone, not demolished, merely swallowed; what he sees is a 'good-sized manufacturing town ... [with] an enormous river of brand-new houses which flowed along the valley in both directions and half-way up the hill on either side'. He asks an old woman the way to the marketplace. She didn't know and answers him in a Lancashire accent.

(There's a lot of them in the south of England now, he thinks.) He tries again, and stops a man who answers him in cockney. Disturbed, Bowling reflects on 'the newness of everything! The raw, mean look! Do you know the look of these new towns that have suddenly swelled up like balloons in the last few years?'

For John Betjeman and Massingham and for many others, it was difficult not to resent this automobile-induced world. Its vulgarities and materialism were deeply obnoxious. Even Orwell himself, most people indeed, resented some part of it. Yet what the travel, the migrations, the new economic configuration had brought about was a profound change in social patterns and relationships. This in the end must be as important a consequence of the motoring age as any. The much respected *New Survey of London Life and Labour*, published in 1930 as a sequel to Charles Booth's classic work of a generation earlier, itself admitting regret for the passing of some of the old originality and colour, commented on how the visible signs of class distinctions were disappearing. How chokers, Derby Coats and ostrich feathers were rarely to be seen, how the cockney dialect and rhyming slang were fading away while the cockney twang was spreading to other classes. It was a change which 'would certainly not have taken place so rapidly had it not been for the much freer mingling of the classes which has resulted from the increase of travel'. Priestley, referring to his 'third England', said that now, for the first time in history, 'Jack and Jill were almost as good as their master'. Another writer of the time put it that the automobile had developed a new type of human outlook and human character.

In fact, it is George Orwell in his *The Lion and the Unicorn*, written as the war started and just before the bombs began to fall, who summed it up best:

> After 1918 there began to appear something that had never existed in England before: people of indeterminate social class. In 1910 every human being in these islands could be 'placed' in an instant by his clothes, manners and accent. That is no longer the case. Above all, it is not the case in the new townships that have developed as a result of cheap motor cars and the southward shift of industry. The place to look for the germs of the future England is in the light-industry areas and along the arterial roads. In Slough, Dagenham, Barnet, Letchworth, Hayes — everywhere, indeed, on the outskirts of great towns — the old pattern is gradu-

ally changing into something new ... There are wide gradations of income, but it is the same kind of life that is being lived at different levels ... It is a rather restless, cultureless life, centred round tinned food, *Picture Post*, the radio and the internal combustion engine. It is a civilization in which children grow up with an intimate knowledge of magnetos and in complete ignorance of the Bible.

10
Aftermath

So, where are we now?

On 7 September 2000 *The Times*, along with other newspapers, warned readers on its front page that by the end of the year the price of petrol was due to hit 87p a litre, of which 70p would be tax. The next day, in its main story, it reported that motorists were upset and were demanding a 2p cut in the fuel tax. Hardly revolutionary, one would have thought, and certainly less intimidating than the French hauliers, out on the roads blocking Calais and Dunkirk to the considerable inconvenience of British tourists on their way home from holiday. Such calls were anyway nothing new, and the British government prepared to follow its standard practice — that is, to ignore the protests at home and to remind the French of their obligation under European Union rules to keep their roads open. What was new, this time round, what caught government and public on the hop, was that the (admittedly long-suffering) British hauliers — claiming 'we are doing this for the people of Great Britain' — took drastic action themselves and, speedily joined by farmers, set up blockades outside the oil refineries. If it was not exactly all hell that broke loose, it was nevertheless a near universal panic, with thirty-mile tailbacks on north of England roads and long, long queues at petrol stations.

Shell announced an imminent disappearance of petrol at the pumps, but they and the other oil companies appeared relaxed, while the tanker drivers made little effort to break through the picket lines. The police too, it was felt, showed little ardour. The Privy Council, meeting at unpolluted Balmoral, backed crisis powers and the Prime Minister declared that he had no intention of following the French government's example of giving way to blockades and cutting fuel taxes. *The Times*, however, was unimpressed, stating that the Prime Minister's attitude was 'a textbook example of appeasement' — and he did later abandon some of the proposed price rises — and accused Stephen Byers, the hapless minister most closely engaged, of talking nonsense.

By 13 September it was over, leaving a number of lessons to be learned. One was how mobile phones enabled protesters to react quickly in face of countermeasures; another was how much 'just-in-time' production methods increased commercial and industrial vulnerability. Above all, the crisis revealed a public utterly dependent on their cars. Virtually addicted in fact. While sympathetic to the blockaders, they demanded a quick solution from the government and, failing to get it, turned for the first time in years to the more or less moribund Conservative opposition, which surged ahead of Labour in the opinion polls. The BBC's *Panorama* programme ran a feature entitled 'Pump Wars —7 days that shook the Government'.

Even a rumour that petrol supplies are at risk is enough to set off a stampede, with the queues forming up at the petrol stations. Immediately demand for petrol accelerates, which of course makes matters worse. This anxiety is not just a British phenomenon. In his book *The Prize* (1991), Daniel Yergin relates a story of the proprietor of an Exxon petrol station in Alaska who, as a sales gimmick, declared that for one day he would offer free petrol. By nine o'clock in the morning the line of cars waiting to fill up stretched for six miles. In January 2003, Michael Meacher, the Environment Minister and the government's champion of green policies, conceded that much of what was desirable from an environmental point of view was out of the question, the political risk of antagonizing motorists was too high. 'In a democracy, you can only go as far as people are willing to go,' said Mr Meacher.

So strong now is the cult of the car in Britain that, according to a report of 2001 by the RAC on motoring habits and attitudes, only a minority of motorists would use their cars less were railway and bus services to improve. Some 90 per cent of drivers said that they would find it very difficult to adjust their style of life were they to be without a car. Part of the trouble is the weakness of the railway system; it is regarded with contempt or, at best, as a joke. Automatically, people's minds fix on a picture of would-be passengers waiting hopelessly on freezing platforms for trains that are either outrageously late or never come at all. There is the tale, perhaps apocryphal, of a frustrated traveller told by a railway employee, 'Anyone would think that the railways were run for you.' Buses are in a better state, but they are usually unprofitable and their services therefore always at risk. It is a familiar story: with public passenger transport, a small drop in revenue can have a disproportionate effect on profits. The trouble is compounded by the very diversity of journeys which people make, the result of wide car ownership, and also of the far-flung and scattered nature of the suburbs in which so many of them live. It is difficult for the public transport to offer a comprehensive service. The whole story of course is familiar: as people get richer (and most people have got richer — more swiftly than did their 1930s predecessors), they want a car, and once they have it, they use it for virtually all their travel, long distance and short. As a result, public transport fares have been forced up; they rose by 20 per cent in inflation-adjusted prices between 1987 and 2000, a rate four times that of the rise in prices overall.

By 1938 car ownership was widespread, penetrating deep into British society. But it was on nothing like the scale of today. In 1938 there were 2,422,000 motor vehicles registered, with one person in every fifteen a car owner. In 2001 there were 29,747,000 motor vehicles registered, of which 25,126,000 were cars. That is, there were 494 cars per 1,000 population. According to the latest statistics, for the first time the average household now spends more on its car than on anything else. Weekly expenditure on all goods averages £398; transport takes £58 (with motoring accounting for some £49), while food absorbs £41.70 and housing £35.90. Commuting by car, unusual before the Second World War, is considerable, as too is the use of cars on business. Just about the only thing not to have risen is the number of road deaths, which is low by international standards; with an increased population and infinitely more automobiles, it is less than half of what it was in pre Hore-Belisha days.

The switch from rail and bus to car has been massive. There have been fluctuations in transport use along the way. In the 1950s and

1960s, for instance, there was a growth in rail travel at the expense of buses. TV has had the effect of keeping people at home. But by the close of the twentieth century 93 per cent of total miles travelled in Britain (leaving out bicyling and walking) were by road. Of these road miles, cars accounted for 85 per cent, bus and rail 6 per cent each, with motor cycles, almost off the statistics, at 1 per cent. As in the inter-war years, not all the increase in motoring has been at the expense of other forms of transport. Cars have created entirely new journeys, encouraging people to undertake trips which, without them, they would not have made at all. Many of those trips are for shopping: it seems that 50 per cent or more of shoppers drive to the shops, which, increasingly, are supermarkets remote from town centres. In prosperous Bracknell in Berkshire, one of a number of new towns built between 1946 and 1970, 80 per cent of those living within ten minutes of the town centre prefer to shop well away for their main purchases. Since bus services are inadequate, it means that most must travel by car. (One disadvantage is the harmful effect on community life.) With freight, the story is the same as ever, a steady transfer from rail to road, encouraged by the arrival on the scene of 'juggernaut' lorries, which permit lower operating costs per ton of goods carried. In 1968 another transport act made another attempt to push freight traffic back on to the railways, but the result was just the same.

The bus is undoubtedly egalitarian, but the car is more ambiguous. Car ownership, as such, unadorned, can hardly now denote more than the most elementary privilege. But then, a step closer and we find a multitude of adornments, whether in the form of larger engines, more splendid bodies, television screens or whatever. And, emphasizing privilege, employers grade the cars they allocate to their staff according to a pecking order. While the experience of Rolls-Royce and the *parvenus* is not to be forgotten, it cannot be doubted that in normal circumstances to drive a Bentley, or any other very expensive car, is prestigious.

The earlier motorists gained esteem through the mere fact of ownership, and they did not look forward to the prospect of mass motoring. The reason was less snobbery than loss of enjoyment. It would mean the end of 'the open road', a favourite and evocative expression. 'There is a joy in the open road, the thin white line stretching afar into illimitable distance, where the miles fly past like the wind,' wrote George D. Abraham in 1929. And in *The Morris Owner's Road Book* the car, the magic carpet, offers 'enjoyment of the kingdom whose portal is the open road'. There are other common expressions, as when J. J. Hissey asks himself, 'I wonder whether our descendants in the far future will ever look back longingly and lovingly on the "good old motoring days".' Charles Jarrott, in the preface to the 1928 edition of his *Ten Years of Motors and Motor Racing*, published originally in 1906, wrote that the romance of the early days of motoring was now forgotten. Max Pemberton in 1907 thought of how motorists dream great dreams of the future, with few of them likely to be justified by 'the slow and unimaginative march of reality'. To Pemberton:

> When every high road is alive with cars, when there is a ceaseless roaring of exhausts and blowing of horns, when the railways are almost forgotten and the reign of the car undisputed, then I venture to question if pleasure will have any say in the matter at all.

Others too, even if they were little more than onlookers, could appreciate the old days. In 1928 H. V. Morton found among the 'ubiquitous museums' of Hull one which contained an 'amusing collection' of motor cars. They will become more interesting and valuable as time goes on, he thought. He was of course quite right. In the 1950s, not that far away from the 1930s, Nicole de Buron wrote a book, *The Bride and the Bugatti*. She (the bride) and her husband bought a 1935 Bugatti, once used for racing, no doors, nowhere for luggage, an almost invisible windscreen, which demanded 'the patience of a saint' for the raising or lowering of the hood, and was very noisy. But the joy — fancy having such a thing in the age of the atom bomb! High prices go now not just for famous cars but for motoring artefacts as well. A recent article in the 'How to Spend It' section of a Saturday edition of the *Financial Times* was devoted to car mascots:

> Could there be anything more romantic, more evocative of the age of Grande Luxe at its most opulent, than gliding through Mayfair in a V12 Hispano-Suiza with a moulded glass 'Victoire' mascot mounted on the radiator cap?

It was a good question, but the thought was of the 'Victoire', not the car. It would be worth £10,000 on its own. But a really rare mascot, a top example by René Lalique, would come in at £160,000.

What is more, automobile manufacturers are now paying increased attention to the motoring past. Daimler Chrysler are producing a rival in luxury to the Rolls-Royce called the Maybach, named after the designer of perhaps the best of all veteran cars, the 1901 Mercedes 35hp. It is to be sold, the information goes, with two sets of personalized matching golf clubs in the boot, a fine period touch. Volkswagen have produced a new Beetle which echoes the design and style of the original, and their forthcoming luxury model is to be called the Phaeton, a name from horse and carriage days. Down the price range is the Tamora, its character that 'of an old-fashioned sports car', built by TVR of (unexpectedly) Blackpool, which while making no more than 1,200 cars a year, produce their own engines and plan to produce their own gearboxes. The tiny Smart Roadster, neither powerful nor expensive, but with 'the most entertaining exhaust bark this side of a Ferrari 360', is intended to be thought of as in the mould of a classic 1960s sports car. There is too, of course, the Morgan, faithful for years to a classic style. Further evidence of the boom for 'retro-motoring' comes with the Chrysler PT Cruiser, its front reminiscent of an old-time Cord. (This return to old motoring days is by no means unique; it is part of a more general nostalgia strongly manifested in the craze for tracing family trees. The good news is that, on the Internet, family-history websites attract more visitors than pornography.)

But to leave their cars (and pornography) and return to the people, how did they visualize the future? Pioneer motorist, Max Pemberton, imagined it with distaste, and with prescience — congested, noisy roads from which the fun has gone. H. G. Wells drew an astonishingly accurate picture at a time when there was still practically nothing to go by. There were utopians, or 'autopians' as the American expression went; 'Greys', 'the big cigarette with the choice flavour' for one, pictured London in AD 2500 as part of an advertising campaign. Here were cars powered by atomic energy driving over the rubber roadways along Piccadilly, selecting the track with the speed limit which suited them best — 50, 100, 150 and 200mph were on offer.

The motoring journalist Leonard Henslowe was no Wells — he would have been astounded by a comparison — but he knew how cars were evolving and their technical possibilities. As a writer, he was, to put it mildly, eclectic, with books such as *The Gospel of*

Health, How to Keep Slim and Fit and *The Folk Lore of Borneo* under his belt. To his *Motoring for the Million* of 1922, he annexed a chapter entitled 'A Dream of 1950'. Henslowe dreams that he wakes to find himself in the middle of a populous garden town. Every house along the 'main boulevard' has a garage attached, some of them built below ground and 'only discernible by a lift entrance on the surface'. There is no corrugated iron or matched boarding to be seen, or even brickwork, for that has been long ago replaced by reinforced concrete. Everything is in keeping with the modern trend of architectural design, which means roller shutters instead of doors. 'I learned,' said Henslowe, 'that traffic was entirely mechanical', with horses, long abandoned, only to be seen at the zoo, where they keep company with other rare specimens from the past such as rats, mice and vermin, species completely eliminated from the civilization of 1950. Cars are of every imaginable kind, from miniature two-seaters in which nurse takes baby for an airing to the most majestic super-limousines, six-wheeled and electrically propelled. The tradesmen's boys and girls are all travelling on motors of one sort or another. 'Self-starters of sorts were evidently fitted to every car, as I saw no one starting up a car by hand. Silence in running was the rule, and I noticed a complete absence of vibration also; while noise from gear changing had been overcome, as the gear box as understood in our day was non-existent.' Nobody carries spare wheels, for they are unnecessary. Fuel is very cheap, but even so private vehicles are mainly powered by electricity, and there are recharging stations on every street. Instruction in mechanics is given in school, with all children taught the elements of traction engineering. Servants are required to be able to drive as part of their training. Spare parts and accessories are standardized, and so interchangeable, whatever the make of car. (Harley Earl and General Motors would have applauded, for it meant creative energy could be directed entirely towards the looks of a car.)

> The law required all cars to carry drip pans under the chassis, which explained why the streets were so extraordinarily clean ... Fuel purity, more perfect combustion, and an ingenious invention in the exhaust boxes had the effect of leaving the air in a much purer condition than it had been ever since the motoring movement began. In fact, I was told that about 1930, so horribly had carbon di-oxide and other exhaust gases from motor vehicles poi-

soned the air of cities, that the health of the community had been greatly endangered ... In this advanced age no oily, smoky, or smelly odour was tolerated under any circumstances whatever, and so, living in town was just as healthy as living in the country.

There are some 1920s period touches. For instance, Henslowe adds that driving cattle in the streets has become almost entirely prohibited. Parking in 1922 was already a worry: Henslowe calls the matter of where to leave cars during lunch or dinner 'a great problem'. In the 1950s restaurant, he says, the whole ground floor and 'sub-ground floors' are occupied entirely as garage space, with the complete frontage open to the street, so that 400 cars can be garaged at once by the aid of turntables. Moreover, while you are eating, your car can be replenished with fuel (or presumably have its battery recharged) and the tyre pressures adjusted, by means of one or other of 100 pipes which protrude at intervals from the floor. But what perhaps is most striking is the attention the author gives, even from the early 1920s, to pollution, which already, as he sees it, is on the verge of 'greatly endangering' the health of the community.

Other predictions of the future assume an integrated transport system, one that would incorporate not just railways but aircraft. In 1913 a German writer, Ernst Seiffert, looked forward fifty years to 1963. The ground level of his city is reserved for pedestrians, who travel on moving sidewalks at 10 or 20 or 30kph as they choose. The next level is for cars, and the one above that for the elevated railway. The top level of all is for 'airship and aviation operations'. (It is a city close to Fritz Lang's *Metropolis*.) Then there is an astonishing conceit presented by H. G. Wells back in 1893 in the *Pall Mall Gazette* entitled, 'The Advent of the Flying Man'. People do not realize, he wrote, how extremely close we are to the art and mystery of flying. Not, he stresses, just ballooning. Wells foresees a time — in the far future — when in the City of London at the stroke of five o'clock

a vast cloud of winged figures will begin to erupt from among the grimy roofs of the crowded business houses, and hang for a moment eddying and circling in the air after the cramping labours of the day. The dome of St Paul's will be covered with the fathers and sons of suburban families [each carrying, says Wells, his inseparable bag and umbrella], poising themselves for their homeward flight.

If aviation and automobilism grew up at close to the same time, it was none the less obvious that in terms of technology the automobile was the junior partner. Winston Churchill in 1909 had reassured Wilfrid Blunt that his worries about the danger to children on Sussex roads were exaggerated, since in ten years' time flying machines would have superseded motors as an amusement of the rich. In September 1923 the *News of the World*, announcing to it readers that small aeroplanes could now be bought for around £250 (less than £10,000 today), forecast that the day was rapidly approaching when the man in the street would own and drive his little aeroplane, just as in 1923 he drove his motor cycle and light car. It became understood, particularly among the young, that the car was merely a forerunner, and that the future of passenger transport, except perhaps for short runs, lay with the helicopter and light aircraft. It was an opinion shared by experts who visualized a world full of the most marvellous innovations — flying cars, amphibious cars, rocket- and nuclear-powered cars.

If motoring and electricity worked in harness as instruments of social and economic change, motoring and aviation were united as symbols of the scientific imagination, and of the aesthetic imagination as well. The classic aesthetic figuration of the automobile is generally considered that of the Italian poet Marinetti in his 'The Founding and Manifesto of Futurism', published by the *Figaro* in February 1909:

> A racing car whose hood is adorned with great pipes, like serpents of explosive breath — a roaring car that seems to ride on shrapnel — more beautiful than the *Victory of Samothrace.* We want to hymn the man at the wheel, who hurls the lance of his spirit across the Earth, along the circle of its orbit.

Other artists of the earlier part of the century were exhilarated by the power and speed of the automobile. Countless writers, as we have seen, and painters and sculptors such as Picabia, Balla, Derain, who described his Bugatti as more beautiful than any work of art, and later Henry Moore, a Jaguar fan who spoke of his car as 'sculpture in motion'. Just as in Britain a number of the leading figures in motoring were fliers — Rolls, Moore-Brabazon, Lanchester for example — so was it the same everywhere, particularly in France, which took the lead in aviation as it had in motoring. Wilbur Wright

in 1908 developed his Flyer at Léon Bollées's factory at Le Mans, and Gabriel Voisin, another important French car manufacturer, was a pioneer aircraft designer and even flew over the Seine in one of his own aircraft as early as 1906. Marinetti himself wrote on the aeroplane and, in the same year that he composed the piece quoted above, dedicated a play to Wilbur Wright. And H. G. Wells, who, in his *Anticipations* of 1902, wrote so perspicaciously of the automobile and its effects, not least on the 'probable diffusion of great cities', is more famous for his interest in the air, as for example in his *The First Men in the Moon* and *The War in the Air*.

The model for a 'flying car' designed by Norman Bel Geddes, 1945. Geddes, 'a phenomenon of continuous reinvention', was one of a number of inventors intent on constructing a multipurpose vehicle.
© Harry Ransom Humanities Research Center, University of Texas at Austin, the Norman Bel Geddes Collection.

Together aviation and automobilism influenced the design of all sorts of commonplace objects. Moreover, the aircraft influenced car design. An obvious example is the fins that decorated (they were of no practical use) American cars in the 1950s, which were based by Harley Earl on the Lockheed P-38. Tail lights were modified to resemble flaming rocket exhausts. A completely revolutionary car, the Dymaxion, which never progressed beyond prototype, was by intention multifunctional — to act as automobile, aircraft or hovercraft. It was designed by Richard Buckminster Fuller, an inventor with a background in the aviation industry. The eminent designer Norman Bel Geddes, 'a phenomenon of continuous reinvention', predicted that in 1960 'the average person will be flying about in a small mosquito plane, the roadster of the air'. His last project was a 'flying car'. From the early 1950s Molt Taylor, another American aviation enthusiast, built a dozen or so flying cars, which could be driven to the airport with wings and fuselage towed in the form of a trailer. In the 1930s there was also a British prototype of a futuristic car in the Burney Streamline, built at Maidenhead.

Nevertheless, for many years the automobile held place as the definitive representation of the machine age. An expert in 1972 wrote, 'The automobile industry stands for modern industry all over the globe. It is to the twentieth century what the Lancashire cotton mills were to the early nineteenth century: the industry of industries.' It was, of course, nearer to hand, and familiar in a way that the aeroplane was not.

In the 1930s, at any rate the later 1930s, the government was solicitous of aviation and of the British aviation industry, above all as an essential means of defence in an increasingly unstable Europe. But in terms of pressure on land and on social amenity, it was automobilism and its consequences that were the problem. Another act of Parliament tightened up the rules on ribbon development, and the Green Belt Act of 1938 made possible the construction — or at least the start of construction — of a green belt around London, a girdle to constrain suburban outflow and to create a barrier between town and country. Not everyone was enthusiastic: the Council for the Preservation of Rural England was opposed, afraid that developers would leapfrog the belt and put more countryside at risk than would be rescued. Still, it was generally felt, in the years following the Second World War, that the scheme was a success. Indeed, one view was that the legislation was passed only just in time.

The most positive reaction to the environmental and demographic anxieties of the 1930s and to the studies and reports that followed, not least the Barlow Report, was a package of legislation carried through by the 1945 Labour government, of which the New Towns Act and the Town and Country Planning Act were just two examples. A distinguished authority on planning, Sir Peter Hall, has put it that between 1945 and 1952 Britain set up one of the most comprehensive and powerful planning systems in the world. Restriction on development was stringent, with all proposals vetted to make sure that they were in accordance with the published plans issued by local authorities. A heavy tax was laid on development gains.

Motoring was embedded in the minds of politicians and civil servants for other reasons as well. The war had left Britain in a parlous economic state; massive exports were vital, with no industry better placed to contribute than the motor industry. The background was favourable. Britain had recovered from the Depression more strongly than other countries. In 1938 its motor industry had built 447,000 vehicles, many fewer than the Americans but more than the Germans at 340,000, the French at 227,000 and the Italians at 67,000. Even comparison with the Americans was encouraging, for, in the admittedly (for them) especially poor year of 1938, United States production was half what it had been in 1929, while the British was nearly double. More important, the foreground was promising as well; with much of Europe in ruins, its motor industries were in no state to compete. In 1950 Britain took a 52 per cent share in world automobile exports.

A great deal was done by the government to encourage the industry's drive for exports. Materials required for automobile construction were controlled centrally and allocated in favour of exporters. New cars were made available to the home market very slowly, and petrol rationing, at times very strict indeed, remained in force until 1950. At the end of that year, less than one-third of the 2.25 million cars on the road had been registered since the war. The government also changed the method of motor taxation, dropping the link with horsepower. This tax, long controversial, discouraged imports but also militated against exports, since it encouraged a type of engine unpopular with overseas buyers. (In its heyday this tax was higher for the Model T than for a 4.5-litre supercharged Bentley.)

Yet fifty years on, it is a sad story: of the immense number of motor vehicles on British roads very few are British. Many certainly were made in Britain, but by foreign-owned companies. Governments must take some of the blame for what has happened. While they were supportive of the industry in some ways, there were conflicting interests at work, one of which was the need to revive the distressed areas which had suffered so harshly before the war. The remedy of the 1945 Labour government was to unravel, so far as they could, the pre-war pattern, to enforce a reverse migration, a

253

relocation of industry, away from the south-east and the West Mid-lands to the north and Wales. Building of industrial plants, whether on new or existing sites, was controlled by industrial development certificates. For the motor industry the effect was higher transport costs, rather worse industrial relations and a delay in the reorganization which would be needed badly once the favourable circumstances of the 1940s were passed.

More serious yet, and for which governments again can be only partly blamed, was the fundamental weakness of the British economy over the decades, the tendency of any boom to get out of control and to end in tears. Thus the policy of 'Stop-Go', the frequent changes in interest rates and tax, particularly purchase tax and hire purchase costs. In such circumstances motor manufacturers, like others, found it difficult to anticipate consumer demand and so the appropriate level of investment. An example of the process was the Maudling Boom, named after the Chancellor of the Exchequer. In late 1962 the economy was let rip in a dash for growth; just short of two years later there was a serious economic crisis and a run on the pound. To avoid devaluation the newly elected Labour government initiated a credit squeeze and raised income tax, and the motor boom brought into being by the 1962 measures collapsed and was followed by five years of decline. The perennial financial problems meant the abandonment of many good intentions. There was an urgent need for road improvements, not only because of neglect during the war years but because of the increase in automobile use. The planned expenditure for the 1948 roads programme was reduced by 80 per cent; the first part of the M1 motorway was opened only in 1959. The slow speeds generally possible on British roads gave manufacturers less incentive to produce cars capable of the sustained high-speed cruising, which by the 1950s was easily obtainable abroad.

The immediate post-war success did not rely just on the lack of competition, for many British cars still had a fine reputation. In 1951 New York's Museum of Modern Art exhibited eight cars chosen for excellence of design. They were a 1930 Mercedes Model SS, a 1937 Cord, a 1941 Lincoln Continental, a 1939 Bentley, a 1939 Talbot three-seater, Pininfarina's 1949 Cisitalia coupé, a 1951 Jeep and a 1948 Model TC MG. Three out eight was pretty good. However, such distinction was on the wane. British cars — with exceptions — looked increasingly out of date, to an extent merely reflecting the unenterprising and dull atmosphere of the time. A recent book on the motor car and popular culture has drawn attention to an odd 1950s advertisement in the *Field* which features in 'an oily pastiche of middle class manners' Giles and Charles, dressed in dinner jackets, engaged in a stilted dialogue about the merits of their Wolseleys beneath the awning at the entrance to a nightclub. Their wives in evening dress and fur wraps stand waiting, smiling indulgently. (Wolseleys, best known as police cars, were not natural nightclub habitués.) Surely, one thinks, this must be an advertisement of the 1930s that has strayed ineptly into the post-war world.

Wolseleys were just one of a confusing number of British models bearing good old names but, appearance aside, more or less indistinguishable. Regularly when the Motor Show came round, there were reports in the papers of puzzled foreign buyers. Yet if in one way there were too many models, in another there were too few. Nowadays, if you want more engine power for the same body space, there is no problem. With a Honda Civic, for instance, you order the 1.6 version rather than the 1.4, paying something like an extra £500. In the 1950s you would have had to order (and pay for) a larger car.

Britain was well known for its small cars, and one reason for the motor industry's growth in the 1930s had been their popularity with Depression-hit buyers overseas. The reputation persisted and, in its time, the Mini was to be very successful. However, the greatest small car of all, ready to fall into the British lap, was rejected. After the war, we had the opportunity to take over the Volkswagen factory. A committee that considered the proposal, headed by Sir William Rootes, declared the Volkswagen to have no future: it was ugly, noisy and insufficiently robust for British roads. (Ford also turned it down.) In fact, it was not ugly, it was streamlined; it was not exceptionally noisy, and its ability to cope with roads much more difficult than those in Britain became famous.

With the merger of Austin and Morris in 1952, it appeared that the bewildering diffuseness of models would be rationalized. But it turned out to be one of the most half-hearted mergers ever, with a continuance of separate boards of directors, separate accounts and cars which competed against each other. In 1953, with Volkswagen in the lead, German production overtook the French, in 1956 it overtook the British. The motor cycle industry started to lose out to the Japanese. More mergers. In 1967 Rootes sold out to Chrysler, a year later Morris Austin (British Motor Holdings) were merged with Leyland Motors, the successful commercial-vehicle manufacturers. Successful, but there were depressing indicators. When Donald Stokes (by then in charge of the combined firms) had been appointed managing director of Leyland in 1963, he was the only director under seventy. Again the merger stalled. A manager of the new British Leyland described the situation in the company: 'multiplicity of style, multiplicity of technology, multiplicity of everything ... The organization lacked a common system, a common ethos or culture.'

British productivity levels were very low. The number of motor vehicles produced annually by each British worker in 1955 rated at 4.1 to Germany's 3.9; in 1965 it was 5.8 to 6.4, and in 1973, while Britain was still at 5.8, Germany had risen to 7.7. On another measure of efficiency, the fixed assets per worker, the comparison was even more grim. British Leyland in 1974 accounted for £920, with Ford (UK) at £2,657, Renault at £2,694, Volkswagen at £3,632 and Volvo at £4,662.

While commercial vehicle exports were still strong, for cars 1974 marked the first year since 1913 that imports exceeded exports. On top of all its other troubles the industry, with the Kennedy Round reducing import duties, and entry into the Common Market, was obliged to compete without the old tariff protection and without Imperial Preference, which stood behind exports to the Commonwealth.

Low productivity and low investment. One very important reason was the atrocious relations between management and workforce and the quite excessive number of strikes. A source of irritation from the point of view of the workers was the traditional fluctuation of wages. Back in the 1930s, for instance, George Mason, an engineer working at Cowley and a migrant from Lancashire, found that his weekly wage could vary between £3 12s 6d (£3.62) and 8s 5d (£0.42). Motor manufacture was well paid in general terms but it was cyclical. There had of course been strikes in the inter-war years — that of the iron moulders over four months during 1919 and 1920 involving 50,000 men and causing great disruption was long remembered. There had too been a serious strike at Pressed Steel in 1934. However, by and large the unions were weak in the motor industry, wages were good and a lot of people were looking for jobs. The Second World War changed the relationship, for now firms were clamouring for workers. The war over, the unions were more powerful and management controls and skills feeble. The situation was the more unsatisfactory in that the unions were competing with each other for members, complicating negotiations with management. And more unsatisfactory yet, as power shifted to the shop floor, to the shop stewards. Collective agreements, reached with difficulty, were frequently unenforceable, and at times there was near anarchy.

By the 1970s the government could no longer use the motor industry as an instrument to further its policies, be they regional relocation or the heating or dampening of consumer demand. Harold Wilson described it as an essential part of the country's economic base, which meant that every effort must be made to rescue it. British Leyland (BL) was nationalized, the management purged, the shop stewards cowed, but it was past saving; it no longer made sense to go on feeding in money. In the late 1980s it came to an end.

By that time anyway there was a new spirit abroad, a doubt as to whether governments could do more than provide benign conditions for economic management, a belief that no more than King Canute could they hold back the waves, the natural forces. By the end of the 1970s, countries, even those in the still-extant Eastern bloc, were turning towards private enterprise and the introduction of private capital into formerly state-run monopolies. (They were likely, however, still to retain some degree of control, for instance in price setting.) Mrs Thatcher's government was naturally in the van of the movement. Their attention was taken by public road transport, most of which had been in effect nationalized since the beginning of the 1930s. Most, but not all, for the Conservative government of the day had privatized road haulage in 1953. Then it was the turn for the privatization of bus and coach services, and later of the railways. Now there is no more forceful protagonist of private finance for public services than the Labour government in its renovation of the battered London tube.

With or without King Canute, by the end of the twentieth century a sea change was taking place in attitudes towards the automobile. It was not that there was a falling off in degree of car dependence, as the reaction to the refinery blockades was to make clear. It was rather that there existed a more universal awareness of its consequences than there had been back in the times of Professor Joad.

The congestion in towns and country, the evident pollution, were having their effect. There was too a very vocal opposition to the spread of motorways, which were hacking their way through the countryside. An 'unbridled spread' was how John Bolster, a writer on motoring and an ex-racing driver, put it in 1976, noting how dramatically public attitudes towards the private car had changed since the late 1960s. The Automobile Age came to an end in the early 1970s, wrote a leading American authority, James Flink, adding that the automobile had not been 'a historically progressive force in American civilization' since at least the 1960s.

The technical stagnation of the motor industry increased disillusion. James Flink believed that technological stagnation had set in as early as 1925. By then or by a year or two later, apart from automatic transmission, the major mechanical innovations that distinguished cars of the period after the Second World War from the 1908 Model T had been incorporated. Others would allow some progress after that, but would agree that by the 1950s it had come to a halt. The comparison with what was happening in the air was startling and Flink also pointed out that new industries were connected with aerospace or electronics. The anti-automobile movement was buttressed by two books, both American. One was John Keats's *The Insolent Chariots* of 1958, which excoriated American car design. 'Since 1900', Keats wrote, 'American automobiles have grown longer, lower, wider, faster, jazzier, more complicated and more, much more expensive — but far less efficient — and no safer.' Then in 1965 there burst on the scene a famous diatribe against American cars and those who made them. Not only had there been no advance technologically, but cars were not even safe to drive, was the message rammed home eloquently by Ralph Nader in his *Unsafe at Any Speed: The Designed-in Dangers of the American Automobile*, with its violent attack on a particular car, the Chevrolet Corvair.

It was not only the automobile itself which, from a technical point, was advancing slowly. Little progress was being made towards the solution of old problems. One most unpleasant discovery was that road improvements (the old panacea of the RAC and AA) delayed congestion only for a short time: traffic expanded to fill the road space available. It is often difficult to compare traffic congestion, pre-war and post-war, without verified figures, for opinion on the subject is likely to be highly subjective. Rudyard Kipling, wintering in Monte Carlo in 1926, considered that 'the motor car has made the Riviera an hell — and a noisy, smelly one'. How bad it really was by later standards is hard to judge; the observation was jotted down in his diary, and could well amount to no more than the sort of off-the-cuff remark one makes when irritable. Nevertheless, that congestion in London was taken very seriously in the inter-war period is evident in a warning made in the authoritative *New Survey of London Life and Labour* of 1930, which states that 'unless some definite policy with regard to the main traffic arteries in the central area is adopted soon, the growth of street traffic in London, and with it probably the growth of London itself, must be checked and restricted'. *The Economist* in 1936 observed that 'possibly a general ban on the poor patient horse [in central London] may be followed by the prohibition of private cars in the centre of our cities, if the interests of reasonably speedy public transport are to be adequately served'. (Nearly seventy years later we may have a congestion charge but we have not gone as far as that. We are, though, reverting, in principle, to a form of Road Tax: the surplus from the London congestion charge is to be put to transport improvement.)

The Economist also came out with some startling figures, reporting that 57 per cent of sentences given in English and Welsh courts were in respect of traffic offences, a statistic to give extra pertinence to the joke about the small girl who asks her mother what policemen did when there weren't any motors. One answer was that in those days whatever they did was unlikely to be bothersome to the upper and middle classes. Disagreeable and frequent contacts with the police were another by-product of motoring. Efforts were made of course to avoid them: just as in our time you can, if you wish, buy radar devices to give warning of approaching police, the early motorists could purchase 'Dunhill's Bobby Finders', magnifying spectacles which enabled the wearer to spot a police constable at half a mile even if he were 'disguised as a respectable man'.

One early and ambiguous expression of a counter-culture was the hot-rod craze, in the main an American phenomenon, though through cinema, particularly through such films as James Dean's *Rebel without a Cause* and the motor cycling *Easy Rider*, it was influential elsewhere. Young men, with or without girls, would meet to race on empty stretches of road, preferably with beefed-up engines to their cars. By the 1960s it became part of a general youth protest against society and the cars involved were intentionally battered and stripped down, without the least pretence to conventional appearance. Yet, at the same time, life revolved around the cars; they symbolized 'the feverish freedom of breaking loose and getting away'. This sounds like an expression of motoring in its sociable role. It could be the opposite, motoring as the solace of the lone wanderer. Jack Kerouac's *On the Road* is famous, but in this quotation the wanderer is the sad hero of Paul Auster's *The Music of Chance*:

> Speed was of the essence, the joy of sitting in the car and hurtling himself forward through space. That became a good beyond all others, a hunger to be fed at any price ... The car became a sanctum of invulnerability, a refuge in which nothing could hurt him anymore. As long as he was driving, he carried no burdens, was unencumbered by even the slightest particle of his former life.

In something of the same mood a British writer has described the car as a place where 'you are physically cocooned', and — an unusual comparison — the nearest we get to the lavatory at the bottom of the garden, where people once went to have a little time to themselves. Perhaps too, relief at solitude explains the patience of drivers — their eyes from time to time skipping over the mendacious speedometer which pretends that their car is capable of 150mph — in the interminable rush-hour queues that wait to enter or to leave the big cities.

The car as sanctuary and, as always, but now more explicitly, the car as menace. Violence (with sex) appears in macabre form in J. G. Ballard's horrifying *Crash,* and, less extreme, in Andy Warhol's 'Car Crash' prints. Sometimes, though, aggressive appeal is taken to absurdity, as when Chrysler, taking over Rootes, tried to give a kickstart to sales by calling their very ordinary new model the Avenger.

Descriptive writing is sharper than it used to be. To Heathcote Williams the automobile is a credit card on wheels — it demonstrates the size of your salary:

> And you want that automobile to be *overpowering,*
> Feed people's fantasies about your success
> And breed even more success.
> > Impress. Success.
> > > Let safety suck.

In a witty book published in 1991, he goes on to interpret what car advertisements mean behind the flannel. He renders Volvo's 'Drive it like you hate it' as 'Car as enemy. The enemy only you can control'. For Saab's 'Nothing performs like a Saab' read 'The car as stud' and for Honda's 'For people who lead the good life. A car that leads the simple life' read 'How to radiate a high-minded Vegan glow while eating steak tartare'. Heathcote Williams's book is entitled *Autogeddon*, an example of the puns which collect around motoring subjects — the old one, 'Autopia', and then 'Motopia', 'Carmageddon' and 'Autokind' as in another book, *Autokind vs. Mankind*.

Reality was coming home. The familiar anxieties — congestion, pollution, destruction of the physical environment — were embraced by the anti-motoring movement. In fact, damage to the environment was opposed so vigorously (with civil disobedience not excluded) that at one time the preservationists succeeded in thwarting the motorway programme. An especially bitter fight, and one where the protesters failed, was over the proposed M3 at Twyford Down near Winchester. It was a test case, since the area was officially designated as one of 'Outstanding Natural Beauty'. The environmentalists argued for a tunnel, a proposal rejected on grounds of cost. The road crashed through. So, people might well ask, what value was to be put on protective labels? There was also now concern about the social effect of mass car ownership on country villages once liberated by bus and car from their centuries-old confinement. One village — examined briefly in Chapter 4 — was Swanbrooke Down in East Anglia. By 1990, the blacksmith's forge with its well in the yard, formerly the village meeting place, was a secondary home belonging to a London merchant banker. Ironically the internal-combustion engine had ended up by making transport more difficult for many people, so an old inhabitant told Rosamond Richardson, author of the village's history:

> When I first come here, there were five butchers and three grocers delivering, and two bakers doing a round, so we weren't dependent on transport. The motor car was the end of village life; if you haven't got your own transport now, you've had it.

Bus services had gone and, years before, the railway branch lines. Outings fostered by charabanc and bus dwindled. And the drawbacks to some of the charms of motoring so attractively set forth in the old Badminton book became clearer. The much more interesting social life that enabled you to escape your 'near neighbours of whom you have seen almost too much', of which Lord Montagu had written, could lead to the dissolution of local ties and communities. Margaret Ward at Rottingdean, writing in 1993, reported that neighbours no longer mixed so well as they did in the old days, no longer for instance did they walk together to fetch children from school. Doubt was cast on a standard conception of the car, that through its power to open up the countryside, it acted as a stimulant to the imagination. A writer on a Fen village, while conceding that cars and television had greatly eased the old isolation, declared that they had also had the effect of dulling the imagination of the inhabitants.

Old solutions may no longer work. There is, for instance, the admired and cherished green belt to London, the fragility of which is all too evident. The population of London continues to grow and in the next ten years is expected to rise by 700,000. The M25 motorway that encircles the metropolis was constructed almost entirely on green-belt land, and housing (justified on the grounds of 'exceptional need') steadily devours more land. In south-east England as a whole it seems that in each of the last few years an area of green-belt land three times the size of Hyde Park has been annexed. Again in London, plans are in hand to replace with traffic lights hundreds of the zebra crossings, the old Belisha Beacons, because they are now deemed unsafe for pedestrians. 'Sleeping policemen', the road humps so popular with local authorities as a means of 'calming traffic' (a masterful euphemism) are, so we are told, actually dangerous in that they delay ambulances. What is more, they increase car emissions, and also damage automobile suspension, to the extent that Brighton taxi drivers have added a supplement to their fares to pay for the cost of repair. A novel return to the past as a way of reducing road accidents is being taken by Italy, where the accident toll is very high. From 2004 the speed limit on three-lane motorways is to go up from 130kph to 150kph. The transport minister is reassuring, stating that 'all psychologists and doctors say people who go faster drive better and are more careful'.

For what has happened on the road to Autopia or, to borrow from the evocative title of Emma Rothschild's 1973 book, the road to Paradise? This book, *Paradise Lost: The Decline of the Auto-industrial Age*, argued that in the 1930s and 1940s the automobile, instead of remaining a practical and efficient means of transport, became a symbol of wealth and power. She attacked the fantastical cars of the day and, quoting Nader, the failure of motor company engineers, and their inability to overrule stylists and cost-efficiency experts. The trouble was, though, that the public liked these cars, and were determined to buy 'overornamented, overchromed, overly expensive' gas guzzlers. For, as Keats pointed out, in 1954, when Chrysler brought out a shorter, sturdier, frill-less, easier-to-park car, it was a dreadful flop and sales dropped by half. So Chrysler back-tracked, replacing it with a bigger affair, blazing in three colours and with huge tail fins. Sales soared.

Finally, the message got across, mainly to the benefit of the Japanese motor industry. In any event the problem was not really a British one. Ours was, and is, worse: for we are a small country with an affluent population packed closely together, and with a rail system that has so deteriorated as to be quite inadequate, and, from the look of it, whatever is done, likely to remain that way for a long time. It was not that we had not been warned. Lewis Mumford, in Sir Peter Hall's words, 'almost the bible of the regional planning movement', for years urged that the emergence of the automobile made essential a more comprehensive and analytical approach to the transportation system. As early as 1930 Mumford had written that the American dream of a nation on wheels, which began with the covered wagon, had come to 'a dreary terminus'. In his preface to the 1964 British edition to his *The Highway and the City*, he observed that though the virtues of Britain and the United States are highly individualized, our vices are indistinguishable, for they are those common throughout Western civilization. Why had we not learned from American experience?

> Our disastrous American experience with mono-transportation by automobile, which has already gutted out the interiors of our great cities, should be of some service, if only your planners and administrators would take note of the dire results. Unfortunately, your leaders in transportation are now, with the smiling confident faces and the tightly closed eyes of sleepwalkers, extravagantly planning to imitate all our mistakes ... The great promise of the automobile forty years ago was that, with its flexibility of movement and its ease in climbing grades that the railroad train balked at, it would round out the rail system and produce a complex

regional transportation network that would provide for a more even distribution of population and industry, instead of the prevailing 'apoplexy at the heart and paralysis at the extremities'.

In his chapter on London, Mumford goes on to say:

> If motor transportation is to be the liberation and pleasure it should be, we should plan every part of a whole region, from the relatively close-built central neighbourhood to the most sparsely settled rural area, so as to reduce the number of unnecessary journeys, to transfer as much long-distance freight as possible from roads to railroads and canals, and to lessen the length of daily journeys to work by multiplying the industrial and business sub-centres within a metropolitan and regional area.

It is worth noting that Mumford's mentor, the Scotsman Patrick Geddes, had proposed the construction of rail and roads from the centre of the city 'to delineate paths of development' which would restrain the fabrication of amorphous suburban sprawl.

To have adopted a regional plan on the scale demanded by Geddes and Mumford would have entailed a profound reform of local government. In fact in the 1960s a royal commission recommended the establishment of city regions, incorporating hinterland and catchment area, but the plans were watered down when it came to legislation. Nevertheless, central government and local government together have introduced many measures to deal with motor traffic. Examples are annual tests for older vehicles, the 70mph speed limit, extensive use of one-way streets, legislation against drinking and driving, parking meters, pedestrian precincts in cities, 'park and drive' facilities, which allow mobility but protect city centres. The government has attempted, sometimes with EU prodding, to put 'green' measures into effect. Indeed, the fuel tax which triggered the September 2000 fuel crisis, and which rose automatically by more than the rate of inflation, was established by the previous Conservative government with the justification that it was necessary for the best of green reasons.

Governments — in Europe pressed by or pressing Brussels — have tightened rules against vehicle emissions. Partly as a result, automobiles are safer and, with the use of new technology such as catalytic converters and low sulphur fuels, much less polluting than they were thirty years ago. They are also more reliable. Like the road humps, though, there are penalties; higher safety standards can mean higher fuel consumption.

And what happens if the fuel runs out? The question has been discussed with varying degrees of intensity since the internal-combustion engine was invented. Since the Empire, apart from Burma, appeared to have little in the way of oil resources, Britain was vulnerable, not just to a general exhaustion of supplies but to the disposition of foreign governments, an unpleasant change to the old days when the massive coal fields made us rich in sources of energy. The importance of oil supplies — not least for the Royal Navy — guided much of our foreign policy, including of course the humiliating Suez campaign. Efforts were made to find domestic oil or oil substitutes which might reduce our dependence on others. There was drilling for oil in Derbyshire, and in Dorset the government encouraged the raising of Jerusalem artichokes in the hope that they might produce enough alcohol for use as automobile fuel. During the Second World War cars were fitted with gas containers, without a satisfactory result. The latest attempt was very recent, made in Wales just before the 2000 panic. An ingenious motorist discovered that diesel-powered engines flourished on a mixture of conventional diesel oil and unconventional (at least for this purpose) cooking oil. When the tanker drivers and farmers blockaded the Milford Haven refinery, this new mixture became locally famous. But the experiment came to an abrupt end, not because it was in itself illegal, but on grounds of alleged tax evasion since cooking oil was bought free of tax.

Naturally oil is far more important now than it was in earlier days — for instance, in 1921, when, in response to momentary anxiety, the Fuel Research Station at Greenwich was established. In that year Britain consumed 1.04 million tonnes of motor fuel; in 1999 it was 21.5 million. While the country's general dependence on oil has actually declined (with natural gas taking over for many purposes), transport is still almost totally dependent. The North Sea fields of course made it unnecessary to experiment with Jerusalem artichokes and the like, but they are now past their peak, as are other sources on which the world relies. But forecasts say that in ten years' time the world will be consuming 20 per cent more oil than it is does today.

The future of oil reserves, however, is extremely difficult to judge.

In 1979 a Canadian book with the title *Running on Empty* raised the prospect of rapidly dwindling oil supplies and rapidly rising oil prices. In 1970 Esso forecast that global production would peak about the year 2000. Happily, these prophecies proved premature, as the huge North Sea and Alaskan fields and others proved their worth. And now in the *Financial Times* (22—23 March 2003) Daniel Yergin, chairman of Cambridge Energy Research Associates and Pulitzer prize-winner for his history of the world oil industry, takes a much more relaxed view, believing that technology and immense new fields in Russia and Canada will at least alleviate the problem.

Whatever the answer, though, there is no sign that people are about to tighten their belts; rather it is the other way round. Despite rising petrol prices, large-engined cars and SUVs are selling well. It is not that motorists have rediscovered the open road, but that when they can afford them, they love powerful cars even if they seldom have the opportunity to drive them as they are built to be driven. In the 1980s one writer pointed out that there were probably more Porsches per head in Guernsey than anywhere in Britain despite a speed limit on the tiny island of 35mph. Even though Japanese motor manufacturers have been selling very well and regularly win reliability tests, their cars are deemed dull to look at. The chief executive of Mitsubishi in Europe has recently stated that he wants to 'create emotions, passion and a smile by giving our cars a spirited design'. Temperamentally we are at one with the old General Motors and the 'motoring age', not at all possessed of the more puritan mood appropriate to oil shortages. Whether it is the sort of mood which will attach us to trams, now making a tentative comeback, remains to be seen. At Blackpool trams run eleven and a half miles along the coast. At Manchester they cover nineteen and a half miles, from Bury in the north to Altrincham in the south, passing through the centre of the city, while another company operates an approximately twelve-mile service from the centre of Birmingham to Wolverhampton. There are other lines too, although the tram company at Croydon has been having difficulties.

Still, electricity, used in another way, is clearly coming back to motoring. Toyota and Honda are producing hybrids in which electricity and internal combustion work alongside each other to provide the motive force. The Toyota Prius, on sale for several years already, uses electricity in town and petrol in the country, the selection recommended by Lord Montagu one hundred years ago but now combined in a single car. Perhaps this will overcome the sort of dislike that met Clive Sinclair's electric C5 with its engine produced by Hoover. Yet the hybrid may merely provide a bridge to the future, a stage on the road to the hydrogen fuel cell. Sheikh Yamani, the feared Saudi oil minister at the time of the great oil price rise in the 1970s, believes in it, and President Bush has declared that 'the first car driven by a child born today could be powered by hydrogen and pollution-free'. He accompanied his speech with a $1.2 billion federal research grant.

However, that is all sometime away yet. In the mean time we may get the 'Thinking Car':

> The queue's long, the engine temperature's rising, it's warming up outside and in, and the kids are getting noisier and you're about to boil over. Almost imperceptibly soothing music starts to play, the colour of the dashboard fades to a calming pastel green and a cool breeze with a hint of the sea wafts around cabin.

Thus, the *Sunday Times* on 2 February 2003. Very comfortable, so long of course as the pessimists are wrong and fuel prices do not go through the roof and shortages give us less luxuriant commodities with which to concern ourselves. In the cabin of the 'thinking car', computer-linked sensors are at work examining the driver's eyes in case a momentary burst of anger is the result of drink, drugs or lack of sleep. When it is dark, the night-vision sensors display an infrared view on the windscreen. When you are out of the car, perhaps a thief gets in ... It matters little: he stays in, locked up. (Anyway, his electronic image has already reached the police.) Already a system is in operation which recognizes the signs of imminent impact and automatically tightens safety belts and shifts seats to their safest position. In the car of the future, you switch on indicators, or climate control, lighting or music, by speaking to them. Material progress is indeed, as George Orwell surmised, making life safer ... and more soft.

We are a long way now from the horseless carriage and floundering around in the mud changing tyres. We are a good way too from the 1930s, when you were supposed to show your intentions by sticking a hand out of the car window and flapping it about. We are now in a time of new industrial techniques as thoroughgoing as those with which Henry Ford influenced manufacture in his day. Japanese motor firms pioneered the system of 'lean production'; they are being followed by all the big companies. In motor-vehicle construction 'flexible manufacturing' generally entails the re-equipment of assembly lines with computer-controlled robots that can be switched by computer command from making one vehicle type on the same line to another within minutes. It means that manufacturers are able to respond very quickly to change in customer demand. If it is the end of Fordism, it goes out with a flourish. *Le Monde*, in its 'Initiatives' supplement for March 2003, described the revolution as 'le nouveau taylorisme', the new Taylorism, but since it was Henry Ford who most famously put the ideas of Frederick Winslow Taylor into practice, it might equally be called the 'the new Fordism'. For anyone feeling a touch of nostalgia, it is agreeable to learn that at the Detroit Motor Show in January 2003 Ford unveiled a 'concept car' to be powered by hydrogen fuel cells and constructed of recyclable materials. Its lubricating oil will be made from sunflower seeds. With deliberate symbolism it was named the 'Model U'. A new age begins, with a glance back at the old.

Sources

General

For the history of individual makes of cars, see D. Culshaw and P. Horrobin, *The Complete Catalogue of British Cars* (1974); G. N. Georgano, *The Complete Encyclopaedia of Motor Cars* (1973); and Lord Montagu of Beaulieu, *Lost Causes of Motoring* (1960) and *Lost Causes of Motoring: Europe*, vol. 2. (1971).

1: Prelude

For old London, see F. E. Huggett, *Carriages at Eight* (1979); M. Constanduros in N. Streatfeild, *The Day before Yesterday* (1956); J. Bone, *London Perambulator* (1926); and Frederick Willis, *101 Jubilee Road* (1948). For the 'less enthusiastic' version, see A. H. Beavan, *Imperial London* (1901); and Thomas Burke, *London in My Time* (1934). For commuting, see H. J. Dyos, *Journal of Transport History*, vol. 1, May 1953. Cresswell is in the December issue. The 'Dalmatian Dog' reference is from R. Turvey, 'Street Mud, Dust and Noise', *London Journal*, vol. 21, no. 2, 1996. For Duncan, see his *The World on Wheels* (Paris, 1926). For Jarrott's description, see his *Ten Years of Motors and Motor Racing* (1906).

St John Nixon wrote this description of the first Brighton Run in *Veteran and Vintage Magazine*, October 1956 and January 1957. See also M. E. Ware's chapter in M. Jeal (ed.), *London to Brighton Run Centenary* (1996); and T. R. Nicholson, *The Birth of the British Motor Car*, vol. 2 (1982). Also Jarrott, as above. For the quotation from Edison, see M. Adeney, *The Motor Makers* (1988). For earlier motoring, see Nicholson, as above, vol. 1; and C. D. Buchanan, *Mixed Blessing* (1958); and H. Perkin, *The Age of the Automobile* (1976). For the Great Eastern, see Duncan, as above. The George Eliot quotation is from *Felix Holt*. For Carnegie, see his *An American Four-in Hand in Britain* (US, 1933 edn).

Strachey was writing in the Badminton Library book referred to in Chapter 2. J. J. Hissey deplored the state of the inns in his earlier books. S. F. Edge, *My Motoring Reminiscences* (1934). The number of traction engines at work in the 1890s is given in T. Barker (ed.), *The Economic and Social Effects of the Spread of Motor Vehicles* (1987). Willis remembers the Crystal Palace in his *Peace and Dripping Toast* (1950). The general history of British motoring in these early days comes from Buchanan and Perkin, as above. For Edge, see his reminiscences, as above. The Hewetson anecdote is taken from P. Tritton, *John Montagu of Beaulieu* (1985). For Salomons, see general histories of motoring; and D. J. Jeremy, *Dictionary of Business Biography* (1984); and also Ware, as above. For Gottlieb Daimler, see C. Johnson, *The Early History of Motoring* (no date given), both for the counterfeiting and the quotation. For Henry Chaplin, see *Parliamentary Debates*, 30 June 1896. The description of Chaplin is from E. F. Benson, *As We Are* (1932).

2: Mr Toad and Kindred Spirits

Martin Harper, *Mr Lionel* (1970); A. F. C. Hillstead, *Fifty Years with Motor Cars* (1960); J. J. Hissey, *Untravelled England* (1906); and O. Sitwell, *The Scarlet Tree* (1946) and, for his travel book, 'In the Train', from *Winters of Content* (1932). For the German reference, see W. Sachs, *For Love of the Automobile* (English trans., 1992). Percy Richardson's experience is recorded in R. D. Paul, 'Selling Cars in the late 90s', *Motor* 29 January 1929. The excitement on going out to dinner is taken from *The Autocar: Biography of Owen John* (1927). For Sturmey, see his *On an Autocar, through the length & breadth of the Land* (1898). S. F. Edge, *My Motoring Reminiscences* (1934), with the affair of the whip in C. Jarrott, *Ten Years of Motors and Motor Racing* (1906). The 'timid women' and the 'old women' anecdotes are drawn from M. Pemberton, *The Amateur Motorist* (1907).

R. Kipling, *Something of Myself* (1937). Montagu from Lord Montagu, *The Motoring Montagus* (1959). *The Motor Maniac* is by Mrs Kennard, 1902. For King Edward VII, see K. Middlemas, *The Pursuit of Pleasure* (1977); and C. W. Stamper, *What I Know* (1913). The extracts from *Car Illustrated*, sometimes known simply as *The Car*, relate to various issues during 1902 and 1903. For Escott, see his *Society in the New Reign* (1904); the date of *The Motoring Annual* ... is also 1904. For Lonsdale, see R. Garrett, *Motoring and the Mighty* (1971); for the Duke of Bedford and other grandees, see Lord Montagu of Beaulieu and F. Wilson McComb, *Behind the Wheel* (1977); and for the Duke of Portland, see A. C. Bird, *Roads and Vehicles* (1969). *The Wind in the Willows* was published in 1908. Mrs Campbell was writing 'To Scotland on a Lanchester' for *Car Illustrated*, 10 December 1902. For the price correlation with guns and jewellery, see J. Foreman-Peck et al., *The British Motor Industry* (1995). E. F. Benson describes the motoring habits of Lord Battersea in his *Final Edition* (1940); Sir Henry Wilson figures in Garrett, as above; and the 'the Motor Lie' in A. B. Filson-Young, *The Complete Motorist* (1904). The 'archbishop' is from A. R. Lucas, *Motor Dealing* (1922). Mrs Peel, *Life's Enchanted Cup* (1933); G. W. E. Russell in *Social Silhouettes* (1906); C. G. F. Masterman, *The Condition of England* (1909); and *Contemporary Review*, vol. 81, February 1902. For the *Tatler* reference, see J. Camplin, *The Rise of the Plutocrats* (1978). For the French Revolution, see P. Brendon, *The Motoring Century: The Story of the Royal Automobile Club* (1997).

Woodrow Wilson is quoted in D. Gartman, *Auto Opium* (US, 1994), and Walter Long in W. Plowden, *The Motor Car and Politics* (1971). The story of the parson is from the Badminton volume, 1902; G. F. M. Cornwallis-West, *Edwardian Heydays* (1930). For King Edward VII, see Stamper, as above; and for Benson, *As We Were* (1930). Lord Ernest Hamilton is quoted from his *Halcyon Era* (1933). Mr Eliot's trouble is recounted in D. Keir et al. (eds.), *Golden Milestone: 50 Years of the AA* (1955), and Mr Sampson's in H. Barty-King, *The AA* (1980). For Jarrott, see above. The history of the Automobile Club is given by Barty-King and Brendon, as above. For Dillon, see his *Motor Days in England* (1908). The duke who shut his park is referred to in J. E. Vincent, *Through East Anglia in a Motor Car* (1907). For J. J. Hissey, the references are *Untravelled England*, *An English Holiday with Car and Camera* and *The Charm of the Road*. For Kipling, see above. Also as above, Mrs Campbell and Lanchester. For the Brabazon quotation and descriptions, see Lord Brabazon of Tara,

The Brabazon Story (1956). For Brooklands, see Brendon, as above. F. Hedges Butler, *Fifty Years of Travel* (1920). For Churchill, see W. S. Blunt, *My Diaries*, part 1 (1919). For foreigners in the Mercedes, see Parliamentary Debates on Motor-Cars Bill 1903, House of Lords, and, more generally, in the House of Commons. The Local Government Board's circular was dated 19 September. For numbers of cars, see B. R. Mitchell and P. Deane, *Abstract of British Historical Statistics* (Cambridge, 1962); *Country Life*, 2 May 1913; Lowes Dickinson appears in *Independent Review*, vol. 11, October 1906. A letter from Lady Jeune quoted in Filson-Young, as above. Accident statistics from Department of Transport. *Road Accidents Great Britain 1990: The Casualty Report* (1991). Osbert Sitwell, *The Scarlet Tree* (1946).

3: Upheaval

D. Marsh, *The Changing Social Structure of England and Wales* (1958). B. R. Mitchell and P. Deane, *Abstract of British Historical Statistics* (Cambridge, 1962); *Spectator*, 11 October 1902; and Lord Montagu of Beaulieu and F. W. McComb, *Behind the Wheel* (1977). For Albourne Green, see M. Ware in M. Jeal (ed.), *The London to Brighton Run Centenary* (1996). Old habits are recorded in J. Bridges, *Early Country Motoring* (1995). M. Harper, *Mr Lionel* (1970). Sir J. Clapham, *An Economic History of Modern Britain* (1938). J. Ridley and C. Percy (eds.), *The Letters of Arthur Balfour and Lady Elcho* (1992). For peaked caps, see P. Brendon, *The Motoring Century* (1997). The salesman anecdote comes from M. Pemberton, *The Amateur Motorist* (1907). Mrs Simpson, in *The Times*, 30 January 2003. For Hissey, see his *The Charm of the Road* (1910). Craig's book was published in 1905. For the horse and carriage trade, see F. E. Huggett, *Carriages at Eight* (1979); and also G. A. Oliver, *A History of Coachbuilding* (1962). For Lanchester, see P. W. Kingsford, 'The Lanchester Engine Company Ltd', *Business History*, vol. 111, June 1961; and M. Adeney, *The Motor Makers* (1988).

J. Tilling's *Kings of the Highway* (1957) gives a full description of this firm. Also see L. A. G. Strong, *The Rolling Road* (1956). Salomons and his garages are considered in K. Richardson, *The British Motor Industry, 1896—1939* (1977), and Lutyens by M. Girouard, *Country Life*, vol. 70, and J. Brown, *Lutyens and the Edwardians* (1996). The French visitor was Léon Faucher, who recorded his impressions in his *Etudes sur l'Angleterre* (Paris, 1856). For Captain

Sampson and London mews, see B. Rosen and W. Zuckermann, *The Mews of London* (Exeter, 1982), and *The Survey of London*, vol. 39. The history of Coventry is related in a number of books and journals: those used here are *Illustrated London News*, 15 August 1896; J. B. Priestley, *English Journey* (1934); W. H. G. Armytage, *A Social History of Engineering* (1961); D. Thoms and T. Donnelly, *The Motor Car Industry in Coventry since the 1890s* (Beckenham, 1985); and B. Lancaster and T. Mason (eds.), *Life and Labour in a Twentieth Century City* (1986). For Lady Ripon, see E. F. Benson, *As We Were* (1930).

For investment, see A. E. Harrison, 'Joint-Stock Company Flotation in the Cycle, Motor-Vehicle and Related Industries, 1882—1914', *Business History*, vol. 23, 1981; and S. B. Saul, 'The Motor Industry in Britain to 1914', *Business History*, vol. 5, December 1962. All histories of the early British motor industry refer to Harry Lawson. The 'Swiss Admiral' comment comes from Ware in Jeal, as above, and he is discussed thoroughly in Nixon, Jeremy and Bird, in publications listed under Chapter 2, and also in a book by Nixon on the Daimler company. *The Economist's* warning is dated 28 November 1896 and that of the *Stock Exchange Gazette* 15 February 1896. For the second-hand car comment, see Adeney, as above. For Oxford the principal books consulted here are Adeney again; P. Snow, *Oxford Observed* (1991); R. C. Whiting, *The View from Cowley* (Oxford, 1983); and J. M. Mogey, *Neighbourhood and Family* (Oxford, 1956). For the skirmish with the Great Western Railway, see E. W. Gilbert, 'The Industrialization of Oxford', *Geographical Journal*, vol. CIX, 1947. For William Morris, see in particular his biography by M. Adeney, *Nuffield* (1993). For the East Anglian motor industry, see J. F. Bridges, *Early Country Motoring* (1995). For the rise and fall of manufacturers, see Saul, as above. Balfour, as above. For electric cars, see J. J. Flink, *The Automobile Age* (US, 1988). For the unfortunate French nobleman, see W. Sachs, *For Love of the Automobile* (English trans., 1992).

For the *Country Life* woman, see issue of 8 March 1913. For Rolls-Royce and prices, see I. Lloyd, *Rolls-Royce* ... (1978). For Dorothy Levitt, see her *The Woman and the Car* (1970 edn). For earnings, see Sir A. Bowley, *Wages and Income in the United Kingdom since 1860* (Cambridge, 1937). On Henry Ford there are innumerable books or sections of books; quoted here are some of those which are particularly relevant to Britain: R. Batchelor, *Henry Ford* ... (Manchester,

1994); K. Richardson, *The British Motor Industry* (1977); R. Crabb, *Birth of a Giant* (1969); and D. Lewis, *The Public Image of Henry Ford* (US, 1976). W. Lewchuk, *American Technology and the British Vehicle Industry* (1987), and D. Hounshell, *From the American System to Mass Production* (US, 1984) are very helpful on the more technical side.

4: The Rediscovery of Arcadia

The *Mayfair Magazine* is quoted from J. Camplin, *The Rise of the Plutocrats* (1978). The war in J. Keegan, *A History of Warfare* (1993). Curzon in J. J. Flink, *The Automobile Age* (US, 1988). For Cugnot, see T. R. Nicholson, *The Birth of the British Motor Car* (1982). For Rivaz, see H. Michelet, *L'Inventeur Isaac de Rivaz* (Switzerland, 1965). The East India Company's experiments are mentioned in Nicholson, as above. Simms's armoured cars figure in L. Field, *Bendor, the Golden Duke of Westminster* (1983). The *Autocar: Biography of Owen John* (1977) records the author's experiences in the Motor Reserve. For owner-drivers to France, see M. Adeney, *The Motor Makers* (1988). For the Duke of Westminster, see Field, as above. The Duchess of Sutherland described her time in France in her *Six Weeks at the War* (1914). The pompous officer comes from D. J. Mitchell, *Women on the Warpath* (1966). See Pat Beauchamp's *Fanny goes to War* (1919). Olive Turney's life as a driver forms part of J. Bridges, *Early Country Motoring* (1995). For car registrations, see B. R. Mitchell and P. Deane, *Abstract of British Historical Statistics* (Cambridge, 1962). Kipling wrote of the purpose of motoring in a letter printed in A. B. Filson-Young, *The Complete Motorist* (1904). Advice on touring is by L. Henslowe, *Motoring for the Million* (1922). The quotation on the 'fairy tale world' is taken from W. Sachs, *For Love of the Automobile* (English trans., 1992). Prioleau's book was published in 1929, and those of H. V. Morton in 1931 (England), and in 1932 (Scotland and Wales). The letter to *The Times* about the Lake District was published on 9 September 1907.

The references for ancient monuments and their visitors are the Public Record Office, WORK14/2314 and WORK14/2315. The reference is to the 1927 edition of *Baedeker* (*Great Britain*). For Bray, see P. F. Brandon, 'A Twentieth-Century Squire in his Landscape', *Southern History*, vol. 4, 1982, and in Surrey Archaeological Collections, vol. 39, G85/37—38. For Bennett on Sturt, see A. Bennett, *Books and Persons* (1917). E. Mackerness has published *The Journals of George Sturt*, vols. 1 & 2 (Cambridge, 1967). Ford Madox Ford's life in the country is described in his *Return to Yesterday* (1931) and *It was the Nightingale* (1934), while the incident with the tourists is recorded in A. Judd *Ford Madox Ford* (1990). Life in Rottingdean is remembered in S. M. Moens's *Rottingdean* (Brighton, 1952); Margaret Ward's *Memories of Rottingdean* (Brighton, 1993) and her *One Camp Chair in the Living Room* (Brighton, 1988); and in Bob Copper's *Early to Rise* (1976). For villages, see R. Richardson, *Swanbrooke Down* (1990); O. Rice, *Village Memories* (Milton Keynes, 1982) for Woughton-on-the-Green, and J. Robins, *Elmdon: Continuity and Change* (Cambridge, 1980). For village life and transport, see also T. C. Barker and C. Savage, *An Economic History of Transport in Britain* (1974 ed.); and K. Innes, *Life in a Hampshire Village* (1944, privately printed). For Laurie Lee, see his *Cider with Rosie* (1960). For L. T. C. Rolt, see his *Landscape with Machines* (1971).

For the effect of buses in the country there is J. Hibbs, *The Country Bus* (1986) and also *The History of British Bus Services* (Newton Abbot, 1968). The Birmingham Bus Company's reconversion is mentioned in R. Fulford, *Five Decades of B.E.T.* (1946). For London taxis, see G. N. Georgano, *A History of the London Taxicab* (1972). *The Economist's* views on early investment in bus services are given on 11 March 1905, 26 August 1905 and 18 November 1905. Studies of Sir George White are provided in *Journal of Transport History*, vol. 9, September 1988, and by D. J. Jeremy in his *Dictionary of Business Biography* (1984). For the projected Guide, see C. F. Klapper, *The Golden Age of Buses* (1978). For excursions, see A. Delgado, *The Annual Outing and Other Excursions* (1977). For Laycock, see Hibbs, *History ...*, as above. For Turnham, see Klapper, as above. Thomas Burke expressed his enthusiasm in his *The London Spy* (1925 edn). *Holidays: Where to Go, What to See — and the Cost*, published by Cassell in 1921, enthuses about resorts. For Blackpool, see J. K. Walton, *Blackpool* (1998); and J. A. R. Pimlott, *The Englishman's Holiday* (1947). Barry Band's *Blackpool's Century of Stars*, book 1, (Blackpool, 1998) is invigorating. Don Haworth's memories are recorded in his *Bright Morning* (1990). For the congestion on roads, see A. Crosby, *Leading the Way* (Preston, 1998). The excursion coaches and their improvements are discussed in the books on buses above, while Richard Hoggart's description comes from his *The Uses of Literacy* (1957). For Gourmont, see his *Promenades Philosophiques* (Paris, 1925). The *Autocar* quotation is taken from *Holidays* above.

5: The Roaring Twenties

Patrick Hamilton, *The West Pier* (1951), and 'The Siege of Pleasure', which was published as part of his *Twenty Thousand Streets under the Sky* (1935). Don Haworth, *Bright Morning* (1990). D. Gartman, *Auto Opium* (US, 1994). *Sylvia's Chauffeur* is by Louis Tracey. For the reference to S. F. Edge, see A. J. Smithers in *Dornford Yates* (1982). The dust menace is described in *Adele and Co.* and the race through the Landes in *Jonah and Co.* For Churchill on Lawrence, see R. Blythe, *The Age of Illusion* (1983). F. M. Ford's view comes from *It was the Nightingale* (1934) and the 'timeless St Martin's Summer' from J. Brooke, 'The Military Orchid', published as part of *The Orchid Trilogy* (1981). V. S. Pritchett, *Midnight Oil* (1979). Tom Wolfe is quoted in C. G. Dettelbach, *In the Driver's Seat* (US, 1976); C. Posthumus, *Vintage Cars: Motoring in the 1920s* (1973). Ogilvy in his *Our Times* (1953). For motor cycles and the young, see B. R. Mitchell and P. Deane, *Abstract of British Historical Statistics* (Cambridge, 1962); and D. Fowler, *The First Teenagers* (1995). Patrick Balfour in his *Society Racket* (1933). De Mille in D. L. Lewis and L. Goldstein, *The Automobile and American Culture* (US, 1980). George Formby is criticized in R. Bergan, *Sports in the Movies* (1982).

For movie stars, see Gartman, as above; F. Clymer, *Cars of the Stars* (US, no date); and P. Marsh and P. Collett, *Driving Passion* (1986). For Malcolm Campbell and Henry Segrave, see G. Campbell and M. Meech, *Bluebirds*; and R. Garrett, *Motoring and the Mighty* (1971). Garrett also describes the Bentley Boys, as does P. Brendon, *The Motoring Century* (1997). The J. J. Hissey book in question is *A Leisurely Tour in England*. The necessity of golf clubs is stressed by G. D. Abraham in his *Motor Ways in Lakeland* (1913). The trip to Romania is described in T. R. Nicholson (ed.), *The Age of Motoring Adventure* (1972). A thorough and analytical study of women and motoring is made in Sean O'Connell's *The Car in British Society: Class, Gender and Motoring 1896—1939* (Manchester, 1998). The Riviera scene is described in Francis Rose, *Saying Life* (1961), and in M. Blume, *Cote d'Azur* (1992). For Delaunay and Baker, see F. Basham and B. Ughetti, *Car Culture* (1984). For Paul Whiteman, see Lewis and Goldstein, as above. Also excellent on fashion is D. B. Tubbs, *Art and the Automobile* (1978).

For Lonsdale, see Garrett, as above. For Burgoyne, see *Journal of the Royal Society of Arts*, vol. 74, 1 January 1926. The date of the reference to 'the billiard room' is 10 January 1932 in *The Motoring Encyclopedia* (1932). The Benz advertisement is included in W. Sachs, *For Love of the Automobile* (English trans., 1992). See M. Frostick, *Advertising the Motor Car* (1970). For Auburn, see J. Laux et al., *The Automobile Revolution* (US, 1982). For Rolls-Royce, see I. Lloyd, *Rolls-Royce: The Years of Pleasure* (1978). For the demise of the Ford Model T, see Dettelbach and Gartman, as above. For the change in styling, see D. Hounshell, *From the American System to Mass Production* (US, 1984), and E. Cray, *Chrome Colossus* (US, 1980). Mumford, *The Culture of Cities* (1940).

6: The Open Road to Brighton

The Proust quotation is from 'Journées en Automobile' in *Pastiches et Mélanges* (Paris, 1919). For Sitwell, see *Great Morning* (1948). For the hum of the six-cylinder motor, see L. Henslowe in the *Gentlewoman and Modern Life*, 30 January 1926. For songs of sex, see P. Wollen and J. Kerr, *Autopia: Cars and Culture* (2002). For Laramie, see P. Marsh and P. Collett, *Driving Passion* (1986). For Arnold Wilson, see *Walks & Talks* (1934). For 'Brighton meant sex', see N. Richardson, *Breakfast in Brighton* (1998). For Byng, see *The Torrington Diaries*, vol. 1 (1934). The background is set out in O. Sitwell and M. Barton, *Brighton* (1935), and in T. Burke, *The London Spy* (1922). *Roadhouses and Clubs* was published by Sylvan Publications without its author named. Other books on roadhouses relevant here are B. Oliver, *The Renaissance of the English Public House* (1947); J. Stevenson, *British Society 1914—1945* (1984); G. Long, *English Inns and Road-Houses* (1937); and W. G. McMinnies, *Signposts to the Road Houses, Country Clubs ...* (1935). The Crawley Reference Library also provided useful information. *England, Ugliness and Noise* was written by A. Darby and C. C. Hamilton. See A. D. King, *The Bungalow* (1984). The despoiling of south-east England and the coast is brilliantly described in D. Hardy and C. Ward, *Arcadia for All* (1984). See also D. Seward, *Sussex* (1995), and Sue Farrant's 'London by the Sea', *Journal of Contemporary History*, vol. 22, 1987. The reference to typewriters comes from P. Brandon and B. Short, *The South-East from AD 1000* (1990).

For Dickens, see *The Tugges at Ramsgate*. The (unpublished) Brookfield thesis was submitted to the University of London, and the Prioleau quotation is taken from O'Connell, as above. The 1931 census is quoted from E. Brunner, *Holiday Making and the Holiday Trades* (Oxford, 1945). For Joad, see *Horrors*. The background to Eastbourne comes from D. Cannadine, *Lords and Landlords* (Leicester, 1980). Councillor Clarke figures in J. Collier and I. Lang, *Just the Other Day* (1932). The Brighton court cases were reported in the *News of the World*, 18 February 1922 and 11 September 1921. For St Ives, see J. K. Walton, *The British Seaside* (2000). For the effect of railways and then of buses, see King, as above, and E. W. Gilbert's *Brighton: Old Ocean's Bauble* (1954). For Trevelyan, see his *An Autobiography and Other Essays* (1949). *Progress at Pelvis Bay* was published in 1936. Laurie Lee's life is continued here in his *As I Walked out One Midsummer Morning* (1969). For Mrs Stawell, see her *Motoring in Sussex and Kent* (1926); for Jaywick, see the *Star*, 22 June 1932; and for 'Bohemia', see Denis R. Mills (ed), *Twentieth Century Lincolnshire* (Lincoln, 1989). Peacehaven (and its syndrome) are reported in *Guardian* 3 May 1969; in Farrant, as above; and in an article, 'A Disgusting Blot on the Landscape', published in *New Society*, 17 July 1975. The beach hut gets full treatment in *The Times*, 3 January 2002.

7: Road against Rail

For redundancy of farm workers, see A. Armstrong, *Farmworkers* (1988); and M. Adeney, *The Motor Makers* (1988). See also the German visitor Karl Silex's *John Bull at Home* (1931). For modern equipment, see J. Thirsk (ed.), *The Agrarian History of England and Wales*, vol. 8 (Cambridge, 1978); and I. Niall, *To Speed the Plough* (1977). For Crompton, see his *Reminiscences* (1928), and L. T. C. Rolt, *Great Engineers* (1962). For the early development of goods-carrying vehicles, see, as well as Pratt, M. Seth-Smith in his *The Long Haul* (1975); T. Barker and D. Gerhold in *The Rise and Rise of Road Transport* (1993); and C. Dunbar in his *The Rise of Road Transport* (1981). G. Turnbull in *Traffic and Transport* (1979) studies Pickfords. The source for the 1919 strike is *The Times*. The number of goods vehicles in 1919 and 1926 is given in T. C. Barker and C. Savage, *An Economic History of Transport in Britain* (1974 edn). For Jempson, see Barker and Gerhold, as above. For Dearman, see C. Dearman, *Up and Down the Hertford Road*, published by the Edmonton Hundred History Society in 1979. The history of Wordie & Co. has been published by E. Paget-Tomlinson, *The Railway Carriers* (Lavenham, 1990). For a contemporary account of the attitude to road and rail cooperation, see

C. T. Brunner, *The Problem of Motor Transport* (1928). *The Ruin of Rural England* was written by J. W. Martin. The examples of railway delays come from *The Times* 2 September 1919 and S. V. Pearson, *London's Overgrowth and the Causes of Swollen Towns* (1939).

For Trafford Park, see D. A. Farnie, *The Manchester Ship Canal and the Rise of the Port of Manchester* (Manchester,1980); and T. H. G. Stevens, *Some Notes on the Development of Trafford Park* (1947). For Eric Geddes and Marshall Stevens, see D. J. Jeremy, *Dictionary of Business Biography* (1984), and for Geddes's attitude, J. Hibbs, *The History of British Bus Services* (1968). The rivalry of road and rail is described in H. Perkin, *The Age of the Automobile* (1976); and D. H. Aldcroft's *British Transport since 1914* (1975) and *British Railways in Transition* (1968). Employment figures are derived from D. J. Jeremy, *A Business History of Britain* (1998). The Royal Commission's report is filed as Command Paper 3751. The miles covered by various forms of transport are given in Aldcroft, *British Transport since 1914*, as above, and revenue in R. Stone and D. A. Rowe, *The Measurement of Consumers' Expenditure and Behaviour in the United Kingdom 1920—1938*, vol. 2 (Cambridge, 1966). For 'rationalization', see D. Kynaston, *The City of London: Illusions of Gold* (1999); and S. Pollard, *The Development of the British Economy 1914—1950* (1962). For Churchill, see R. Jenkins, *Churchill* (2002). For Stamp, see Kynaston, as above, and his own *Industrial and Railway Amalgamations* (1928). For 'Troubles of the Road Carrier', see *Listener*, 25 May 1938, and for road haulage more generally, see M. R. Bonavia, *Railway Policy between the Wars* (Manchester, 1981); and G. Walker, *Road and Rail* (1942). For 'grandfather's rights', see A. Townsin, *The British Bus Story: Early Eighties* (1992).

8: Coming to Terms

Types of car are described by L. Henslowe in *Motoring for the Million* (1922) and 1930 prices in his *Car Buyers Annual* of that year. For the Duke of Bedford, see John, Duke of Bedford, *A Silver Plated Spoon* (1959). The return to Brighton description is given in L. T. C. Rolt in his *Landscape with Machines* (1971). For the Speedy Car, see P. S. Bagwell, *The Transport Revolution from 1770* (1974); and *The Times* 13 September 1919. Market share is set out in D. H. Aldcroft, 'A New Chapter in Transport History: The Twentieth-Century Revolution', *Journal of Transport History*, ns, vol. 3, February 1976. Lord Shrewsbury is mentioned in F. E. Huggett, *Carriages at Eight* (1979). Motorcycle statistics are to be found in B. R. Mitchell and P. Deane, *Abstract of British Historical Statistics* (Cambridge, 1962). For the chairman of Raleigh, see D. Thoms et al., *The Motor Car and Popular Culture* ... (1998). The enthusiastic motor cyclist was Joseph Pennell, writing in *Contemporary Review*, vol. 81, February 1902. (Books on motor cycling include C. Posthumus et al., *The Motorcycle Story* [1979]; M. Partridge, *Motor Cycle Pioneers* [1976]; and C. Ayton et al., *The History of Motor Cycling* [1979].) Cyclecars are discussed in J. J. Flink, *The Automobile Age* (US, 1988); M. Adeney, *The Motor Makers* (1988); and M. Worthington-Williams, *From Cyclecar to Microcar* (Beaulieu, 1981,) as well as in standard reference books for automobile listings. The 'cement mixer' quotation is from S. O'Connell, *The Car in British Society* (1998).

On the question of affordability, see also Bagwell, as above. *The Economist* estimate is taken from Adeney. Colin Clark's calculation can be found in S. V. Pearson, *London's Overgrowth and the Causes of Swollen Towns* (1939). The Morris quotation is given in Bagwell. For the price index, see Aldcroft in *Journal of Transport History*, as above. For national income per head, see B. R. Mitchell and P. Deane, as above. O'Connell, as above, makes a close study of hire purchase. Other sources consulted here are S. Bowden and M. Collins, 'The Bank of England ...', *Economic History Review*, vol. 45, 1992; S. Bowden and P. Turner, 'The Demand for Consumer Durables ...', *Journal of Economic History*, vol. 53, June 1993. D. E. W. Gibb, *Lloyd's of London* (1957), provides a detailed study of the problem at Lloyd's. See Bagwell, as above, for persons per car. Component manufacturers are considered in D. J. Jeremy, *A Business History of Britain* (1998); see also J. Foreman-Peck et al., *The British Motor Industry* (Manchester, 1995). For Austin, see R. Church, *Herbert Austin* (1979). The contact of Henry Ford with Triplex is recounted in Adeney, with Dillinger in T. Burness, *Cars of the Early Thirties* (US, 1970), and with Clyde Barrow in J. Pettifer and N. Turner, *Automania* (1984). The government's attitude generally is discussed in W. Plowden, *The Motor Car and Politics* (1971). For roads, see R. E. Crompton, *Reminiscences* (1928); A. Crosby, *Leading the Way* (1998); R. M. C. Anderson, *The Roads of England* (1932); Lord Montagu of Beaulieu and F. W. McComb, *Behind the Wheel* (1977); and A. Bird, *Roads and Vehicles* (1969). The *Spectator* registered its approval on 15 August 1925. For

Burgoyne, see *Journal of the Royal Society of Arts*, vol. 74, January 1926. Again Plowden, as above. The motor-led recovery in Germany is recorded in R. J. Overy, *War and Economy in the Third Reich* (Oxford, 1994).

Sources for projected motorways are the report in the *News of the World*, 27 May 1923, the Public Record Office MT 39/295 (for Manchester's view) and H. Clunn, *Famous South Coast Pleasure Resorts* (1929). For Lord Cecil, see Parliamentary Debates, House of Lords, vol. 75. The RAC's acceptance of the government's position is drawn from P. Brendon, *The Motoring Century* (1997). The AA's policy on filling stations comes from H. Barty-King, *The AA* (1980), and S. Cooke, *This Motoring* (1931). For the preservationist movement, see J. Sheail, *Rural Conservation in Inter-War Britain* (1981). The indignation which greeted Brighton's plans for the Downs is shown clearly in the *Listener*, 27 December 1933. For the Box Hill affair, see Sheail and the entry for J. Chuter Ede in the *Dictionary of National Biography*. The references for the Ministry of Transport and its attempts to address the problems of the moment are Public Record Office refs. FD 1/4017, MT 34/155, MT 34/221 and MT 34/216. See also on traffic lights K. Silex, *John Bull at Home* (1931). The claims that pedestrians are making themselves a nuisance are found in the *Listener*, 14 September 1932, 29 January 1930 and 6 April 1932. Moore-Brabazon is quoted in Plowden, as above. For the *Practitioner*, see issue of September 1937, and the conflicting interests of the National Safety First Association in O'Connell, as above. The Belisha board game is described under British Library ref. 85/1856.G13(112). The Blackpool reaction is referred to in O'Connell, as above.

For Hore-Belisha, see also R. J. Minney, *The Private Papers of Hore-Belisha* (1960); K. Robins (ed.), *Blackwell Biographical Dictionary of British Political Life in the Twentieth Century* (1990); and, for his earlier life, an entertaining sketch in C. Hollis, *Oxford in the Twenties* (1976). The Mersey Tunnel speech is quoted in *The Times*, 14 September 1934. *The Times* (10 July 1934) reports the near disaster on the pedestrian crossing. For the *Spectator*'s 'fifth rate carnival', see R. Graves and A. Hodge, *The Long Week-End* (1940 edn). Hore-Belisha's report of his conversation with the Prince of Wales is to be found under ref. HOBE 4/5 in the Hore-Belisha papers in the possession of the Churchill Archives Centre at Churchill College, Cambridge. Hore-

Belisha's correspondence with MacDonald and Chamberlain is recorded in HOBE 4/3, HOBE 4/4 and HOBE 4/19. The letter from Sir David Cameron is dated 28 May 1937. The road plan for London — in which Sir Charles Bressey was prominent — is included in C. M. Buchanan, *London Road Plans*, published in 1970 as the Greater London Research Intelligence Unit's Research Report No. 11.

9: Metroland Magnified

For the wireless talks, see J. B. Priestley, *Postscripts* (1940). *English Journey* was published in 1934. Richard Hoggart is quoted from his *A Local Habitation* (1988) and Don Haworth from his *Bright Morning* (1990). For population figures, see B. R. Mitchell and P. Deane, *Abstract of British Historical Statistics* (Cambridge, 1962). For Coventry, see B. Lancaster and T. Mason, *Life and Labour in a Twentieth Century City* (1986). L. Lee, *As I Walked out One Midsummer Morning* (1969). For migration to the south, see B. Thomas, 'The Movement of Labour into South-East England, 1920—32', *Economica*, ns, vol. 1, 1934. Sir Arnold Wilson, *Walks & Talks* (1934). The Barlow Report is filed as Command Paper 6153, and Scott as Command Paper 6378. Priestley's reaction to trams is from *English Journey*. E. D. Smithies, 'The Contrast between North and South in England 1918—1939', unpublished thesis submitted to the University of Leeds in 1974 and in the possession of the Brotherton Library at the university. For the struggle in the LCC, see O. J. Morris (ed.), *Fares Please* (1953). For transport in London, see T. C. Barker and M. Robbins, *A History of London Transport*, vol. 2, (1974). The *Economist* article is dated 8 May 1937. A. Sutcliffe (ed.), *Metropolis 1890—1940* (1984), provided urban population figures. For Metroland, see Metropolitan Railway's 1932 edition of its annual guide, introduced by O. Green. Also D. Edwards and R. Pigram, *Metro Memories* (1977), and *Golden Memories ... Metro-land Dream* (1983), both published at Tunbridge Wells. The Great Western Road is discussed in M. Simpson's 'Urban Transport and the Development of Glasgow's West End', *Journal of Transport History*, ns, February 1972. The effect of cheap tickets is related in A. A. Jackson, *Semi-Detached London* (1973). For Hamilton, see her *Modern England* (1938). For buildings getting smaller, see G. Weightman and S. Humphries, *The Making of Modern London, 1914—1939* (1984). For Goldring, see his *A Tour in Northumbria* (1938).

For Wythenshawe, see T. W. Freeman, *The Conurbations of Great Britain* (1959) and Sir E. D. Simon, *The Rebuilding of Manchester* (1935). For Birmingham, see Sir Peter Hall, *The Containment of Urban England*, vol. 1 (1973). For the spread of suburban expansion everywhere, see T. Sharp in C. Williams-Ellis (ed.), *Britain & the Beast* (1937). The quotation from Abercrombie is taken from Jackson, as above. For Becontree, see T. Young, *Becontree and Dagenham* (1934); K. K. Liepmann, *The Journey to Work* (1944); and S. V. Pearson, *London's Overgrowth and the Causes of Swollen Towns* (1939). For the increase in housing development, see J. T. Coppock, *Greater London* (1964). The (New) Fabian booklet was F. J. Osborn, *Transport, Town Development and Territorial Planning*. For Glasgow, see Liepmann, as above. For industrial concentration and separation from workplace, see H. W. Richardson and D. H. Aldcroft, *Building in the British Economy between the Wars* (1968). J. M. Richard's book on the suburbs is *The Castles on the Ground* (1948). Paul Vaughan's *Something in Linoleum* was published in 1994. The car prices given here are from the *Motor Car Index 1928–1939*, published by Fletcher & Son of Norwich in 1939. (The 1930 figures are at odds with those by Leonard Henslowe, mentioned earlier, probably because Henslowe's included extras.) Graham Robson in his *Motoring in the 30s* (Cambridge, 1979) mentions the choice between a Baby Austin and the baby carriage. For the Austin Seven, see R. Church, *Herbert Austin* (1979); and R. J. Wyatt, *The Austin Seven* (1968). The 'gnat' comparison was made by the Earl of Cottenham in his *Motoring To-day and To-morrow* (1928). The close association of the Austin Seven with the suburbs was stressed in a BBC2 progamme shown on 2 March 2001.

For the destruction of old Middlesex, see J. Betjeman, *Ah Middlesex* (1984), but originally published in *Punch*. 'Slough' by J. Betjeman is taken from *Collected Poems*, John Murray (Publishers) Ltd. H. J. Massingham, *London Scene* (1933). The quotation from Orwell on the effect of mechanical progress is taken from his *The Road to Wigan Pier* (1937). Huxley refers to the subject in *Along the Road* (1925). The 'other writer' referred to is C. Delisle Burns.

10: Aftermath

Meacher reported in *Financial Times*, 15 January 2003. For motorists' devotion to their cars, see *Financial Times*, 24 January 2001, quoting *RAC Report on Motoring*. See also G. Lyons and K. Chatterjee,

Transport Lessons from the Fuel Tax Protests of 2000 (Aldershot, 2002), which includes references to increase in public transport fares. For car usage, see *Social Trends* (2000 edn). For proportion of household spending, see *The Times*, 23 January 2003. Shopping statistics were given by Stephen Glaister in his (published) 1997 AA Lecture. For Bracknell, see *Financial Times*, 27—28 July 2002. D. Starkie, *The Motorway Age* (1982), deals with the effect of juggernaut lorries. Abraham in *Motoring in the English Lakeland*; M. Pemberton, *The Amateur Motorist*. For Tamora, see *Sunday Times*, 19 January 2003; and for the Smart Roadster, *The Times*, 7 February 2003. For family history websites see *Financial Times*, 6—7 July 2002. The Greys Cigarettes advertisement is to be found in *Holidays: Where to Go, What to See* ..., published by Cassell & Co., 1921. H. G. Wells, in an anonymous article 8 December 1893. Seiffert is quoted in W. Sachs, *For Love of the Automobile* (English trans., 1992). *News of the World*, 9 September 1923. For Marinetti, see J. Pettifer and N. Turner, *Automania* (1984). For early flying, see R. Wohl, *A Passion for Wings* (1994). For Harley Earl, see P. Wollen and J. Kerr (eds.), *Autopia* (2002), a book with reference also to the Dymaxion car and to Norman Bel Geddes. Also for Geddes, see I. Margolius, *Automobiles by Architects* (Chichester, 2000). (For experimental cars, see too R. Brandon, *Auto Mobile* [2002].) Molt Taylor is recorded in Pettifer, as above. The Burney Streamline reference is taken from P. Collins and M. Stratton, *British Car Factories from* 1896 (Godmanstone, 1993).

The 'cotton mill' quotation is from D. Thoms et al., *The Motor Car and Popular Culture in the* 20th *Century* (1998). For CPRE and planning generally, see Sir Peter Hall, *The Containment of Urban England*, vol. 2 (1973), and his *Urban and Regional Planning* (4th edn, 2002). Statistics on pre-war production of automobiles are provided by R. J. Overy, *War and Economy in the Third Reich* (1994). For postwar, see R. Church, *The Rise and Decline of the British Motor Industry* (Cambridge, 1994). For political background, see W. Plowden, *The Motor Car and Politics* (1971). For the poor industrial relations, see P. J. S. Dunnett, *The Decline of the British Motor Industry* (1980), and, more generally, Starkie, as above. The New York exhibition is described in Margolius, as above; the Wolseley advertisement comes from Thoms, as above. The rejection of the Volkswagen is recorded in J. J. Flink, *The Automobile Age* (US, 1988). Productivity levels are compared in Church, as above, and assets per company in Dunnett, as above. 'Multiplicity in everything' is quoted from Church. For George Mason, see G. Lanning et al. (eds.) for Television History Workshop, *Making Cars* (1985). For the reaction in favour of private enterprise, see K. Button and D. Pitfield (eds.), *Transport Deregulation* (1991). J. Bolster, *The Upper Crust* (1976). The reference to Kipling's diary is Julian Barnes's article http//books.guardian.co.uk/review/story of 3 February 2003. The *Economist* article on the horse and traffic bans comes from the edition on 15 August 1936; the statistics on traffic sentencing from 7 August 1937. For 'Bobby Finders', see P. Brendon, *The Motoring Century* (1997). For hot-rodding, see Wollen, as above, and for 'physical cocooning', see D. Miller (ed.), *Car Cultures* (Oxford, 2001). The Heathcote Williams extract is taken from his book entitled *Armageddon*, published by Jonathan Cape. Reprinted by permission of The Random House Group Ltd.

For preservationist campaigns and civil disobedience, see C. Mosey, *Car Wars* (2000); for Swanbrooke Down, R. Richardson, *Swanbrooke Down* (1990); and M. Ward, *Memories of Rottingdean* (1993). For road humps, see the *Sunday Times*, 2 February 2003, and for Italy, *Sunday Times*, 9 February 2003. The Patrick Geddes reference comes from M. Dalbey, *Regional Variations and Metropolitan Boosters* (2002). Yergin was writing in the *Financial Times*, 22–23 March 2003. Early attempts to achieve independence of fuel supply are described in G. Jones, *The State and the Emergence of the British Oil Industry* (1981); D. Yergin, *The Prize* (1991); and S. Cooke, *This Motoring* (1931). For Porsches in Guernsey, see S. Bayley, *Sex, Drink and Fast Cars* (1986). For Mitsubishi, see *Financial Times*, 8 January 2003; for Toyota and Honda, *Financial Times* Auto in *Financial Times*, 4 March 2003. For trams, the author's direct enquiries and on Croydon, for one instance, *Financial Times*, 6 February 2003. For Sinclair, see Collett, as above, and for Sheikh Yamani, see Brandon, as above. Detroit and the Model U are reported in *Financial* Times, 30 January 2003.

Index